EVANGELICALS AND CULTURE

Evangelicals and Culture

DOREEN M. ROSMAN

CROOM HELM
London & Canberra

© 1984 Doreen Rosman
Croom Helm Ltd, Provident House, Burrell Row,
Beckenham, Kent BR3 1AT

Croom Helm Australia, PO Box 391, Manuka,
ACT 2603, Australia

British Library Cataloguing in Publication Data

Rosman, Doreen
    Evangelicals and culture.
    1. Evangelistic work – England – History – 18th century
    2. Evangelistic work – England – History – 19th century
    3. England – Civilization
    I. Title
    269'.2'0942   BV3777.G7

ISBN 0-7099-2253-1

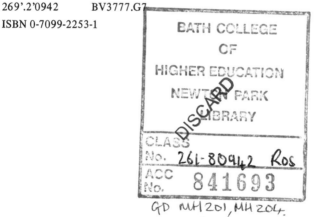
Printed and bound in Great Britain by
Biddles Ltd, Guildford and King's Lynn

CONTENTS

Contents

ABBREVIATIONS

Societies

BFBS   British and Foreign Bible Society
BFSS   British and Foreign School Society
BMS   Baptist Missionary Society
CMS   Church Missionary Society
LMS   London Missionary Society
RTS   Religious Tract Society
SPCK   Society for the Propagation of Christian
                                       Knowledge
SPG   Society for the Propagation of the Gospel
WMS   Wesleyan Missionary Society

Periodicals

BM   Baptist Magazine
CO   Christian Observer
EM   Evangelical Magazine
ER   Eclectic Review
MM   Wesleyan Methodist Magazine

Note

The practice of the British Library Catalogue has been followed for the citation of volume numbers of periodicals. Thus the series and volume number is supplied for BM and ER, whereas the volumes for BM, CO and MM are numbered consecutively from the beginning with no series division.

ACKNOWLEDGEMENTS

The publication of this book has been assisted by a grant from the Twenty-Seven Foundation for which I am most grateful.

Chapter 8 incorporates a revised version of an essay on evangelicalism and the novel, originally published in D. Baker (ed.), <u>Renaissance and Renewal in Christian History: studies in Church History</u> xiv (Blackwell, 1977). I am grateful to the Ecclesiastical History Society for permission to reprint this material, to the Cambridge University Press for the quotations from T. Pinney (ed.), <u>The Letters of Thomas Babington Macaulay</u>, and to the Columbia University Press, who hold the copyright of P.E. Shaw, <u>The Catholic Apostolic Church</u>. I am glad to acknowledge the use of a number of unpublished theses, the work of Dr. I.C. Bradley, Mr. T.F. May, Dr. H.C. Morgan, Dr. I.S. Rennie, and Dr. P.E. Sangster, and am particularly indebted to Dr. H. Willmer, who lent me a copy of his unpublished Hulsean prize essay.

During the years in which I have worked on this subject I have received help from many people. I am grateful to the ever-co-operative staff of the Dr. Williams's Library, to the Rev. W.M. Jacob and the late Mr. D. Jacobs, who sought out manuscript material for me, and to members of the Bacon family, whose ancestor's diary proved most illuminating. As a research student I was kindly invited to the homes of Canon M.M. Hennell, Dr. A.G. Newell, and Dr. Ann Saunders (nee Cox-Johnson), to discuss matters of mutual interest, and I have since benefited from conversation with Professor A. Pollard. Particular thanks are due to my colleagues, Dr. B.J. Atkinson, Dr. H. St. C. Cunningham and Professor D. Read for their comments on the manuscript at various stages of production, and to my research

Acknowledgements

supervisor, Mr. J.H.Y. Briggs, without whose patient
encouragement over many years this work would not
have been completed. The final copy was typed by
Miss Sheila Hawkins and Mrs. Barbara Holland and I
want them to know how much I appreciate their
constant forebearance and ready co-operation.
    Above all, I want to thank my parents for the
opportunities they have given me, and for their
unfailing love and support. This book is dedicated
to them.

Doreen M. Rosman   Rutherford College
                    University of Kent at Canterbury

PROLOGUE

> On one of its sides Victorian history is the
> story of the English mind employing the energy
> imparted by Evangelical conviction to rid
> itself of the restraints which Evangelicalism
> had laid on the senses and the intellect; on
> amusement, enjoyment, art; on curiosity, on
> criticism, on science. (G. M. Young)

A study entitled 'Evangelicals and Culture' must of
necessity begin with reference to Matthew Arnold's
Culture and Anarchy, a work which through its
scathing denunciation of mid-nineteenth century
nonconformity, has done much to establish the
legend of evangelical philistinism. Dissent of
his day, Arnold believed, encouraged 'a life of
jealousy of the Establishment, disputes, tea-
meetings, openings of chapels, sermons', a life
signally lacking in 'culture'.[1]
     Arnold defined culture as the pursuit of
total - not merely religious - perfection, and
claimed that it fostered an interest in 'the
development of all sides of our humanity'. It was
therefore incompatible with 'the over-development
of any one power', such as the moral sense, 'at
the expense of the rest'.[2] The truly cultured man,
he argued, was aware of 'the variety and fullness
of human existence', familiar with 'the best that
has been thought and said in the world', able
because of his breadth of vision to turn 'a stream
of fresh and free thought upon our stock notions
and habits ...'[3] The nonconformist environment
seemed to Arnold peculiarly unconducive to the
nurturing of culture thus defined. Indeed he
maintained that to be cultured a man had to be in
contact with 'the main current of national life',
which found its natural home within the established

1

church; dissenters who wilfully excluded themselves from the national establishment were by definition archetypally uncultured.

Arnold's description of dissent should not be dismissed as mere polemic unsupported by observation. As a school inspector he met numerous dissenters whose interests seemed to him more narrowly and exclusively religious than those of many Anglicans. While he may have been wrong to imply that their philistinism resulted from their churchmanship, his charge that nonconformists 'have developed one side of their humanity at the expense of all the others and have become incomplete and mutilated men in consequence' merits examination.4

So does the possibility that Arnold's charge was too narrow. Arnold focused his attack upon nonconformity because he believed that it epitomised the ills of his age, but other critics have similarly censured evangelical Anglicans for their narrow outlook on life. Was Evangelicalism, as Arnold's theory might seem to imply, any less philistine than dissent?5

Although Arnold was writing in the second half of the nineteenth century, his essay prompts questions which can appropriately be applied to evangelicalism of an earlier era, traditionally subject to similar criticism. Were evangelicals as Arnold and other detractors have suggested interested only in religion? How far did they accept non-religious interests as character-forming and life-enhancing? Were they willing to develop other facets of their personalities than the purely spiritual? Did they, as Arnold assumed, disregard the cultural heritage of their society in favour of a narrow sectarianism? Were they prepared to bring critical acumen to bear upon their own 'stock notions and habits' or did they despise such intellectual activity?...

These questions may give some indication of the scope of the word 'culture' in the title of this book. While not carrying the weight of meaning with which Arnold invested it, 'culture' is used here, in some respects as he used it, as an umbrella term: its primary reference is to literary, aesthetic and intellectual interests, but it denotes too an inquisitive and affirmative attitude to life as a whole.

* * * * * * * * * *

When G. M. Young claimed that evangelicalism
exercised a restraining influence upon 'the senses
and the intellect; on amusement, enjoyment, art;
on curiosity, on criticism, on science', he was
writing within a tradition which predated Arnold
and can be traced back to the earliest days of the
revival.[6] Particularly common was the allegation
that evangelical faith was antagonistic to intellectual activity: 'Pure METHODISM' complained an
anonymous writer in 1781, 'requires of its votaries
to commit themselves to the guidance of the Spirit,
with an utter contempt of reason and all human
learning'.[7] Equally common was the charge that
Methodists were killjoys despising even the most
reputable cultural pursuits. Thus according to
Sydney Smith

> The Methodists hate pleasure and amusements;
> no theatre, no cards, no dancing, no punchi-
> nello, no dancing dogs, no blind fiddlers;
> all the amusements of the rich and the poor
> must disappear wherever these gloomy people
> get a footing. It is not the abuse of
> pleasure which they attack; but the inter-
> spersion of pleasure, however much it is
> guarded by good sense and moderation; it is
> not only wicked to hear the licentious plays
> of Congreve, but wicked to hear Henry the Vth
> or the School for Scandal ...[8]

If many critics spoke primarily of Methodism,
their reproof was by no means restricted to the
connexions established by Wesley and the Countess
of Huntingdon. The term 'Methodist' was often used
generically to the intense annoyance of evangelical
Anglicans who shunned what they regarded as
Methodist excesses. But the same sort of criticism
was levelled specifically at them. Thus the
Edinburgh Review maintained that the Evangelical
system demanded the continual suppression of
intellectual questions.[9] Evangelical Anglicans were
themselves very conscious of such censure: 'Every
man of the world' wrote Hannah More, leading
Evangelical laywoman, 'naturally arrogates to
himself the superiority of understanding over every
religious man'.[10]
Those who moved away from Evangelicalism
frequently criticised the movement for disparaging
learning and the arts. W.E. Gladstone, tracing the
history of the Evangelical party, commented:

> It must be remembered that the massive
> learning which never wholly deserted the
> Church, and the preponderating share of
> purely intellectual force were never theirs,
> and perhaps were not in all cases adequately
> viewed among them.[11]

More forcefully, Mark Pattison, who had suffered a
strictly evangelical upbringing, argued that
evangelicalism 'insisted on a "vital Christianity",
as against the Christianity of books. Its instinct
was from the first against intelligence. No text
found more favour with it than "Not many wise, not
many learned"'.[12] In the next century another son
of evangelical parents, E. L. Woodward, claimed that
the evangelicals' weakness 'was on the intellectual
side', while A. V. Dicey, a descendant of Clapham,
noted that 'Evangelicals assuredly did not
exaggerate the value of the aesthetic side of human
nature, and the High Church movement, looked at
from one side, was a revolt against that underestimate of taste ...'[13]
    Even those who remained more consciously
within the evangelical tradition accepted and
perpetuated similar criticisms. Dicey's uncle,
James Stephen, praised much that he saw to be of
worth in 'The "Evangelical" Succession', but drew
attention to its failure to produce scholars or
authors of note. Indeed he suggested that the
Church of England had suffered during the
Evangelical ascendancy from 'intellectual barren-
ness' for

> her most popular teachers had not merely
> been satisfied to tread the narrow circle
> of the 'Evangelical' theology, but had
> exulted in that bondage as indicating
> their possession of a purer light than
> had visited the other ministers of the
> Gospel.[14]

The complaint that Stephen made of Anglican
evangelicalism, R. W. Dale, leading Congregationalist, made of dissent. Evangelicalism had much to
commend it, but it had destroyed the older puritan
type of Independency, which was characterised by a
'keen interest in theology ... a delight in books
and in intellectual pursuits of the severer kind'.
With the influx of revival converts 'the
intellectual earnestness ... disappeared'.[15]
Vision was limited for there was 'no eagerness to

take possession of the realms of Art, Science,
Literature, Politics, Commerce, Industry, in the
name of their true Sovereign and Prince'. Moreover,
although evangelical leaders were often 'men of
learning, men of great intellectual vigour and
keenness', they lacked a disinterested love of
truth: they cared for it not for its own sake but
merely as an instrument in conversion.[16]
   Dale's view is implicitly accepted by Donald
Davie, whose 1976 Clark lectures constitute one of
the most recent contributions to the study of
evangelicalism and culture. On the one hand
Professor Davie is concerned to reinstate eighteenth
century dissent, and even Methodism as propagated by
the Wesley brothers, as the locales of an important
and neglected form of genuine literary culture:
he rightly calls for further studies which will
analyse the hymns of Watts and Wesley not as an
isolated corpus of material but as part of the
literature of their day.[17] On the other hand he
accepts with little question the strictures levelled
against nineteenth century dissent by men such as
Arnold, of whose arrogance he is however properly
critical: dissent, he argues, sadly became 'as
philistine as the Church had always said it was'.
That evangelicalism in its Anglican form was
similarly tarnished is, he believes, fully
established: 'of the philistinism of the
Evangelicals there can be no doubt'.[18]
   Historians have widely concurred in such
labelling of evangelicalism. Thus the suggestion
that evangelicals were antagonistic to learning is
repeated by Geoffrey Faber who writes of 'the
stupid party', by J. H. Plumb who suggests that
'there was an anti-intellectual philistine quality'
about Methodism 'which attracted the dispossessed
but was dangerous for society ...', and by E P
Thompson who argues that Methodism taught men to
read but was 'a religion hostile to intellectual
inquiry and artistic values, which sadly abused
their intellectual trust'.[19] Even W. E. H. Lecky,
whose judicious and perceptive treatment of
evangelicalism holds its own against many more
recent works, concluded that intellectual incapacity
was one of the greatest weaknesses of the movement.[20]
   Given such concordance of opinion the
traditional depiction of evangelicalism as anti-
intellectual, ascetic, and philistine appears too
well established for effective challenge. Nevertheless there is evidence to suggest that it may be
open to dispute. J. A. Froude, brother of the

Tractarian leader and anti-ecclesiastical historian,
was surprised into respect for the Evangelical
family with whom he stayed in the summer of 1842,
commenting

> There was a quiet good sense, an
> intellectual breadth of feeling in this
> household, which to me, who had been bred
> up to despise Evangelicals as unreal and
> affected, was a startling surprise. I had
> looked down on Dissenters especially,
> as being vulgar among their other
> enormities; here were persons whose creed
> differed very little from that of the
> Calvinistic Methodists, yet they were easy,
> natural, and dignified ...[21]

That evangelicals and dissenters in particular have
suffered an unduly bad press from those 'bred up to
despise' them has been more recently stressed by
Valentine Cunningham who has shown how nonconformity, _Everywhere Spoken Against_, has been grossly
misrepresented by those who have relied on the
testimony of novelists. Other historians have
argued that evangelicals were no more antagonistic
towards cultural and intellectual interests than
other religious groups, while many have cited
individual instances of evangelical culture which
challenge the traditional picture.[22] Thus Amy
Cruse has described the Anglican evangelical leaders
as scholars and cultured men, a depiction accepted
by A. O. J. Cockshut who suggests that Clapham
parents encouraged 'an active love of the best
literary culture'. Similarly Owen Chadwick points
out that notwithstanding austerities in other
spheres the children of evangelical pastors 'were
given the run of good libraries' and 'were encouraged to varied interests of natural history or
music or good literature'. While not rejecting the
time-honoured charge of evangelical intellectual
naivety, Professor Chadwick implies that it needs
qualification, as does Charles Smyth who writes

> Where the Evangelical party was weak, by
> comparison for example with the Tractarians,
> was on the intellectual side. This is the
> more surprising, because it always contained
> a number of individuals of outstanding
> intellectual ability among the clergy and
> even among the laity. The simplicity and
> sincerity of the Evangelical piety captivated

many extremely able men in every walk of
life. It has also to be said, I think,
that the quality of such scholarship as
the Evangelical party did in fact produce
has been habitually under-estimated,
whether because it is out of date or
simply because it is forgotten.[24]

Implicit in such statements is the challenge
to test general allegations against the hard
evidence of particular and neglected sources.
Evangelicalism has suffered from the failure of
historians to give due attention to its special
literature which as Lecky and more recently Donald
Davie have pointed out, 'has scarcely obtained an
adequate recognition in literary history'.[25] It
has suffered too from a shortage of individualised
and localised studies which increasingly reveal the
fallacy of treating the movement as a homogeneous
entity. Biographies and group histories clearly
prove that not all evangelicals and not all
evangelical groups can be tarnished with the same
anti-intellectualist, philistine brush. Relying
on local source materials for his book, So Down to
Prayers: studies in English nonconformity 1780-
1920 (1977), Clyde Binfield points to the existence
of a cultured nonconformity all too frequently
ignored by earlier writers. Work such as his
exposes the need for a detailed examination of the
validity of the traditional thesis.

****

At least two distinct approaches can be
identified in the plethora of recent studies of
nineteenth century evangelicalism. A number of
historians, following G. M. Young, have been
concerned to examine the contribution of the
movement to the emergence of an identifiably
Victorian frame of mind. In The Call to Seriousness: the evangelical impact on the Victorians
(1976) Ian Bradley argues that evangelical
principles were peculiarly suited to the exigencies
of an increasingly complex industrial society,
within which they were therefore widely accepted.[26]
Kathleen Heasman similarly stresses the extensiveness of evangelical influence, which she suggests
operated to the benefit of society in philanthropic
activity.[27] While Ford K. Brown agrees that

7

evangelicalism was pervasive, he like John and
Barbara Hammond condemns it as pernicious,
attributing to evangelicals the responsibility for
all those nineteenth century developments which he
regards as most deplorable.[28] Notwithstanding
their differing assessments of the value of
evangelicalism, these historians unite in a common
aim, to analyse the influence of the supposed
Fathers of the Victorians upon their descendants.

Other historians have adopted a very different
approach. Rather than viewing evangelicalism as a
cause of social change, they have studied it as the
product of a particular environment. Moreover,
rather than assuming an initial distinction between
evangelicalism and the rest of society (which
according to Brown et. al. was ultimately to be
transformed for good or ill into the evangelical
image), they have stressed the similarities
between early evangelicals and their contemporaries.
Thus whereas evangelicalism was once regarded as a
reaction against eighteenth century life and
thought, now its congruity with the society which
gave it birth is increasingly recognised. The most
substantial work adopting this perspective is
W. R. Ward's Religion and Society in England 1790-
1850 (1972) which examines the way in which the
churches were affected by new social pressures
characteristic of society as a whole. For an
earlier period recent essayists have stressed the
continuity between Methodism and a traditional
folk-culture, under attack from the new mobility
of labour and the enclosure movement: in so doing
Arnold Rattenbury implicitly challenges the view
that evangelicalism was hostile to traditional
pleasures which he suggests found new expression
within it.[29] Whereas he concentrates on Methodism,
rooting this form of evangelicalism within the
folk-practice of the age, Haddon Willmer is
concerned primarily although not exclusively with
Evangelicalism, which he sees as an essentially
eighteenth century form of religion, growing out
of latitudinarianism, the basic assumptions of
which it shared and developed. The thesis of his
Hulsean prize essay 'Evangelicalism 1785-1835'
(1962) is that evangelical theology was not, as is
often assumed, simply a reaction against the age of
reason but on the contrary manifested many of its
traits.

This study builds upon the work and follows
the approach of such historians. If, as they
suggest, evangelicalism was a recognisable product

of the eighteenth century, reflecting the values
and traumas of society as a whole, then it seems
probable that its adherents shared the cultural and
intellectual attitudes of their contemporaries to a
far greater extent than Arnold and many other
writers have been prepared to admit. The chapters
that follow attempt to discover how far evangelicals
were influenced by and participated in the thought
and taste of their age.

****

The age in question is the forty years between
the death of Wesley and the death of Wilberforce.
Evangelicalism has suffered from the tendency of
adherents and denigrators alike to treat the
movement as an unchanging entity, assuming that the
attitudes of any one generation are typical of all
time. In contrast Michael Hennell has suggested
that the period 1770-1870 saw 'an increasing
strictness and rigidity with regard to "the world"',
as practices permitted by earlier evangelicals were
condemned by their successors.[30] His brief
prologomenon to the study of evangelicalism and
culture testifies to the need for a more detailed
examination of each generation's attitudes.
Sympathetic and unsympathetic historians alike
accept that the pre-Victorian generation was less
philistine than that which followed. The latter,
Ford K.Brown writes, 'had lost to a distressing
extent ... the taste, culture and intellectual
interest that had marked many of the dominant
Evangelicals of Wilberforce's generation' among
whom 'there was always a less bigotted Puritanism
than developed at the end of the reform period and
was a notable mark of the Bleak Age'.[31] His
admission provides both the incentive to and the
justification for a study of evangelicals and
culture between 1790 and 1833.

****

But what was meant by the designation
'evangelical' in this period? Historians concerned
to examine the contribution of evangelicals to
society have sometimes used the term very loosely,
thereby exaggerating evangelical influence. David
Newsome has criticised Ford K.Brown for describing
as 'peculiarly Evangelical sentiments and beliefs

which were certainly not peculiar to Evangelicals'
and for enlisting within an evangelical party all
who supported the organisations which the movement
spawned.[32] While it is probably true that most
evangelicals were involved in such societies, this
involvement by itself cannot be used as a test of
evangelical commitment: in the absence of
comparable bodies evangelical foundations gained -
and indeed solicited - the support of many who did
not profess evangelical belief but who could find
no other context for their religious activity.

Evangelical belief however cannot easily be
defined, for as Haddon Willmer has shown the
doctrines propounded by evangelicals in the late
eighteenth century conformed far more closely to
those of other churchmen than has always been
admitted. Twentieth century identification of
evangelicals by reference to a conservative approach
to Scripture and the proclamation of some form of
substitutionary atonement is of little use when
applied to an age in which neither characteristic
was peculiar to evangelicals. In many respects
evangelicals' claim to be simple 'Bible Christians'
was more a war-cry than a means of distinguishing
them from their contemporaries, many of whom also
identified revelation with the record, believed that
the Bible was self-authenticating and the Genesis
story historical and factual. Moreover, non-
evangelicals such as the natural theologian William
Paley stressed the sacrificial character of Christ's
death, and in a sermon on 'The efficacy of the
death of Christ' quoted numerous Biblical texts
supportive of this view.[33]

Nevertheless some doctrinal differentiation
between evangelicals and their contemporaries can
be attempted for the former gave far more weight to
original sin and the need for redemption than did
Paley and other non-evangelical Christians.
Evangelicalism centred upon soteriology and its
soteriology centred upon the Cross. Thus in 1811
Charles Simeon, the most influential of all
Evangelical clergymen, entitled a university
address 'Christ crucified, or evangelical religion
described', and proposed that the description
'evangelical' could only properly be applied to
those who like St. Paul 'determined not to know
anything among you, save Jesus Christ and him
crucified'.[34]

Simeon would not have denied that others
preached about the atonement, but he was critical of
the nature and emphasis of their preaching. Arguing

against salvation by works, Paley pointed out that
even the best of men were painfully aware of the
selfishness of their motives and the poverty of
their service: 'all men stand in need of a redeemer'
and the Scriptural teaching that God had met this
need was 'much more satisfactory' than uncertain
reliance upon human merit.[35] With all this
evangelicals could agree but their belief was
expressed in much starker terms. Rather than
arguing that men could not be sure that they
deserved heaven, evangelicals maintained that they
were positively bad, estranged from God and under
his condemnation: through the death of Christ
individuals were not only freed from the guilt of
their sin and thereby admitted to heaven, but were
also brought into a restored relationship with God
that profoundly affected their immediate lifestyle.
Paley was concerned that men should live moral and
godly lives but he did not on the whole relate this
demand to his belief about the atonement: the
death of Christ was for him primarily the means of
facilitating man's entrance to heaven. In contrast
the Cross was for evangelicals the lynchpin of
their faith, affecting not only their future but
their present state, constraining them to that
obedience which they believed would lead to
increasing holiness. Whereas redemption was for
Paley a transaction within the godhead, efficacious
whether or not men know of it, for evangelicals it
was a potentially present experience demanding
personal response.

It followed that evangelicals were characterised by a belief in conversion - from estrangement
into relationship. But conversion was not necessarily instantaneous. The biographies of Anglican
evangelicals and old dissenters reveal that many
never claimed the sudden experience of religious
certainty, so lauded within early Methodism. On
the contrary they agonised over months and years
wondering if they were truly Christian and
eventually attained peace of mind in the gradual
awareness that they were manifesting those fruits
of the Spirit, which they regarded as the only
proof of true conversion.[36] Their doctrine was
again articulated by Simeon who explicitly
repudiated the allegations

> that we require a _sudden_ impulse of the
> Holy Spirit ... to convert the soul to
> God; and that we require this change to
> be so sensibly and perceptibly wrought

11

that the subject of it shall be able to
specify the day and hour when it took
place ... It may be so gradual that the
growth of it, like the seed in the parable,
shall at no time be particularly visible,
either to the observation of others, or to
the person's own mind...[37]

Nevertheless Simeon insisted that conversion,
whether a recognisable or imperceptible experience,
instantaneous or gradual, was an essential part of
the spiritual progress of all men. Herein he
differed from Paley who maintained that while some
men, including some churchgoers, needed to be
converted, conversion was not necessary for all.[38]

The disagreement over the universal need for
conversion found its focus within Anglican circles
in a protracted debate on baptismal regeneration
which spanned much of the second decade of the
nineteenth century. In an attempt to refute
highchurch affirmations some Evangelicals lapsed
into negative and minimalising language.[39] Others
however stressed the value of baptism, agreed that
it could sometimes effect the new birth, and
challenged the highchurchmen only in so far as they
implied that this automatically took place. The
sacraments, one writer concluded, should be highly
esteemed but 'popish error' should be avoided.[40]
This aptly sums up evangelical views on Holy
Communion, for both Evangelical and dissenting
writings reveal a concern for proper preparation
prior to receiving the sacrament and an awesome
appreciation of its value and significance. On
the other hand just as the atonement was not central
to Paley's teaching, so sacramental practice was
not central to that of evangelicals: there are
comparatively few references to the Lord's Supper
in the first edition of Simeon's multi-volume set
of sermon outlines, Horae Homileticae, and no sermon
is included on the most detailed New Testament
exposition of the sacrament, 1 Corinthians xi.[41]
Evangelicals admitted that in practice the Lord's
Supper was a peculiarly effective means of grace,
but they had no doubt that it was but one of a
number of means that the Spirit of God might use.[42]

It was this emphasis upon the activity of the
Spirit that most obviously differentiated
evangelicals' beliefs from those of their fellows.
While evangelical Anglicans by no means disregarded
and in some cases highly valued the ordinances –
and also the order – of the established church, they

refused to limit the Spirit, believing that in the essential converting and nurturing of each individual he used other instruments alongside the discipline and sacraments of the Church of England. Even in the frenzied years following the French revolution when Evangelicals consciously eschewed the irregularity of some of their forebears and became highly solicitous of church order, they still co-operated with only slight qualm with dissenters in the interdenominational societies which they believed to be the work of the Holy Spirit.

Their contemporaries certainly regarded a marked interest in the activity of the Holy Spirit as a distinguishing feature of early evangelicalism. The term 'fundamentalist' characterising evangelicals by their approach to Scripture dates only from the 1920s. Older synonyms such as 'enthusiastic' define by reference to the Spirit rather than the Word. Indeed evangelicals' approach to the Bible itself can best be differentiated from that of others by reference to their belief in the Spirit. In no doubt that the Holy Spirit guided the sincere reader of the Old and New Testaments, they assumed with the early nonconformists that 'the Lord hath yet more truth and light to break forth from his Word'. Thus William Carey, the first Baptist missionary, was galvanised by the challenge 'Go ye into all the world', neglected by previous generations. Similarly John Wesley came to believe that the Word was challenging the existing formularies and practices of the Church through which orthodox Anglicans assumed it was properly expressed. Scripture was for Carey and Wesley as for the latter 'the truth once and for all delivered to the saints' but it was dynamic as well as authoritative.

Their firm conviction in the work of the Spirit gave rise to both the worst and the best in evangelicalism. On the one hand believing in the personalised guidance of the Holy Spirit evangelicals tended to assume that the Spirit had directed them into all truth and that others must deliberately be setting themselves up against God. The title of Wilberforce's famous book, <u>A Practical View of the Prevailing Religious System of Professed Christians in the Higher and Middle Classes of this Country contrasted with Real Christianity</u> (1797), is indicative both of evangelical exclusiveness and of the lack of tact which was sadly characteristic of much evangelical apologetic. On the other hand evangelicals' belief

in the Spirit carried with it a concern for spirituality which could result in a way of life admired
even by those who despised their doctrine. 'If the
test was personal holiness', J.A. Froude wrote of
the family who so impressed him in 1842, 'I for my
own part had never yet fallen in with any human
beings in whose actions and conversation the Spirit
of Christ was more visibly present'.[43] Well might
Hannah More speak of 'those writers, whom it is the
fashion to call evangelical; but which you and I
had rather distinguish by the name of spiritual'.[44]

While her statement reinforces a definition of
evangelicalism which lays stress upon an interest
in the work of the Holy Spirit, it introduces
further complications. Hannah More was writing to
Alexander Knox, a man who with his friend Bishop
Jebb of Limerick has been described as a forerunner
of the Oxford Movement: holding decidedly Catholic
views on church and sacraments, they were highly
critical both of individual evangelicals and of
evangelical dogmatic theology.[45] But they were
among a number of highchurchmen intimate with
evangelicals: the effective founder of the Clapham
community, Henry Thornton, appointed the
conservative highchurchman Robert Inglis as guardian
of his children and, prior to the premature death
of John Bowdler, had hoped that this son of a
highchurch family might worthily carry on the
Clapham tradition.[46] Just because evangelicals laid
such emphasis upon spirituality they were likely to
establish close relations with others who shared
this preoccupation: 'Though doubtless, in certain
points, I entertain a view different from them'
wrote Knox, 'I say now, what I should desire to
say on my deathbed, sit mea anima cum istis'.[47]

The close association between these
recognised highchurchmen and the Clapham sect
provides a timely warning to any historian who
attempts to define evangelicalism too rigidly. If
the imprecise use of terminology misrepresents so
too does the overprecise use of that same language.
The history of opinion does not permit categoric
classification. The preceding description of
characteristic evangelical belief must serve as a
guide rather than a plumbline, for some who do not
altogether conform to the general pattern were
clearly included by association within the
evangelical fold.

On the other hand it can readily be admitted
that some were more centrally within that fold than
others. In an analysis of evangelical attitudes it

seems appropriate to restrict discussion to those
who saw themselves and have been seen over a
considerable period of time as being unquestionably
within the evangelical tradition. In the discussion
that follows it is assumed on doctrinal grounds that
at this time all dissenters save Quakers and
Unitarians were evangelical, and periodicals
representing mainstream dissent constitute a major
primary source. Evangelical Quakers, most notably
J. J. Gurney, can easily be identified, for unlike
other Friends they were active in evangelical
organisations such as the Bible Society. The
Anglicans are the most difficult to distinguish:
in practice the title 'Evangelical' will be used
primarily of those who were accorded obituaries in
the recognised Evangelical periodicals and who have
featured in the old hagiographical histories which
evangelical writers have from time to time produced
for the edification of the faithful. Uncritical
though these sometimes are, they provide an unparalleled guide to those whom through the ages it
has been 'the fashion to call evangelical ...'.

NOTES

   1. M. Arnold, Culture and Anarchy (1869, C.U.P.
edn. 1960), p. 58.
   2. Ibid., p. 48.
   3. Ibid., pp. 6, 14.
   4. Ibid., p. 11.
   5. In accordance with the general convention
'evangelical' and 'evangelicalism' are used as
generic terms while 'Evangelical' and 'Evangelicalism' refer to the Anglican branch of the movement.
   6. G. M. Young, Victorian England, Portrait of
an Age (1936, 1966 edn.), p. 5.
   7. Quoted A. M. Lyles, Methodism Mocked (1960),
p. 23.
   8. Edinburgh Review, xi (1808), p. 357.
   9. Ibid., lii (1831), p. 449.
   10. H. More, Thoughts on the Manners of the
Great (1798), Works (1834 edn.), ii, p. 269.
   11. W. E. Gladstone, 'The Evangelical Movement;
its parentage, progress, and issue', British
Quarterly Review, lxx (1879), p. 7.
   12. M. Pattison, 'Learning in the Church of
England' (1863), Essays ed. Nettleship (1889), ii,
p. 268.
   13. E. L. Woodward, The Age of Reform 1815-1870
(1938, 2nd edn. 1962), p. 504; A. V. Dicey, Lectures
on the Relation between Law and Public Opinion in

England (1905), p. 404.

14. J. Stephen, Essays in Ecclesiastical Biography (1849), ii, pp. 169-72.

15. R.W. Dale, History of English Congregationalism (1907), pp. 590-91.

16. R.W. Dale, The Old Evangelicalism and the New (1889), pp. 19-20.

17. D. Davie, A Gathered Church, The literature of the English dissenting interest, 1700-1930 (1978), lectures ii and iii.

18. Ibid., pp. 56-58, 77-82.

19. G. Faber, Oxford Apostles (1933, 2nd edn. 1936), p. 74; J.H. Plumb, England in the Eighteenth Century (1950), p. 95; E.P. Thompson, The Making of the English Working Class (1963, Penguin edn. 1970), p. 44.

20. W.E.H. Lecky, A History of England in the Eighteenth Century (1878-90, 1913 edn.), iii, pp. 150-52.

21. J.A. Froude, Short Studies on Great Subjects (1894 edn.), iv, p. 295.

22. For comparison with others see for example L.E. Elliott-Binns, The Early Evangelicals, a religious and social study (1953), p. 434; G. Best, 'Evangelicalism and the Victorians' in A. Symondson (ed.), The Victorian Crisis of Faith (1970), p. 50.

23. A. Cruse, The Englishman and his Books in the Early Nineteenth Century (1930), p. 71; A.O.J. Cockshut, Truth to Life: the art of biography in the nineteenth century (1974), p. 73.

24. O. Chadwick, The Victorian Church, i (1966), pp. 444, 450-51; C. Smyth, 'The Evangelical Discipline' in H. Grisewood (ed.), Ideas and Beliefs of the Victorians (1949, 1966 edn.), p. 102.

25. Lecky, op. cit., iii, p. 120.

26. Bradley, op. cit., p. 33.

27. K. Heasman, Evangelicals in Action, an appraisal of their social work in the Victorian era (1962).

28. F.K. Brown, Fathers of the Victorians (1961); J. and B. Hammond, The Town Labourer 1760-1832 (1917), chs. x and xi.

29. A. Rattenbury, 'Methodism, Commonsense and Coincidences of 1751', paper read at a conference on 'The Working Class and Leisure: class expression and/or social control', University of Sussex, November 1975. Cf. from the same conference J. Rule, 'Methodism and Recreational Conflict in West Cornwall'. Revised versions can be found in E. and S. Yeo (eds.), Popular Culture and

Class Conflict (1981) and R.D. Storch (ed.),
Popular Culture and Custom in Nineteenth Century
England (1982) respectively.
30. M.M. Hennell, 'Evangelicalism and Worldliness 1770-1870' in G. Cuming and D. Baker (eds.),
Popular Belief and Practice, Studies in Church
History, viii (1972), p. 229.
31. F.K. Brown, op. cit., pp, 6, 404.
32. D. Newsome, 'Fathers and Sons', Historical
Journal, vi (1963), p. 298.
33. The Works of William Paley D.D. (1838,
new edn. 1842), pp. 772-74.
34. A. Pollard (ed.), Let Wisdom Judge,
University addresses and sermon outlines by Charles
Simeon (1959), p. 110.
35. Paley, op. cit., pp. 775-77.
36. See for example the biographies of such
notable Evangelicals as Hannah More, William
Wilberforce and Zachary Macaulay, and among
dissenters, I. Taylor (ed.), The Family Pen,
Memorials ... of the Taylor Family (1867), E.R.
Conder, Josiah Conder, a memoir (1857). Josiah
Conder was editor of the dissenting Eclectic Review
which maintained 'we would not attempt to fix the
date of any man's conversion', ii series xviii
(1822), p. 489. A similar stance was maintained
in the more enthusiastic Evangelical Magazine, ii
series vi (1828), p. 477, where it was stressed
against Calvinist assertion that no-one could be
sure that he possessed an 'interest in Christ'
until his faith had been tested by its fruits.
This belief led to a widespread suspicion of
deathbed conversions which, while sometimes
genuine, could not be so proved, e.g. EM, i series
xix (1811), p. 167; ii series ii (1824), p. 438.
37. Pollard (ed.), op. cit., 'On the New
Birth', p. 51.
38. Paley, op. cit., 'On the doctrine of
conversion', pp. 737-42.
39. See for example the discussions in the
Evangelical periodical the Christian Observer, xv
(1816), p. 172, 228ff.; xvi (1817), p. 309.
40. Ibid., xiv (1815), p. 286. Cf. xi (1812),
p. 370.
41. An omission belatedly rectified by three
sermons in the 1832-33 edn.
42. See for example CO, xii (1813), p. 518
where a reviewer criticised a highchurchman for
attributing 'exclusively to the Lord's Supper'
'that ... which though eminently due to it, is still
shared in common by every other act of worship'.

43. Froude, op. cit., iv, pp. 296-97.

44. W. Roberts, Memoirs of the Life and Correspondence of Mrs. Hannah More (2nd edn. 1834), iii, p. 238.

45. Y. Brilioth, The Anglican Revival, studies in the Oxford Movement (1925), ch. iv; CO, xxxiv (1834), pp. 691ff.

46. S. Meacham, Henry Thornton of Clapham (1964), pp. 57-58, 183.

47. Brilioth, op. cit., pp. 39-40.

Chapter One

THE STORY OF EVANGELICALISM 1790-1833

The dates chosen to demarcate the different periods
of evangelical history are often arbitrary, used
more for the historian's convenience than to reflect
any definite watershed. As soon as any attempt is
made epigrammatically to entitle an age, it becomes
evident that supposedly distinguishing characteristics were equally prevalent in the following era.[1]
Moreover as W. L. Burn has stressed, any succinct
description of a period 'suffers from being pre-
selected from a particular angle of vision', a
complaint which can be levelled against the practice
of periodisation itself.[2] On the other hand it is
significant that most who have attempted, however
tentatively, to distinguish between the different
phases of evangelical development, have treated the
years between the 1790s and the 1820s and '30s as
a distinct unit. More than most it was a time that
can meaningfully be differentiated from that which
went before and that which followed.

The death in 1791 of John Wesley, the most
dominant figure of the eighteenth century revival,
inevitably marked the end of an era: Methodism
could not but enter a new phase of development,
signified by the adoption of an oligarchic rather
than a monarchical form of government. The Countess
of Huntingdon died in the same year as in 1793 did
the Rev. John Berridge, one of the last great
exponents of an irregularity that was rapidly becoming less common. New leaders who were to dominate
the evangelical stage for the next thirty years were
coming into prominence: the community at Clapham
dates from 1792 in which year Henry Thornton bought
a house and invited Wilberforce to live with him,
while John Venn with great trepidation accepted the
living; Hannah More, who had been emerging into
evangelical conviction during the late 1780s, had

begun her educational work at Cheddar and in 1793
published the first of her many religious tracts
for the poor, a signal event in the history of
popular literature; in 1790 Charles Simeon held
his first sermon class; Joseph Hughes, doyen of
the future Bible Society, was a youthful tutor at
Bristol Baptist College...
        More significantly the 1790s marked a new
expansiveness of evangelicalism and hence a new
co-ordination of evangelical effort. The hyper-
Calvinism of old dissent which had precluded any
interest in evangelism was seriously challenged
when in 1785 a leading Baptist Andrew Fuller
published The Gospel Worthy of All Acceptation.[3]
With the preaching of moderate Calvinism came the
birth of the modern missionary movement: the
Baptist Missionary Society was founded in 1792 and
the Missionary Society (later known as the London
Missionary Society) in 1795. As the vision grew of
extended evangelistic activity, at home and abroad,
so it became necessary to pool resources to achieve
that vision. Hence the setting up of bodies at
county and national level to give effect to the
aspirations of previously localised groups. The
activities of newly formed county associations
and itinerant societies were reported in the
Evangelical Magazine, founded in 1793 and itself
an expression of growing consciousness that
evangelicalism was a nationwide movement. Hand in
hand with expansion and co-ordination went an
increased systematization of evangelical charity.
The Evangelical Magazine recorded the establishment
of numerous organisations concerned with every
aspect of human welfare. The great age of
evangelical societies dates back to the 1790s.
        While the 'nineties were thus characterised by
a proliferation of undenominational activity, they
saw too a new hardening of denominational divisions.
W.R.Ward has argued that in the face of social
divisiveness and the dispersion of authority
consequent upon revolutionary influence, church
leaders sought to consolidate their own position by
asserting control over undenominational institutions
such as Sunday Schools and itinerant societies.[4]
Hence arose a new denominationalism. The belief
that Church and State as in France would stand or
fall together created in Anglicans a stronger
allegiance to the establishment while orthodox
dissenters suffered disparagement by association,
on account of the political and religious radicalism
of Unitarians. New problems arose as the first

heady days of the revival gave way to a more sober period of consolidation. Allegiance to a church and disregard of its discipline could not coexist interminably. Thus it became increasingly difficult for Wesleyanism to masquerade as a society within the established church and Conference moved cautiously but expediently towards effectual separation.[5] Evangelical Anglicans too began to define their loyalties more exactly, and the once common, but never universal, tendency towards irregularity became a thing of the past: far from scorning the limitations placed by the parish structure upon the salvation of souls, as had Berridge, the new Evangelical leaders were scrupulous in their ecclesiastical obedience.[6]

The growth of denominational consciousness was accompanied by the foundation of yet more societies. Whereas in the early days of the revival some evangelicals had chafed against denominational limitations, as time went on there was increasing awareness of the inadequacies of undenominational bodies: beliefs held dear by particular groups were neglected, in some cases challenged. Thus, Anglican evangelicals felt that there was need for a missionary society and a periodical which would propagate both Anglican and evangelical principles, founding in 1799 the Society for Missions to Africa and the East (later the Church Missionary Society) and in 1802 the Christian Observer.[7] Similarly in 1809 a group of Baptists, irritated by the assertion of paedobaptist principles in the Evangelical Magazine, established the Baptist Magazine.[8] The early undenominational foundations, the Missionary Society and the Evangelical Magazine, came increasingly under Independent leadership and ceased to represent the whole gamut of evangelicalism.

The pages of the latter provide ample evidence of the divisions that continued to beset the evangelical world. The bitterness evoked by the Calvinist controversy of the 1770s had long since died down and evangelicals of different schools were prepared to recognise the faith of others. Nevertheless the debate over hyperCalvinism, moderate Calvinism and Arminianism flourished well into the new century. Much space was accorded too to the continuing argument concerning the proper subjects and mode of baptism. Dissenting dislike of Anglicanism was reinforced by the activities of Lord Sidmouth who attempted to restrict dissenting religious liberty, and of individual clergymen and

magistrates who refused to marry or bury dissenters, were often unwilling to grant licences to dissent- ing preachers, and dealt leniently with offenders who stormed dissenting meeting houses and disrupted services. While Anglican evangelicals did not condone such activities they nevertheless sometimes failed to appreciate that dissenters still had a conscientious objection to establishment and casti- gated them for wilfully inciting others to commit the sin of schism. The growing divergence between the two is clearly revealed in the responses to James Bean's book Zeal without Innovation which received a largely favourable review from the Christian Observer but was criticised by the Evangelical Magazine and the Eclectic Review for misrepresenting dissent.[9] The Eclectic Review, designed as an evangelical counterpart of the Edinburgh and Quarterly Reviews, was founded in 1805 on non-party principles but its sponsors soon found that dissenters would only support them on terms which Anglicans found unacceptable. Dis- claiming their predecessors' belief that they were bound to neutrality on controversial issues, the editors of the second series, launched in 1814, proclaimed 'The proper exercise of charity and candour, is found in the maintenance not in the concealment of a conscientious difference of opinion'.[10]
    Nevertheless the undenominational spirit was far from dead for there was much co-operation between evangelicals of different theological, political and ecclesiastical persuasions. Thus one later commentator recorded that

    For many years it was the habit of the
    Secretaries of some of the chief Missionary
    Societies, the Church Missionary, the
    London, the Wesleyan, to meet at one another's
    offices. They then mutually imparted the
    result of their experience, in the conduct
    of their Missions, in the selection and
    training of Missionary Candidates, and the
    course to be pursued with heathen converts.
    They discussed the methods of avoiding
    collision at home, or any matter which might
    excite jealousy or discontent with their own
    Society in the minds of their Missionaries
    abroad. They were all engaged in one
    great work...[11]

The Story of Evangelicalism 1790-1833

A reading of evangelical wills and subscription
lists reveals that many supported missionary
societies other than those sponsored by their own
denomination, while speakers from other communions
were welcomed to the rostrums at annual meetings.[12]
The Christian Observer, Evangelical and Methodist
Magazines were wide ranging in their reports of
missionary meetings and activities, by no means
restricting their coverage to those societies with
which they were most intimately connected.

New undenominational societies continued to
be founded alongside the more denominationally
orientated bodies: thus 1804 marked the establishment of the Bible Society, the most notable expression of evangelical unity in mission. Like the
missionary societies, the BFBS co-operated very
closely with its continental counterparts, utilising
not only Protestant but Catholic agents to expedite
the effective distribution of the Scriptures.
For in this campaign, as in that to abolish the
slave trade and slavery, early nineteenth century
evangelicals proved to be essentially pragmatic:
they sought and acquired influential patronage,
mobilised mass support by constructing a network
of local auxiliaries, and co-operated with any who
shared their aims regardless of belief.

The resulting success of such campaigns gave
rise to an optimism and excitement abundantly
reflected in eschatological expectation. Apocalyptic
studies were of perennial interest throughout this
period in circles far wider than the purely
evangelical, as men attempted with fearful fascination to deduce the cosmic significance of the
cataclysmic events in France, and of the subsequent
dominance of Napoleon, contender with the Pope for
the popular title of anti-Christ.[13] Britain's
stance against this embodiment of evil gave rise to
much patriotic exultation. The Evangelical Magazine
of 1810 proclaimed ecstatically

> Thou art the barrier alone that stays the
> ravages of military despotism, and puts bounds
> to insatiable ambition!   Like the rocks
> which encircle thy sea-girt shores, against
> thee the rage of Corsican malignity foams,
> dashes, and impotently retires.[14]

If such eulogistic invocation was in part an
expression of relief after the paralysing fear of
imminent invasion which had occasioned fasts and
prayer meetings during 1803, it also reflected the

belief that God was graciously at work using the
British as his chosen people. No period in British
history, the same writer continued, had been more
auspicious than the last ten years: godliness had
substantially increased at home, the slave trade had
been abolished, and Britain had led the way in the
diffusion of light and truth throughout the world.
The unprecedented expansion of Christian preaching
and activity confirmed evangelicals in the common
belief that mankind was living through the last
days. In 1808 the Christian Observer devoted many
of its leading articles to eschatological inquiry
while other periodicals likewise engaged in apocalyptic arithmetic and prophetic interpretation,
seeing in the events of the day the long-expected
fulfilment of biblical predictions concerning the
final establishment of the kingdom.

     As time went on however evangelical confidence
and optimism became tarnished, for within the
churches, as within the nation at large, euphoria
was replaced by depression, as victory was followed
by hardship. The commercial crisis of 1825, the
cholera epidemics of the early 'thirties seemed to
evangelicals clearly to prove that the British were
no longer in God's good books. On the contrary
an Evangelical Magazine contributor of 1831, who
listed the national sins of a people who were free
and highly favoured but not godly, expressed no
surprise that they should be suffering the out-
workings of divine judgment. [15]   While the short-
comings he cited were those of the nation at large,
evangelicals were uneasily aware that they were
not themselves exempt from censure. Success
appeared to have taken its toll of the original
spirit of the movement: by the 1820s respectability
and even a measure of respect had been achieved,
but in consequence there was widespread fear that
the distinctiveness of evangelicalism had been
diluted, that the religious were becoming contam-
inated by worldliness, that the impetus of the
revival had been lost. Such unease prompted a
yearning for former glories and many began to look
for further revival: prayer meetings were held
to this end, articles on the subject proliferated
in the Evangelical Magazine of 1828 and 1829, and
considerable attention was paid to reports of
contemporary American awakenings.

     Their dissatisfaction led evangelicals to
exult less over what they believed God had
achieved through them, and to worry more about the
massive task that lay ahead. The continent was

still predominantly Catholic while European Protestants seemed to evangelicals to be mere Socinians.
Horrified by the state of the European churches
which he visited in 1816, the affluent and influential Scottish itinerant preacher, Robert Haldane,
joined with an enthusiastic young patrician, Henry
Drummond, to form a Continental Society for the
evangelisation of Europe. At home too the supposed
prevalence of Socinianism was a cause for concern,
while the campaign for Catholic emancipation, which
spanned the 1820s, evoked much latent anti-Catholic
feeling.[16] In 1827 the British Reformation Society
was formed to convert Catholics. In England however
the main evangelistic task was not to counteract
beliefs regarded as unchristian but to reach the
unchurched millions. Faced with the mushrooming
growth of industrial towns and above all of London,
evangelicals became aware that many, even in their
own land, had never heard the gospel. In 1826/27
the Evangelical Magazine contained articles 'On the
present state of our large cities', while a Christian Instruction Society was formed with the aim
of christianising the masses by systematic house-
to-house visitation and the distribution of Christian literature. Immense though the task was, some
evangelicals believed in the self-critical temper
of the late 1820s that they had been culpably
indolent in failing to convert the nation.[17]
    The pessimism of this period like the euphoria
of earlier decades was reflected in apocalyptic
studies. Ian Rennie has pointed to the emergence
of a less optimistic eschatology which maintained
that the last days would be marked not by evangelistic success but by the decline of the church;
the millenial period of Christian victory, far from
heralding the second coming, as the older post-
millenialists had argued, would only be inaugurated
when the Lord returned. According to the new
premillenialist school the second advent would
precede the millenium.[18] The propagation of these
beliefs was both the product and the cause of an
intensified interest in Biblical prophecy, manifested in periodical discussions and in the summon-
ing in 1826 of the first of a series of annual
conferences at Albury, the home of Henry Drummond.[19]
But while the premillenial scheme became increasingly acceptable, there was considerable criticism of
the eschatological obsessions of some of its proponents. Some who attended the first Albury
conference refused later invitations.[20] Edward
Bickersteth, secretary of the CMS, who was himself

to adopt premillenial beliefs, was among those to
criticise the spirit in which they were promulgated:

> Men get full of their own views, and press
> them as all-essential, and speak as positively
> as if futurity were as open to them as what
> is past; and then others speak publicly
> against them; and so the dividing spirit
> of the age increases and spreads.[21]

Charles Simeon and the Christian Observer protested
that undue attention was devoted to prophecy at the
cost of central doctrines of the faith, while even
the Evangelical Magazine, which had devoted much
space to such discussions, reduced its coverage in
the years after 1829. Its contributors contrasted
the 'wild effusions' of the Albury school with
'sound and temperate' discourses on the subject,
which it, like Simeon and the Christian Observer,
continued to regard as proper.[22]
    Disagreements over eschatology were part of a
wider and more fundamental division of evangelical
opinion over the nature of present Christian
activity, a matter for much debate as men sought
to diagnose and counteract the acknowledged worldliness of the movement. Albury participants were
among those who laid the blame upon pragmatic
policies which they equated with worldly compromise:
the premillenialist belief that Christ would
personally supervise the evangelisation of the
world was but one expression of the growing conviction that divine sovereignty had been unduly sub-
ordinated to human endeavour, faith to human
machination. Most vocal exponent of such views
and outspoken critic of evangelical worldliness was
the Scot, Edward Irving, intimate of Albury,
minister of the metropolitan Caledonian church and,
paradoxically, the most popular preacher in
fashionable London. In his notorious LMS sermon
of May 1824 Irving protested

> This is the age of expediency, both in the
> Church and out of the Church; and all
> institutions are modelled upon the principles
> of expediency, and carried into effect by
> the rules of prudence. I remember, in this
> metropolis, to have heard it uttered with
> great applause in a public meeting, where the
> heads and leaders of the religious world were
> present, 'If I were asked what was the
> first qualification for a Missionary, I

> would say, prudence; and what the second?
> Prudence; and what the third? Still
> I would answer, Prudence'. I trembled
> while I heard, not with indignation but with
> horror and apprehension, what the end would
> be of a spirit, which I have since found
> to be the presiding genius of our activity...[23]

The antithesis of such worldly wisdom seemed
to be renewed reliance upon divine provision.
Irving challenged Christian missionaries to obey
the dominical command, going out without 'purse
or scrip' in reliance upon the true weapons of
Christian warfare which were 'not carnal, but
spiritual'.[24] In accordance with similar beliefs
some of Irving's contemporaries in due course
formed Brethren assemblies and encouraged 'faith
missions', attempts to eschew institutionalisation
and to emulate the supposed direct dependence upon
God of the early church.[25] More immediately such
thinking proved congenial to the emergence of a
short-lived charismatic revival. Those present
at the Albury conference of July 1830 concluded that
they should pray for the gifts of the Spirit, and
find out more about those already manifested in
some Scottish congregations. The following year
members of Irving's congregation and others began
to speak in tongues and to 'prophesy', practices
which Irving eventually felt bound to permit within
the context of church services, fearing that the
repudiation of the revival for which he had prayed
would constitute disobedience.[26]
Few concurred in his belief that this was the
desired revival. The great had proved to be fickle
supporters and had ceased to attend his ministry in
any great number when the Caledonian church had
moved to Regent Square in 1827. If the excessive
length of services deterred many from regular
attendance, almost all sympathy was forfeited by
the indecorum of the 1830s. Charismatic practice
both within and without Irvingite circles was
widely disapproved, the evangelical press responding
with uniform hostility to glossolalia and the
supposed miraculous healing of Miss Fancourt.[27]
In May 1832 the London Presbytery ruled that Irving
had violated the trust deed by allowing unauthorised
persons to participate in services, and had thus
shown himself unfit to be minister of Regent Square
Church. A year later his views on the peccability
of Christ were deemed heretical and he was defrocked,
dying shortly afterwards, discredited within the

orthodox evangelical world and demoted even by his
own newly formed Catholic Apostolic Church to which
pentecostal practice was now largely confined.[28]
    Charismatic activity was but one response to
the feared worldly expediency of evangelicalism.
Of far greater moment was the attempt to stop the
rot by a more rigid definition of doctrine which
would serve to differentiate evangelicals from
others and hence make the movement more exclusive.
Outraged by the theological liberalism which he had
encountered in Geneva, Robert Haldane and his
nephew Alexander, future mentor of Lord Shaftesbury,
campaigned vigorously to prevent similar developments
in Britain.
    The first major controversy arose over the
continental circulation of Bibles containing the
Apocrypha.[29]   The Bible Society committee had long
been uneasy about apparently sanctioning the Catholic belief that the Apocryphal books were as
inspired and authoritative as those which Protestants
recognised as canonical. On the other hand they
acknowledged that, since European Protestants and
Catholics alike expected Bibles to include the
Apocrypha, only such Bibles would prove acceptable
to the continental Bible societies and their clients.
Distribution of the Apocrypha seemed a small, if
distasteful, price to pay for the widespread
dissemination of the Scriptures. The 1820s saw
protracted discussions and the passing and
rescinding of numerous motions on the subject. A
compromise between principle and expediency was
reached in 1824 when the decision was taken to
refuse grants for the publication of Bibles in which
canon and Apocrypha were intermixed, but to support
the production of Bibles in which the Apocryphal
books were grouped together at the end. British
grants, however, were to be spent exclusively on
the canonical part of the work.
    Such an attempt casuistically to salve
consciences satisfied no-one. The Edinburgh auxiliary argued that the Apocrypha should in no
circumstances be circulated. In contrast twenty-
six Cambridge men, including Charles Simeon, the
patriarchal pamphleteer Legh Richmond, and the
future CMS secretary Henry Venn, maintained that the
new measures violated the society's traditional
principle of uniting with other Christian efforts.
The matter was eventually brought before a special
committee which deferred to the anti-Apocryphal
views of the society's President, Lord Teignmouth:
a resolution was passed that all Bibles printed

partially or totally at the Society's expense at
home or abroad should be issued bound without the
Apocrypha. Despite this victory the Edinburgh auxiliary
was still not satisfied: it demanded that its
opponents should confess that they had violated a
fundamental principle, that the executive should be
replaced and that the BFBS should have no further
dealings with continental societies which continued
to circulate the Apocrypha. The failure of such
efforts caused the secession of most Scottish
auxiliaries, while the virulence of the campaign
waged by the Edinburgh society left a residue of
much hard feeling even among those glad that the
BFBS no longer condoned the production of the
Apocrypha. The Scotsmen had refused to concede
the good faith of those who favoured a course of
action different from theirs, castigating their
opponents as 'Apocrypha-lovers', and manifesting
in the words of the Evangelical Magazine an 'unholy
temper'.[30] Their strident tone and simplistic
attitude became the miserable badge of a new and
increasingly influential form of evangelicalism.
If the Christian Observer typified Anglican evangelicalism of the earlier period, the publication of
the Record can be seen as a token of the new era.
A newspaper founded in 1828, it was at first
moderate and conciliatory in its views; coming
under the control of Alexander Haldane, it became
gradually more rigid in its attitudes, less
catholic in its appeal, and more vituperative in
its tone, frequently in conflict with the older
organs of evangelicalism, the Christian Observer
and the Evangelical Magazine.[31] For even when the
latter agreed with its views they challenged its
spirit. Daniel Wilson, future Bishop of Calcutta
and Christian Observer contributor, commended the
Record for its boldness but regretted its lack of
discretion: 'nothing has more impeded the revival
of a holy and consistent Christianity, than un-
measured charges, over-statements on doubtful
matters...'[32] Similarly the Evangelical Magazine
applauded the opinions expressed in Robert Haldane's
book on the inspiration of Scripture but protested
against the asperity of his tone, particularly when
directed against people who reverenced the 'Word of
God' just as much as he did. The work, the reviewer
concluded, manifested 'Scottish fever'.[33]
Haldane's book was, like the Apocrypha controversy, but one of a number of attempts to safeguard what he regarded as the authentic view of the

authority and inspiration of Scripture. In so doing
he perpetrated a much more rigid and precisely
defined doctrine than had previously been current.
'At the beginning of the nineteenth century',
Charles Smyth has argued, 'the Bible was simply
accepted as authoritative... it was not until its
veracity was challenged that the hypothesis of its
verbal inspiration was adduced'.[34] A number of
early evangelicals such as Simeon seem to have
inclined to the views of the eminent eighteenth
century dissenter Philip Doddridge, who maintained
that the Scriptures were free from factual and
doctrinal error, but contained 'some imperfection
in the style and method'. While not denying that
there were some instances of direct divine guidance,
Doddridge maintained that 'it does not seem reasonable to believe, that every word which the apostles
wrote was dictated to them by an immediate
revelation'.[35]

The Recordites categorically opposed Doddridge's
teaching. Critics of Robert Haldane's early work
on verbal or plenary inspiration were characterised
by his nephew as

> ...those whose minds had been perverted by
> the unwarrantable theory of a graduated scale
> of inspiration, which Doddridge had imported
> from the German innovators who proceeded
> Semler, the father of modern neology.[36]

The assumption that Doddridge's views were tanta-
mount to German liberalism is but one instance of
the Haldanes' tendency to regard all who disagreed
with their doctrine as denigrators of 'God's Word
written' of which they were the self-appointed
champions. The Eclectic Review which was itself
critical of German theology was nevertheless subjected to attack and abuse because it denied plenary
inspiration and cast doubt upon the inspired status
of some canonical books. In the opinion of the
Record to hold such views was to commit sin, for any
critical comment was construed as a culpable con-
cession to neology.[37] The Christian Observer and
Daniel Wilson were therefore similarly assailed
as, in a vehement and strongly worded campaign,
was William Greenfield, whose appointment in 1829/30
to the superintendency of the BFBS editorial
department met with the paper's unqualified disapproval. Greenfield had edited Bagster's
Comprehensive Bible and his annotations were deemed
to be neological in tendency.[38]

An obvious corollary of such efforts to protect
doctrine was the attempt to ensure that only those
who were impeccably sound participated in evangelical activity. The seeds of this attitude too can
be seen in the early controversy, for it was com-
plicity with continental Catholics which in the
strict view necessitated the circulation of the
Apocrypha. Thus the Haldanes had long campaigned
for the dismissal of Leander van Ess, a Catholic
priest who until 1829 served as a Bible Society
agent.[39] Following the attack upon Greenfield, a
further attempt was made to secure a 'purer system
of management' by excluding Socinians. In 1830/31
various auxiliary societies submitted resolutions
urging that the BFBS dissociate itself from any who
denied the divinity of Christ, and when the
committee advised against any such measure, amend-
ments were moved to the annual report for the
introduction at various levels of a Trinitarian
test.
    In the tumultuous debate that followed neither
chairman nor speakers could make themselves heard.
Indeed if the opening of the Exeter Hall in March
1831 symbolised evangelical achievement, the Bible
Society meeting, held there for the first time only
weeks later, exposed the depths of the movement's
divisions. The octogenarian Rev. Rowland Hill,
representative of the older order,

> rebuked the unseemly display of party spirit;
> expressed the wish that all the Roman
> Catholics and all the Socinians in the world
> belonged to the Bible Societies for there
> they would find the truth to convince them
> of their errors...[40]

Against this the isolationist sectarianism, always
latent within evangelicalism, found expression
among those who shared the Record's view that
Socinians should be anathematised: 'God directs
us not to receive a heretic of this stamp into our
house, or to offer him any courteous salutation'.[41]
Almost imperceptibly the evangelistic impulse was
being replaced by an inward-looking desire to
protect what had already been gained. The
exuberantly offensive movement of the 1790s was
becoming self-consciously defensive.
    Nevertheless much of the original spirit
remained: supported by the Record, the attempt to
introduce a doctrinal test met with almost universal
opposition from the rest of the evangelical press.

The Evangelical Magazine stressed that Socinians
contributed to the society for one purpose only -
and that purpose was praiseworthy. The Christian
Observer animadverted upon the impossibility of
devising a universally acceptable test, an argument
developed by the dissenting periodicals, which made
acid reference to the failure of religious tests
to keep the Church of England free from Socinianism.
They added that, while tests would not necessarily
keep out those they were designed to exclude, they
would undoubtedly debar a number of theologically
sound dissenters who disapproved in principle of
credal statements.[42] A similar determination to
maintain the carefully preserved unity of the
society greeted the parallel attempt to introduce
regular prayer into meetings, a practice which, it
was feared, would alienate Quakers.[43] Defeated,
some of the dissentients withdrew from the BFBS
and, with the approbation of the Record, formed
their own Trinitarian Bible Society.[44]
     The venture proved to be short-lived. It
never gained the allegiance of Robert Haldane who
objected to its name, and when it refused to
exclude Irvingites from its committee, it lost even
the imprimatur of the Record, which suggested to
its readers that they dissociate from it. Irving's
charismatic practice and denial of the impeccability
of Christ were no less distasteful to the majority
of evangelicals than the Socinianism which the
new society was at such pains to avoid. When men
began to drift back to the BFBS the Record did not
object.[45]
     Such setbacks show that the new modes of
thought were far from dominant within evangelicalism.
Nevertheless their exponents were sufficiently vocal
to cause considerable discomfort to the editors of
the Christian Observer, who disliked not only the
intense modern interest in prophecy and charismatic
experiment, but also the tendency of some evangelicals constantly and uncharitably to detect heresy
even in the most orthodox. They regretted that
whereas opposition had once emanated from the
bastions of 'worldliness and barren formality', now
it came also from those of 'false zealotry':

          ...We have now to oppose the harsh ultraism
          of those who would make a man an offender
          for a word, and who find heresy and infidelity
          in the best writings of the best men who do
          not respond to all their shibboleths.[46]

The hard line attitude, congenial to those frightened by the proliferation of German doctrine, was to become increasingly common. The gradual change of tone within evangelicalism was evident not only in the religious but also in the political sphere. Ian Bradley has usefully differentiated three distinct groups of early nineteenth century evangelical M.P.s: the activists who rallied behind Wilberforce and kept themselves free of party commitments, the more passive 'conservative evangelicals' who served largely as Tory party hacks, and from 1830-31 the small but vociferous group of Recordites who combined the activism of the former with the conservatism of the latter.[47] The *Record* regarded theological and political liberalism as two facets of one ill, and inveighed vehemently against its manifestation in any sphere of life. The Church and the English confessional state had to be defended against the liberal/infidel threat. Thus the *Record* carried its policy of refusing to co-operate with non-evangelicals into politics: it opposed attempts to admit Jews to the legislature, and upheld Christian faith as the primary qualification for membership of Parliament.[48] Whereas Wilberforce and his friends had worked with and respected Brougham and other non-evangelicals anxious to abolish slavery, the *Record* informed its readers that a determined slave-owner was ten times more worthy of a Christian's vote than an infidel.[49] The popular novelist, Charlotte Elizabeth, whose works were frequently quoted by the newspaper, commented:

> Interested as I was in the abolition of negro slavery, and working with heart and hand for its accomplishment, until it pleased God to crown our efforts with success, still from the moment I heard that Daniel O'Connell had been permitted to stand forth at the anti-slavery meeting, and enrolled with acclamation as a helper in the work, I wholly withdrew from all connexion (sic) with the society, and laboured alone, uncontaminated by so degrading an alliance.[50]

Such alliances were regarded by the Haldanes as part and parcel of 'the system of worldly policy and false expediency' which in every sphere they were concerned to combat. Thus they believed that

> Mr Wilberforce himself, and what has been
> termed 'the Clapham sect', had associated
> too much with Socinians and ungodly men, as
> well as with mere worldly politicians, for the
> purpose of promoting the abolition of slavery
> and other objects of philanthropy.[51]

The pragmatic approach to politics of the
Clapham sect was therefore increasingly challenged
by a more doctrinaire conservatism, as all other
evils faded into insignificance in comparison with
the liberalism which the Recordites could see
looming ominously wherever they looked. Indeed
even the slavery campaign, so long a component
part of evangelical activism, was not above
suspicion of liberalism, for some of the arguments
used to support it smacked of the philosophy of
revolutionary France.[52] Ian Rennie has pointed
out that in the final parliamentary campaign
Buxton's son-in-law Andrew Johnston was the only
evangelical to speak in his support. The carrying
of the slavery bill in 1833 was both the greatest
triumph of the older evangelicalism and a mark of
its increasing debility: in his attempt to achieve
a more absolute emancipation than the government
was prepared to grant, Buxton was supported by
fewer than half the evangelical M.P.s [53]

The year 1833 is frequently chosen to mark the
end of an evangelical era because with the preaching
of Keble's assize sermon church historians transfer
their interest from evangelicalism to the Oxford
movement. The date is however only retrospectively
significant. Evangelicalism was in due course to
react very strongly to the threat of Tractarianism
but in 1833 the barely embryonic movement seemed
a far less potent danger to the Record than liberalism in its various forms. During December of that
year the paper devoted space in several numbers to
a discussion of the first tracts, but maintained
that the 'Oxford business' should not be allowed to
destroy Anglican harmony. How foolish it would
be when the Church was under radical attack to be
divided by arguments relating to the exact value
of apostolic succession. While disagreeing with
Oxford views on this matter the Record expressed
the hope that the movement would be the germ of
much good. Societies should be formed in every town
and village in support of the established church...

Such militant denominationalism inevitably
contributed to a worsening of Church/Chapel
relationships. While members of the Clapham sect

were staunch churchmen, saddened and puzzled by the wilful obduracy of dissenters, they were on the whole content to live and let live. Not so the Recordites, who saw dissent as destructive of the English Church/State, and who launched bitter invectives against it, attacking particularly orthodox dissenters' political and educational unions with Unitarians. Nor was the breakdown in relationship one-sided: dissenters increasingly repudiated the quietism characteristic of their eighteenth century predecessors, and even the Evangelical Magazine which paid little attention to political matters reflected the growing concern over dissenting disabilities. As the 'thirties progressed, the interests of some dissenters centred more and more upon political campaigns, and disestablishment became as much a theological principle for them as erastian conservatism was for some Anglicans. The need to secure dissenting rights was one of the factors making for the foundation of the Congregational Union in 1831 and for the reconstitution of the Baptist Union in the same year. Solicitous though both bodies were to preserve the traditional autonomy of local congregations, their establishment inevitably reinforced growing denominational consciousness. When Rowland Hill, Anglican deacon and minister of a chapel neither established nor strictly dissenting, died in 1833, the older form of united undenominational evangelicalism which he represented was already anachronistic.[54]

The same year also marked the death of Bishop Jebb, representative of another outmoded order. As Tractarianism developed evangelicals could no longer claim that theirs was the only spiritually-minded party: men such as Jebb could in future find a more natural home for their religious activity. Moreover, once the publication of the Tracts began to evoke suspicions of Romanism, the evangelical movement became more stridently low church: the age was past when an evangelical such as Hannah More could identify herself with a scion of the non-juring tradition.

Hannah More was but another of the many evangelicals who died in and around 1833. Those who had come into prominence in the 1790s were frequently mourned in the 1830s. William Wilberforce just survived to hear the glad news that his life's work had been achieved on 25 July 1833. Another indefatigable opponent of slavery, James Stephen, also of Clapham, had died the

previous year while other influential Anglican
evangelicals were nearing death: Lord Teignmouth,
first president of the BFBS, died in 1834, Bishop
Henry Ryder and Charles Simeon in 1836, and Zachary
Macaulay, editor of the Christian Observer, in 1838.
The connexional year 1832-33 'proved to be a
season of great and affecting mortality among the
Wesleyan Ministers of England, no less than thirty
of them being called from their work to their
reward...'[55] Prominent among these were missionary
secretaries John James and Richard Watson, and the
writer and thinker Adam Clarke, who had been three
times President of Conference. The death also
occurred in 1833 of Samuel Drew, Methodist shoemaker
turned scholar, who was predeceased by two years by
the Methodist artist, John Jackson. George Burder,
Independent minister and editor of the Evangelical
Magazine, died in 1833, as did the respected Baptist
Joseph Kinghorn of Norwich. Three other Baptist
ministers, Robert Hall the denomination's leading
intellectual, Joseph Hughes secretary of the BFBS,
and William Carey the first Baptist missionary,
were widely revered outside their own communion
when they died in 1831, 1833 and 1834 respectively.
    Outside the movement there was some suggestion
that evangelicalism was past its prime. In
September 1833 The Times noted that the recent
death of Hannah More would cause a sensation in
'not altogether youthful circles of a religious
character, in which at one time she bore a very
potent sway'. The school of which she was a
leader, the writer continued, was not as flourishing
as it had been for the deaths of Hannah More and
of William Wilberforce had deprived it of two
distinguished names which would not adequately be
replaced by those of Spencer Perceval, Sir Andrew
Agnew and the Earl of Roden.[56] Taking a longer
perspective but writing of the years around 1833
John Henry Newman commented 'the Evangelical party
itself seemed, with their late successes, to have
lost that simplicity and unworldliness which I
admired so much in Milner and Scott'.[57]
    Be that as it may, there was widespread
recognition both within and without evangelical
circles that the movement was changing and that a
generation was passing. In the preface to the
1833 edition of the Evangelical Magazine the
editors commented that the last five years had
seen the deaths of thirteen early supporters,
the last year being more fatal than any preceding.
Now none of 'the fathers' survived... Looking back

over a century of evangelical activity the historian of the Bible Society was to comment 'A natural line of cleavage separates the year 1833-34 from the remainder of the first half century, and may be said to close the era of Early Men'.[58]

NOTES

1. C. Smyth, 'The Evangelical Movement in Perspective', Cambridge Historical Journal vii (1943) criticises the analyses provided by H.C.G. Moule and W.H.B. Proby on just these grounds.

2. W.L. Burn, The Age of Equipoise (1964, 1968 edn.), p. 17.

3. On the decline of hyperCalvinism see G.F. Nuttall, 'Calvinism in Free Church History', Baptist Quarterly xxii (1968). Fuller's counterpart among the Independents was Edward Williams who advocated a moderate Calvinism in the early years of the nineteenth century.

4. Ward, op. cit.

5. While the plan of pacification of 1795 permitted societies and individuals to remain in communion with the established church, it also allowed societies to apply to Conference for the administration of the sacrament by their own preachers, a right of which many (but not all) availed themselves. See R.E. Davies and E.G. Rupp (eds.), A History of the Methodist Church in Great Britain i (1965), p. 288.

6. Hence the significance of the title of Charles Smyth's book, Simeon and Church Order (1940). On the concern for church order of some earlier Evangelicals see John Walsh, 'The Yorkshire Evangelicals in the Eighteenth Century...' (Cambridge Ph.D., 1956).

7. The plausibility of both ventures was discussed at meetings of the largely Anglican and largely clerical Eclectic Society: see J.H. Pratt, Eclectic Notes... (1856), pp. 92-93, 95-103.

8. See the prefaces to BM i (1809); EM i series xx (1812).

9. CO vii (1808), pp. 732-41, 781-92; viii (1809), pp. 30-40, 101-09, 168-77; EM i series xvii (1809), pp. 73 ff; ER i series v (1809), pp. 497-511, 616-29, 850-63, reprinted in The Miscellaneous Works and Remains of Robert Hall (1846). Hall castigated Bean, a staunch churchman, as an 'artful, bigoted partizan'.

10. ER ii series i (1814), Preface. For the founding of and early disputes about the ER see

T.P. Bunting, The Life of Jabez Bunting (1859-87), i, pp. 235ff.
11. T.R. Birks, Memoir of the Rev. Edward Bickersteth (1851), i, p. 388.
12. Wilberforce spoke at the 1819 WMS meeting while William Ward of Serampore, a Baptist, was a leading preacher the following year (MM xlii, 1819, pp. 472-73; T. Jackson, Memoirs of the Life and Writings of the Rev. Richard Watson, 2nd edn. 1834, pp. 295-97). Joseph Hughes subscribed not only to the BMS but also to the LMS, CMS, WMS, Moravian and Scottish Missions (J. Leifchild, Memoir of the late Rev. Joseph Hughes..., 1835, p. 436). In her will Hannah More made donations to the LMS, Moravian and Baptist missions as well as to Anglican and interdenominational foundations (H. Thompson, The Life of Hannah More, 1838, pp. 325-26). The highchurch paper, the Christian Remembrancer, disturbed by such indiscriminate munificence, was pleased to report 'that the various bequests to Dissenting institutions...were not hers, but those of her sister, Mrs. Martha More, who left these sums for Mrs. Hannah's use during her life, and at her death to be assigned as directed in the accounts which have gone abroad' (xv, 1833, pp. 637, 698).
13. R.A. Soloway, Prelates and People (1969), pp. 39ff.
14. EM i series xviii (1810), p. 431.
15. EM ii series ix (1831), pp. 136ff.
16. While Catholic emancipation was supported by some evangelical leaders, there was much popular opposition both to Catholics, against whom the EM inveighed with particular venom in 1825 (ii series iii, pp. 94ff, 111f, 150, 187), and to their emancipation (J. Hexter, 'The Protestant Revival and the Catholic Question in England 1778-1829', Journal of Modern History viii, 1936). Attacks upon Socinianism, indicative of the fears it increasingly aroused, were introduced by Rowland Hill into 1820s editions of his popular Village Dialogues.
17. EM ii series iv (1826), pp. 109, 236f, 290, 375ff, 384f.
18. I. Rennie, 'Evangelicalism and Public Life 1823-50' (Toronto Ph.D., 1962, lodged in Cambridge University Library) pp. 19-22, 54-60.
19. Drummond, M.P. Plympton Earle 1810-13, West Surrey 1847-60, was born an Anglican, asked for believer's baptism at the hands of James Harrington Evans for whom he built John St. Chapel,

and subsequently became a leader in the Irvingite Catholic Apostolic Church.

20. A biographical sketch of Alexander Haldane... (1882) p. 12. A list of those attending the five Albury conferences is given in P.E. Shaw, The Catholic Apostolic Church (1946),pp. 19-20.

21. Birks, op. cit., i, p. 437, ii, pp. 44-49.

22. W. Carus, Memoirs of the Rev. Charles Simeon (1847), pp. 629, 657f; CO xxix (1829) p. 474; EM ii series vii (1829), p. 404.

23. The sermon was expanded in E. Irving, For missionaries after the apostolical school, a series of orations (1825), pp. xiv-xv.

24. Ibid., p. 40. Irving argued that the instructions given in Matt. x 5-42 were of perpetual obligation.

25. For a detailed examination, incorporating discussion of the relationship between the early Brethren, premillenialist thinking, and Irvingism, see H.H. Rowdon, The Origins of the Brethren (1967).

26. M. Oliphant, The Life of Edward Irving (1862), ii, pp. 185ff; A.L. Drummond, Edward Irving and his Circle (1937), pp. 135, 153ff.

27. CO xxx (1830), pp. 810-19; xxxi (1831), pp. 63-64, 109-119, 154-68, 192, 256; ER iii series iv (1830), pp. 417ff; v (1831), pp. 231ff. In a rare error David Newsome suggests that the Evangelical Magazine represented the views of Irving and Drummond (The Parting of Friends, 1966, p. 10). The periodical was however strongly opposed both to tongues and to 'modern miracles' which it suggested were often linked with premillenial belief: EM ii series viii (1830), pp. 437ff, 572ff; ix (1831), pp. 68ff, 486, 522; x (1832), pp. 58f, 476f. The organ of Irvingism as Newsome properly notes was the Morning Watch founded by Drummond in 1829.

28. Oliphant, op. cit., ii, pp. 254-98, 342-50; Drummond, op. cit., pp. 208-20. See also Epilogue, below.

29. For expanded accounts written from different points of view see W. Canton, A History of the British and Foreign Bible Society (1904), i, pp. 334-50; A. Haldane, The Lives of Robert Haldane of Airthrey and of his brother James Alexander Haldane (2nd edn. 1852), chs. xxi, xxii; Lord Teignmouth, Memoir of the Life and Correspondence of John Lord Teignmouth (1843), chs. xxiii, xxiv, appendix 1.

30. EM ii series iv (1826), p. 301.
31. It is significant that half of the
'Retrospect of the Record' reprinted from the
edition of 27 May 1882 in the Biographical Sketch
of Alexander Haldane comprises a list of the
people and practices which the paper over the years
assailed. Considerable use of the Record is made
by Rennie, op. cit.
32. The Record, 11 April 1831.
33. EM ii series ix (1831), pp. 15-16.
34. Smyth, 'The Evangelical Movement in
Perspective', loc. cit., p. 163. While the language
of verbal inspiration was employed prior to the
1820s it should not be assumed that it carried the
connotations it was later to develop. Thus Simeon
could claim that 'the whole Scripture was as much
written by the finger of God, as the laws were,
which he inscribed on two tablets of stone, and
delivered to his servant Moses', while at the same
time allowing that 'there are inexactnesses in
reference to philosophical and scientific matters,
because of its popular style' (Quoted M.M. Hennell
and A. Pollard, eds., Charles Simeon 1759-1836,
1959, pp. 44-46). The connotations of language
depend upon the context of contrasting and
complementary ideas: the language of verbal
inspiration in Simeon's day did not so much define
a mode of inspiration as assert the fact of
inspiration.
35. P. Doddridge, 'A Dissertation on the
Inspiration of the New Testament', Works (1803
edn.), iv, pp. 168-98; 'Lectures on Divinity',
nos. cxxxvii-cxl, ibid., v, pp. 93-106; Rennie,
op. cit., pp. 15-16, 48-53. Doddridge differentiated between three different modes of inspiration:
elevation, whereby scriptural like secular writers
rose above the normal level of human competence,
producing inspiring writings; superintendence,
whereby they were protected from perpetrating error;
and suggestion (i.e. divine dictation).
36. A. Haldane, op. cit., p. 548.
37. The Record, 29 August 1831; ER ii
series xxiv (1825), p. 390; iii series i (1829),
p. 417. The ER questioned the inspiration of
Chronicles, Proverbs, the Song of Solomon, Ezra
and Esther. For a further discussion of the ER's
views and evangelical reactions to neology see
Chapter 9B below.
38. The Record, 3 March, 11, 15 and 25
August 1831 et passim.
39. A. Haldane, op. cit., p. 558-59;

Canton, op. cit., i, pp. 438-41.
40. Ibid.,i, p. 538. Further accounts of the
tests controversy can be found in A. Haldane,
op. cit., ch. xxiii; Teignmouth, op. cit., ch. xxv.
41. The Record, 29 August 1831.
42. The views of the various periodicals
along with its own opinion were summarised in CO
xxxi (1831), pp. 443-46, 532-37, 579, 642-43, 705-07,
822. Cf EM ii series ix (1831), pp. 186f, 255ff,
352f; x (1832),pp. 98ff, 193. While Record
editorials were opposed to Socinian participation
in the society (31 January, 28 April, 5 May 1831)
correspondents expressed views on both sides of
the question.
43. EM ii series ix (1831), p. 199. Again
letters to the Record reflect both points of
view while editorials supported 'public prayer'.
The editors were however anxious that the disputed
issues should be discussed at a special meeting,
rightly fearing that the premature proposal of
the motions would disrupt the general meeting:
like their opponents they thoroughly disapproved
of the resulting 'unbecoming display' (14 and 18
April, 2 and 5 May 1831).
44. The Record,5, 8, 12 and 22 December 1831.
45. Ibid., 16 April, 3 May, 26 July, 13
August 1832. The difficulties of the Trinitarian
society and the growing hostility of the Record
to it were noted with glee by the EM ii series x
(1832), pp. 152f, 196.
46. CO xxxi (1831), preface. The CO was
not altogether just in bracketing together the
Recordite and Morning Watch schools. While Irving,
Drummond and some of their followers had been
involved in various of the Haldanes' campaigns for
doctrinal purity, the Record was highly critical
of Morning Watch theology, and in particular
of the group's high church doctrines and high
regard for prophecy (28 October 1830; 24 March,
24, 27 and 31 October 1831).
47. I.C. Bradley, 'The Politics of
Godliness: Evangelicals in Parliament 1784-1832'
(Oxford D. Phil., 1974) pp. ii, 251ff.
48. The paper described the bill proposing
the admission of Jews to the legislature as the
'national unchristianisation bill'. It noted with
disapproval that it was moved by one son of Clapham,
Robert Grant, and supported by another, Tom
Macaulay. (The Record, 15, 18, 29 April, 27 June
1833 et passim).
49. The Record,15 October 1832 and editorials

throughout December. In contrast the Congregational Board urged electors to vote only for anti-slavery candidates (EM ii series x, 1832, pp. 484ff).

50. Charlotte Elizabeth, Personal Recollect - ions (1841), p. 360.

51. A. Haldane, op. cit., pp. 585-86.

52. The Record, 4 July, 26 August 1833 et passim. For the opposition of the CO to this stance see xxxiii (1833), pp. 636, 710-25.

53. Rennie, op. cit., pp. 198ff.

54. Hill had been refused priest's orders on account of his irregularity. The original trustees of Surrey Chapel were all Anglicans and the full Anglican liturgy was used along with extempore prayer. But increasing Anglican disapproval of Hill can be seen in his failure after 1810 to attract Anglican clerics as supply preachers to one of the best-filled chapels in London. See further P.E. Sangster, 'The Life of the Rev. Rowland Hill (1744-1833) and his position in the Evangelical Revival' (Oxford D.Phil., 1964).

55. T. Jackson, The Life of the Rev. Robert Newton, D.D.(1855) p. 127. Jackson who had started to travel in 1804 was able to take a long perspective.

56. The Times, 10, 11, 17 September 1833. Spencer Percival, son of the assassinated prime minister, M.P. Ennis 1818-20, Newport (Hants) 1827-31, Tiverton 1831-32, was a regular attendant at Albury, a founder of the Trinitarian Bible Society, and a member of the Catholic Apostolic Church. Andrew Agnew, 7th Baronet of Lochnaw, M.P. Wigtonshire 1830-37, was leader of the parliamentary campaign for Sunday observance, while Robert Jocelyn, third Earl of Roden, was active in the Orange Society.

57. J.H. Newman, Apologia pro Vita Suae (1864, Everyman edn. 1966), pp. 52ff. The reference is to the Church historian Joseph Milner (1744-97) and to Thomas Scott (1747-1821) author of the influential The Force of Truth.

58. Canton, op. cit., i, p. 319.

Chapter Two

THE THEOLOGY OF EVANGELICALISM

Evangelicals believed that they were children of
God but, although they less readily acknowledged it,
they were also children of the society that bred
them, and their attitudes to cultural, intellectual,
and recreational pursuits were moulded by the
practices and thought-forms of the day as well as
by the teaching of the Bible. It is the argument
of this book that evangelicals shared in the tastes
and interests of the more cultured of their
contemporaries to a far greater extent that is
always recognised, but were unable to justify their
enjoyment within the terms of their world-denying
theology. Thus one concern of this chapter is to
indicate ways in which evangelical theology
militated against secular activity, while at the
same time strongly encouraging some pursuits in
preference to others.

A second concern is to show how evangelicals'
theology was itself clearly related to that of the
age, for as Haddon Willmer has argued evangelicalism
was firmly rooted in that against which it was
reacting.[1] Evangelicals might condemn 'the world'
in a way that their contemporaries on the whole did
not, but other aspects of their theology, their
beliefs about creation and about man, bore the
common insignia of the eighteenth century. Thus
while some facets of contemporary thought were
clearly and consciously rejected, others formed the
maybe subconscious substructure of evangelical
thinking. Modified in part where they could not
wholly be reconciled with what evangelicals
conceived to be Biblical emphases, they conditioned
both the interpretation of Scripture and the
application of Scriptural precepts to life.

The Theology of Evangelicalism

A. THE WORLD OF NATURE

Nowhere is this dual process of modification and
conditioning more obvious than in evangelical
thinking about creation. Along with the vast
majority of other Christians of their day
evangelicals accepted the work of evidence theologians, believing that if man would only use his
reason and look at the world around him he would
find incontrovertible evidence of a Creator. That
God wrote in two books, his Word and his Works, was
an evangelical commonplace. Paley's Natural
Theology was highly praised in both the Christian
Observer and the Evangelical Magazine, while the
Methodist Magazine of 1801 quoted at length from
it.[2] The assumption underlying the same periodical's
sub-section 'The Works of God Displayed' was that
no reasonable creature having surveyed his works
could disbelieve in God.[3] Evidence theology was
written by evangelicals - by Anglicans such as
Daniel Wilson and Thomas Gisborne, by dissenters
such as Olinthus Gregory, and by Quakers such as
J.J. Gurney.[4]
    But evangelicals were not content with evidence
theology of the type put forward, however well, by
Paley. There were two opposite errors in relation
to evidences, the Christian Observer commented in
1817: it was wrong to undervalue them but equally
it was wrong to conceive of them as constituting
the whole of religion.[5] 'Have you read Paley's
Natural Theology?' Wilberforce asked his parliamentary colleague Lord Muncaster:

        To a mind already pious, it will, I hope,
        be serviceable, by multiplying his
        recollections of the Supreme Benefactor,
        by accustoming him to see God in every part
        of his curious frame, and in all nature
        around him. But the view of the divine
        character which is there exhibited is
        very erroneous and mischievous. His
        wisdom, power and goodness, are indeed
        enforced by many new proofs, but another
        grand attribute of the Supreme Being, as
        He is represented to us in the Scriptures,
        I mean His justice or His holiness, is
        entirely overlooked or neglected.[6]

Nature therefore, as described by Paley, revealed
some but not all of the attributes of God, and
failed to point to man's need of salvation.

Consequently the Evangelical Magazine was afraid
that Paley despite his excellencies might encourage
people to feel oversecure.[7] Natural theology
studied independently of revelation was an
inadequate guide in matters religious. Nor was it
essential to religious understanding. The Methodist
Magazine of 1812 praised Gregory's Evidences but
hastened to point out that a man could live and die
a witness to the truth without ever reading
evidence theology.[8]

A further criticism concerned the assumption
that nature was in its pristine and unspoiled state,
a view that evangelicals were prepared substantially
but by no means entirely to accept. The Christian
Observer questioned Paley's thesis at its weakest
point at which it was subsequently to prove so
vulnerable when confronted with evolutionary claims.
The existence of venomous and predatory animals
could not easily be reconciled with a general
benevolence of design.[9] Biblical hints that the
natural world as well as man had suffered as a
result of human depravity provided evangelicals
with an easy answer to this perennial problem: the
flood was but an archetypal expression of the wrath
of God upon sinful humanity. Thus, in the words of
the Christian Observer

> When Scripture tells us of a curse, the
> curse of God pronounced upon nature ...
> Reason ... looks round, and sees nothing
> to disprove and everything to corroborate
> the fact, that Nature is not as she first
> came forth from the hands of her Maker ...[10]

It was a common evangelical practice to take
this reasoning a stage further and, extending
Paley's work, to find in nature proof not only of
God's creative but also of his judicial and
redemptive activity. Thus, while the intricacy and
beauty of the natural world were assumed to reveal
his benevolence and wisdom, the prevalence of
natural disasters, volcanic eruptions, earthquakes,
and hurricanes, were regarded as equally clear
indications of his wrath. Truly 'acts of God',
they confirmed evangelical teaching about man's
apostasy:

> Can we ... suppose, that so many engines
> of terror and destruction, dispersed over
> every quarter of the globe, are consistent
> with the conduct of a Benevolent Creator

towards an _innocent_ race of men?[11]

Such conclusions were treated with disdain by the _Quarterly Review_ which provided a derisive summary of Thomas Gisborne's argument:

> ... had man been in a state of innocence, and the use of metals been necessary to him in that state, they would have presented themselves on the surface in a fusible state; ... all the labour and research, all the skill of subduing the stubborn qualities of ore by fire or otherwise, are proofs of the wrath of God.[12]

Prepared to accept on Scriptural authority that death and the flood were divine punishments for human sin, the reviewer objected to Gisborne's assumption that all other disasters could be similarly explained. The _Christian Observer_, while vastly more approbatory of Gisborne, an associate of the Clapham sect, was nevertheless concerned lest by filling the gaps left by Paley his work should encourage the assumption that natural theology was of equal value to Biblical revelation: Gisborne, the reviewer noted, could not have made from nature the deductions he did concerning the attributes of God had he not previously imbibed them from the Bible.[13]

On the one hand therefore the role of natural theology, however amplified, was in evangelical eyes never more than corroborative and confirmatory. On the other, the fact that evangelicals such as Gisborne sought to extend Paley's teachings in the light of their own doctrinal emphases is clear testimony to the strong hold that evidence theology had upon them. They might earn the disapprobation of Christians of different theological persuasions in the process, but they still thought and wrote within the same tradition: the natural world, partially - but only very partially - marred by God's punishment of man consequent upon the fall, revealed the character of the Creator to those who had eyes to see.

It followed that it was both right and proper to use eyes and mind to examine and investigate physical phenomena for the study of these could be a means of grace. But while evangelicals' belief about creation thus justified and provoked some forms of cultural and intellectual activity, it

also served to disparage them. Believing that
natural theology was a poor sister to the revelation
of God as redeemer in his Word, evangelicals deprec-
iated the work of creation in comparison with that
of redemption, and, regarding God's activity in
relation to man's salvation as all important,
adopted a paradoxically homocentric view of the
universe: William Cowper marvelled that God should
create

> ... a world
> So cloth'd with beauty for rebellious man.[14]

The evidence theologians' emphasis upon the fitness
of all created objects for their particular purpose
helped reinforce a strictly functional approach to
creation: evangelicals praised the divine
condescension that combined beauty with utility,
implying that beauty was an optional extra kindly
bestowed by the deity for the benefit of his
creatures. 'I am a passionate admirer of whatever
is beautiful in nature, or exquisite in art' wrote
Hannah More. 'These are the gifts of God, but no
part of his essence'.[15] The concept of a God who
delighted in creativity and beauty for their own
sake was alien to evangelical thinking, and even
to that of the most cultured and intellectual of
evangelicals: applying the common belief in a
characteristically idiosyncratic fashion the
Baptist John Foster argued that other planets must
be inhabited for to conceive of them as

> desolate and dead, and merely running
> vast circles in space, would really
> suggest something like the idea (we
> speak with reverence) of the Creator's
> amusing himself with an ingenious
> contrivance.[16]

Human creativity could not be justified by
reference to the character and activity of the
godhead.

B. THE NATURE OF MAN

Nor could human creativity be justified by
reference to the faculties and aptitudes with which
man was endowed at creation. While misrepresenting
the extent of evangelical world-rejection, the
Edinburgh Review of 1817 rightly implied that

evangelicals did not readily sanction the guilt-
free and spontaneous use of created powers:

> ... the entire abnegation of worldly
> views and enjoyments which this creed
> inculcates, being unobtainable by mortal
> man, the belief that it is necessary
> to eternal salvation must be attended
> with misery, unless accompanied by
> frequent self-deception. That no such
> system is agreeable to the analogy of
> the universe, or can be pleasing to the
> Author of our being - the creator of
> all our senses, and feelings, and
> faculties - we hold to be a position as
> certain as that virtue itself is becoming,
> and the pursuit of truth rational.[17]

Thus to justify secular activity as concordant
with the created nature of man was completely alien
to evangelical belief in the ravages wrought by the
fall. Evangelicals rarely referred to man as
originally created by God for they assumed that the
image of God in unredeemed man was entirely erased.
True Simeon admitted that 'all good is not so
obliterated', while a reviewer for the Christian
Observer maintained that 'some traces of our
original greatness' must remain to explain men's
predilection for altruistic activity; but such
suggestions are rare.[18] Few evangelicals were
prepared to presuppose even the slightest contin-
uation of prelapsarian goodness, perhaps out of
fear that any acknowledgment of virtue, albeit of
virtue incapable of effecting salvation, might be
construed as justification by works. The moral
turpitude of man was such that creative grace was a
thing of the past. Thus the virtue of non-
Christians was attributed by the popular evangelical
novelist, Harriet Corp, to education in a Christian
and civilized society which upheld Christian values
for emulation. Civilization and the restraint of
Providence cast a veil over the deformity of total
depravity.[19] The Record was even less prepared to
admit any remnant of prelapsarian grace. Although
originally divine the moral principles of human
nature were now Satanic in origin. Slavery would
not be abolished by 'the high moral principles of
our nature' as some asserted, but by the operation
of divine principles lost at the fall and
subsequently restored.[20] Even Simeon in a sermon
ostensibly on the creation of man laid emphasis not

on human potentiality but on human sinfulness.[21]
In evangelical thinking the only relevant starting
point for the history of man was the fall for in all
save the purely physical world God's creative work
had been diabolically undone.[22]
    Thus, while evangelicals shared the common
belief that the natural order still bore the marks
of divine creation, they differed from their
contemporaries in refusing to make a similar affirmation about man. The dichotomy between their attitudes to the physical world and to the world of
humanity is evident in the assertion of a _Christian
Observer_ contributor that the word 'nature' was
approbatory when used of the former, pejorative if
applied to the latter.[23] Men's 'natural' 'senses,
and feelings, and faculties' severely tarnished by
the fall were no longer 'pleasing to the Author of
our being'.
    But some were more pleasing than others.
Evangelicals' evaluation of the different facets of
the human personality reveal the extent to which
even their view of man reflected the assumptions of
their age. For evangelicals had no doubt that man
was essentially a rational being. Admittedly no
evangelical would give to human reason so unqualified an _imprimatur_ as did some of his contemporaries
for the dangers of rationalism were readily
acknowledged, portrayed graphically in evangelical
novels and more soberly elsewhere.[24] Reason could
wander along paths on which it had no right of way,
and when it did it misled, directing men to
Arianism, Socinianism and deism. Reason, it was
constantly stressed, had no authority to judge the
evangelical doctrines themselves: these were to be
accepted as revealed.[25] But reason might legitimately examine the evidences of revelation: when
the authenticity of a record was established by
reason to accept its contents in faith was to be
supremely rational. Religion was a 'reasonable
service' for the leading apologist of the
eighteenth century, whose works evangelicals read
with avidity, had shown that reason and revelation
were fundamentally congruent.[26] Thus when
periodical writers discussed 'the use and abuse of
reason in matters of faith', they stressed that it
was not reason itself but only its misuse that
challenged the faith of the Bible.[27] Reason,
properly used within its rightful sphere, was, like
evidence theology to which it testified, a handmaid
of religion.
    Such approbation of reason carried with it a

respect for man's rational faculties which were
thought to distinguish him from the beast. Yet
such respect was not always easily compatible with
belief in total depravity. Some evangelicals,
acknowledging that when reason was not obscured by
sin it supported revelation, suggested that only
the regenerate could reason properly since unen-
lightened reason depraved by the fall was untrust-
worthy.[28] Others, however, inclined implicitly
rather than explicitly to the view that the
intellect was not so deeply affected by the fall as
were some other facets of the human personality.
The Christian Observer quoted without any apparent
disagreement the opinion that

> The understanding retains somewhat of
> its original brightness. Reason is not
> wholly extinct. The intellectual faculties,
> in general, even in their fallen and ruined
> condition, may be raised by a course of
> discipline and education to a considerable
> degree of elevation. The mind may be so
> expanded by reading and reflection as to
> form theoretic views of Divine truth, not
> so far from correct. But the heart has
> received a deeper wound and labours under
> a more incurable distemper.[29]

Some of the more educated evangelicals accorded
to the intellect a yet more exalted position by
using the terms 'mind' and 'soul' interchangeably.
In a synthesis of Biblical and Platonic concepts,
the evangelical Quaker J.J. Gurney argued that

> ... we cannot rise too high in a just
> contemplation of the spiritual nature of
> the human mind - a spark of the divine
> intelligence, breathed into man by his
> Creator, and formed after the image of
> his own eternity. Between the known
> capacities of the soul of man, and its
> revealed everlasting existence, there
> is a perfect fitness.[30]

Similarly John Foster maintained that the intellect
alone could apprehend and communicate with the
spiritual world and asked rhetorically whether his
readers would grant

> that the mind, the intellectual imperishable
> existence, is the supremely valuable thing

in man? It is then admitted, inevitably,
that the discipline, the correction, the
improvement, the maturation, of this
spiritual being, to the highest attainable
degree, is the great object to be desired
by men.[31]

If few evangelicals thus regarded 'mind' and
'soul' as synonymous, evangelical language was
sufficiently ambiguous to blur the distinction
between intellectual and spiritual activity. Terms
such as 'serious' normally used of the former were
by evangelicals applied to the latter. In Biblical
terminology words like 'mind' and 'knowledge' took
on a wider meaning than the purely intellectual.
Moreover many evangelicals shared the view that
intellectual development was a necessary part of
human growth and was second only to religious belief
in raising civilized man above the level of beast
and barbarian. A Christian Observer contributor
asserted

> As religion calls upon us to be
> continually advancing in holiness, so
> does the happiness of our nature require
> that society and individuals should be
> going forward in moral and intellectual
> cultivation: and notwithstanding all
> the evils, inseparable from civilization,
> man is most happy in that state ...[32]

The juxtaposition of moral and intellectual
cultivation is illustrative of evangelicals' vague
assumption that the two were somehow, although not
necessarily, associated: the word 'education' was
used to imply at one moment the task of 'laying a
foundation of firm principles', at another the
dissemination of knowledge. Here again the
ambivalence of terminology served to identify
operations that were sometimes distinct.
Many evangelicals further agreed with Foster
and Gurney that the mind was a non-physical
attribute of man and could therefore be assumed to
survive death. Believing that heavenly delights
were non-sensual, evangelicals were forced to
conclude that they were 'intellectual'. Thus the
popular preacher John Styles suggested that

> He who lays greatest restraint on his
> passions and appetites, and contemns
> upon principle, every merely sensual

> gratification, increases, in a
> wonderful degree, his powers of
> intellectual enjoyment, and opens to
> himself boundless resources of spiritual
> delight. His happiness is seated in
> the mind; it is pure and refined; it
> is the happiness of angels.[33]

In contrast, as Styles implied, man's senses
and passions were to be repressed, for they were
believed to relate to physical life alone and to
make no contribution to the well-being of the non-
corporeal everlasting soul. Thus George Burder
quoted the view that

> The most innocent of our carnal
> pleasures, such as eating, drinking,
> sleeping and the like, are the badges
> of our weakness, and a sort of reproach
> upon our nature; and it is our
> inclination to them, rather than any
> excellence in them that makes them
> alluring.[34]

When man was in heaven and resembled the angels he
would not require such pleasures. Few were quite
so disparaging but many were wary of instinctive
action. The senses and the passions, acting under
no clear religious motivation seemed to be closely
associated with man's lower nature and might easily
lead him astray as they had archetypally in Eden.[35]
He had to be constantly on his guard for the devil
and his own depraved nature joined battle against
his religious resolves and his better judgment.
    It followed that cultural activities which
appealed to the senses and the passions were
eschewed by evangelicals as by a number of their
more intellectually inclined contemporaries. At
the same time both groups encouraged those pursuits
which nurtured the mind rather than the senses. In
her pre-evangelical days Hannah More was active in
blue-stocking circles, disapproving of the ethos of
a society which encouraged sensual dissipation. In
the life to come she maintained 'we ... shall be
still less encumbered with body, and flesh, and
sense ... we shall all be pure intellect'.[36] In
the meantime mental activity was the road to moral
reformation: the amendment of life by Florio, the
title character of one of her early poems, begun by
his love of a virtuous woman, was furthered when,
instead of frittering away time or reading trash,

he turned, ironically, to the more serious reading
of the Idler.[37] As an evangelical Miss More
continued to assert the superiority of intellectual
over sensual activity:

> ... to multiply and to exalt pleasures,
> which being purely intellectual, may
> help to exclude such as are gross, in
> beings so addicted to sensuality, is
> surely not only to give pleasure but to
> render service.[38]

Such an attitude cannot simply be attributed to her
unusual background for it was endorsed by
evangelicals of a very different stamp. 'It
deserves our notice' commented the Evangelical
Magazine in 1794, 'that whatever tends to inspire
with a contempt for what is frivolous, and to give
the mind a taste for rational pursuits, promotes
the interests of Christianity'.[39]

Thus evangelicals presupposed a spectrum of
human endowments ranging from the non-corporeal
rational faculties which would still characterise
man in heaven and which were therefore under God to
be cultivated, through to the senses and the
passions. Reason could be of service to religion;
the latters' religious function was more questionable for they were frequently seen to be of service
to the devil rather than to God. While they did
not laud the intellect nor condemn the senses and
the passions without qualification, evangelicals
tended to regard the one as more concordant with
spirituality than the other. And so there was a
tendency to assimilate to the Christian doctrine of
progressive sanctification the more widespread
concept of progression from bestiality to rationality.

C. THE LIFE OF THE WORLD

Contemporary practices and forms of thought, so
often a subliminal influence upon evangelicalism,
became matters of open consideration when
evangelicals turned their attention to the question
of conformity to 'the world'. 'The subject',
wrote a contributor to the Christian Observer

> is indeed not a trifling one, but demands
> the most serious inquiry and examination.
> I, at least, consider it as involving

> within its compass some of the most
> essential points in religious principle
> and practice ...[40]

The subject was important because the New Testament
made clear that Christ and 'the world' were
essentially opposed: Christians renounced 'the
pomps and vanities of this wicked world' at their
baptism. J.B. Sumner, future Archbishop of
Canterbury, produced a series of texts illustrating
the distinction as did George Burder in his sermon
'Nonconformity to the world'. The words of Christ
'They are not of the world even as I am not of the
world', of St. Paul 'We have received not the
spirit of the world, but the spirit which is of
God', of St. James 'Know ye not that the friendship
of the world is enmity with God' all pointed
conclusively to the same end. The way of the world
was the way of destruction. The Gospel both
effected the separation of the Christian from the
world and required him to validate this separation
- 'to keep himself unspotted from the world'.[41]
    The term 'the world' in evangelical parlance
referred both to type (non-Christian as opposed to
Christian) and to time (this world as opposed to
the next). This world with its pomps and vanities
was the kingdom and playground of the devil.
Miranda, a character in the Baptist John Satchell's
novel, Thornton Abbey, utilised Biblical imagery to
convey her belief that she was in an alien land:
Christ was her ark; like Noah's dove she could
find nowhere to rest unaffected by the curse. The
earth, she was told, 'is an enemy's country a
parched wilderness, a barren desert'.[42] Consequently evangelicals were constantly encouraged to look
beyond the perversions of the present. Required to
serve a probationary period on earth, the Christian
was merely a stranger and a sojourner there:
heaven not earth was his home. The time-honoured
analogy of the pilgrim was popular. Like the
pilgrim, John Venn suggested, the Christian merely
passed through this world; like a traveller, he
enjoyed refreshments on the way but he was not
tempted to loiter or to forget that he was still far
from home; looking to his goal he did not seek for
ultimate satisfaction en route. To attempt to do
so could only be abortive: 'God has pronounced a
curse upon the earth, and upon the man who looks to
it for happiness, and foolish is he who thinks to
evade that sentence'.[43] Indeed temporal happiness
was an irrelevance to the Christian whose one task

was to prepare for heaven, and who should live with death and eternity constantly in view. 'The one thing needful' was a favourite evangelical text, the subject of many sermons, of letters from parents to children, and of meditations by individuals. Gladstone's confirmation prayer included the petition that he might live 'not seeking after vain things, but making the One Thing Needful the great, the supreme, the paramount object of my pursuit and my desire'.[44] 'After all', the abolitionist T.F. Buxton wrote to a business acquaintance 'the main purpose of our living here is to prepare for eternity. It matters little how we fare in this world providing a better awaits us'.[45]

The belief that this world was but 'the ante-chamber of the next', and the accompanying conviction that eternal life was essentially a future experience, caused many evangelicals seriously to devalue secular activity.[46] Ultimately only religious pursuits were important for anything that pertained to this world alone was vanity. The pastimes of mankind seen in the light of eternity were mere trivia. Burder, deeply affected by the death of one of his daughters, noted that all her improvements and accomplishments were now of no consequence. In the last resort only grace mattered.[47]

Indeed, as the Christian grew in grace, so, evangelicals believed, the depraved nature's delight in the things of earth was replaced by the new nature's delight in the things of heaven. Exuberance and utter satisfaction in heavenly joys are reflected in the writings of J.V. Hall, author of a best-selling tract, who recorded that in June 1823 he

> ... spent half an hour at the bedside of a dying saint, who said he was happier than a king. To behold a dying saint beckoning death to approach, and looking upon his dart with unutterable delight, what a pleasure! No murmurs, though nothing but bare walls and parish-allowance! One cannot call this dying. Happier than a king! I think I shall never forget these words and the animation with which they were uttered. This is the grandest sight I ever beheld - better than a coronation![48]

The Theology of Evangelicalism

John Newton was equally enthusiastic:

> Glorious things of thee are spoken,
> Zion, City of our God ...
> Let the world deride or pity,
> I will glory in thy name.
> Fading is the worldling's pleasure,
> All his boasted pomp and show;
> Solid joys and lasting treasure,
> None but Zion's children know.[49]

Newton's hymn is a characteristic statement of evangelical otherworldliness. Here is the tendency to look to heaven for satisfaction, the antagonism to the hostile world, the dissatisfaction with earthly joys. But this is no mere negative rejection but rejection resulting from the positive affirmation of something believed to be far better. Newton's words convey the exhilaration of the vision of eternity, the invigorating challenge of a battle in which one fought on the minority but victorious side, and the fulfilling satisfaction of joys which evangelicals believed to be lasting, in contrast to which the provisions of earth were essentially vacuous.

Fade worldly pleasure might, but this did not mean that it was totally illegitimate. There were some passages in Scripture which seemed to encourage enjoyment of the things of this world. In a sermon on 1 Corinthians iii 21 - 23, 'All things are yours ...', John Venn argued

> Yours is the world, who use it for those
> ends for which its gracious Creator
> formed it, who survey its delightful
> scenery, its mountains, its valleys, its
> rivers, and feel that they are yours, who
> receive the bounty of heaven with a
> thankful heart, and employ it, as God
> intended, to your own lawful advantage and
> the good of others. The world is yours to
> enjoy it with moderation, thankful for the
> convenience it affords you while a pilgrim
> and a stranger in it, in your way to a
> better and heavenly country.[50]

Similarly, when Simeon preached on 'Vanity of vanities, all is vanity', he insisted on qualifying his text:

> If we give ourselves up to creature comforts,

> we shall be dreadfully disappointed ...
> But if we enjoy them in subserviency to
> God, and in subordination to higher
> pursuits, we shall not find them so
> empty as may be imagined. For God has
> 'given to his people all things richly to
> enjoy' and provided only we enjoy God in
> them, they are both a legitimate and an
> abundant spring of pure delight ...
> Our enjoyments are elevated and sanctified
> ... Only let them be sought in their
> proper place, and they are comforts in
> the way to heaven, though they can never
> stand to us in the place of heaven.[51]

He was even more positive when advising the young
men who attended his conversation parties:

> Serve God in your recreations, and enjoy
> him; but we are too often like the Jews
> or like the monks, afraid of God's
> blessings. We have the spirit of 'touch
> not, taste not, handle not', but this is
> wrong. 'God giveth us richly all things
> to enjoy', (1 Tim vi 17), and we ought to
> do so ... our rule should be to enjoy God
> in everything; to feel the delight of
> affluence, science, friends, recreations,
> children, in fact, of everything, as
> coming to us from God, who gives its
> sweetness, and for whose sake and glory
> it is.[52]

That Simeon found it necessary to speak in such
a way is indicative of the ascetic emphasis of most
evangelical theology, an emphasis evident even in
his preaching and that of John Venn. Their pulpit
appeals to evangelicals to enjoy themselves were
placed within the context of otherworldly teaching:
'creature comforts' were to be enjoyed only 'in
subordination to higher pursuits'. While they
possessed a coherent doctrine of world rejection,
evangelicals laid too little emphasis upon the
creation of man and upon the incarnation of Christ
to develop a balancing doctrine of world affirmation, a process which in any case demands a
deductive rather than a literalistic approach to
Scripture. In consequence the rare appeals to
evangelicals to embrace the things of this world
tended to be based upon isolated texts. Nor was
evangelical language of world affirmation inclusive

of even the majority of secular activities: no
evangelical would have assumed that Simeon was
giving sanction to theatre-going when he said that
God had given men all things richly to enjoy.
'Whatsoever you do do all to the glory of God' was
used to show that many activities were illegitimate
since they could not be done to God's glory.[53]
Interpretations in terms of renunciation thus came
more readily to evangelicals' minds than those of
a more positive nature. Indeed it would not have
occurred to them as it did to Alec Vidler to
endorse 'the Jewish saying that "a man will have to
give account on the judgment-day of every good
thing which he has refused to enjoy when he might
have done so"'.[54]

Evangelicals' sense of accountability operated
in exactly the opposite direction. It was itself
in part the product of their otherworldliness:
although they regarded this life as a mere prelude
to the next, they were not able to dismiss it as an
unfortunate irrelevance which God might well have
omitted from his schema, or at least reduced from
the traditional three score years and ten.
Evangelicals did not desire to 'depart and be with
Christ' prematurely: one had to be prepared for
death. Thus, the otherworldly view of life as a
time of probation in which man prepared himself and
was prepared for heaven created an intensive
concern for the way in which this life was spent.
Time, evangelicals believed, was a sacred trust
from God, and God 'expects his own with usury'.[55]
In consequence many took the belief that each
moment should be profitably used to a near pathol-
ogical extreme - particularly in the early days of
their discipleship. Hannah More who eschewed
almost all non-religious pursuits in the 1790s
rebuked herself for not meditating during a
migraine.[56] 'I have lived twenty-two years' wrote
Edward Bickersteth, as he began to feel his way
towards evangelical faith,

> that is near two hundred thousand hours
> and twelve million minutes; for the
> employment of every one of those minutes
> I am accountable to God. In every minute
> it was my bounden duty to love God with
> my whole heart and strength. What a
> mountain of iniquities does this at once
> discover ...[57]

Evangelicals were therefore firm believers in

the ordered day and in constant self-examination as
a means of monitoring personal progress. Nightly
analyses of the way in which time and talents had
been spent were universally encouraged, and many
attempted to facilitate this enquiry by keeping
spiritual journals. The activities of each day were
carefully scrutinised so that their legitimacy and
spiritual utility might be determined. Even
practices deemed innocent in themselves were
sometimes eschewed on the grounds that time might
thus be redeemed for matters of greater moment:
Jabez Bunting, leading Methodist of the generation
after Wesley, maintained that men should ask not
whether there was any harm but whether there was
any good in a particular pursuit; Daniel Wilson
regretted even the kind visits of friends because
they interrupted his reading and meditation, while
Adam Clarke noted that by giving up tea and coffee
over some four decades he had saved several years
of time.[58]
   If tea-table chatter with the godly marked a
misuse of time in the eyes of some evangelicals,
leisure time association with the ungodly was
universally construed as a much more serious misdemeanour, for, in the words of Henry Thornton of
Clapham,

> Religion consists much in ... passing
> over from the company and fellowship
> of wicked and worldly men, to the
> society and communion of those who fear
> and love their God ... We should care-
> fully observe who are truly religious,
> in order that we may choose them for
> our friends; and we should flee from
> the wicked doers.[59]

That not all non-Christians were downright wicked
was recognised by at least some evangelicals:
Thomas Babington, close friend of the Clapham sect
and Christian Observer contributor, acknowledged
that there was much in their lives that was
commendable. Nevertheless he urged that the
distinction between decent and even religious
'worldly characters' on the one hand, and the truly
religious on the other, should not be overlooked:
the one class lived; the other though it appeared
to live was dead.[60] To the chagrin and perplexity
of their contemporaries evangelicals used the
language of theological state to describe actual
practice: hence they tended to describe their own

(pre-conversion) lives and those of non-Christians as heinously depraved.[61] To mix unnecessarily with such company was to endanger one's soul. 'Familiarity with worldly men' George Burder maintained, 'has a bad influence upon the mind ... if professors needlessly associate with wicked and vain persons, they will soon resemble them, learn their manners, and go back from Christ'. It followed that 'as ... there is in general but little probability of doing good to carnal men by our company, it is far wisest and safest for us to keep our distance'.[62] John Clayton, dissenting member of the Eclectic Society, took the argument a stage further and sought, unconvincingly, to justify 'Scriptural separation' as evangelistically beneficial:

> We lessen our influence by losing our decision of character. The jackdaw is seen in all companies. This separation is calculated to do good to others. It is a specimen of the future and eternal separation. An anticipation of that eternal separation. It is calculated to set men thinking.[63]

'You need to have, and you must have, <u>no intimacy</u> with <u>those that fear not God</u>', Joseph Benson, a Wesleyan minister, wrote to his undergraduate son John, 'If I thought you formed intimacies of that kind it would induce me to withdraw you from Cambridge; because it would be a certain sign that you had not true religion ...'[64] Abstention from non-Christian company thus became an evangelical shibboleth.

To those who thought in this way the fact that Christ had joined in the festivities of publicans and sinners was a matter of some embarrassment, requiring careful explanation. Christ mixed freely with the world, Thomas Babington admitted to his son, but 'he mixed with it only to lead it to God, and to perform the sacred duties for the sake of which he came upon earth'.[65] So effectively did evangelicals convince themselves of this that they frequently argued that Christians should not frequent places of popular amusement to which Christ could not also go.[66] 'The Holy Spirit', John Styles maintained,

> is infinitely delicate. If his first motions are not welcomed ... he silently withdraws. If we rush into situations

where devotion receives a check, and
the spiritual tone of the soul is
relaxed by the foul polluting damps of
the world, our holy guide and monitor
is offended, and the want of his cheering
presence indicates to us the mournful
fact.[67]

The dichotomy between religion and the world was
such that God was thus assumed to absent himself
from parts of his own creation. Evangelicals who
ventured into the Godforsaken haunts of the worldly
did so at their peril.
     As far as was possible therefore evangelicals
believed they should keep themselves to themselves.
While they failed to recognise the insidious
cliquishness which resulted from their desire for
esoteric society, their critics were quick to draw
attention both to it and to the unfortunate
terminology in which it found expression. Attempts
to provide a weekly packet for the use of 'the
followers of a crucified Redeemer who are in the
habit of visiting the Isle of Thanet' were among
the practices derided by Sydney Smith in a damaging
compendium of extracts from the Evangelical and
Methodist Magazines.[68] But if evangelicals were
thus ludicrously scrupulous in their attempts to
avoid promiscuous gatherings, they were well aware
that avoidance of worldly company did not automatically carry with it avoidance of worldliness.
The danger, preachers reiterated, lay in a worldly
spirit, that was in vanity, pride, self-indulgence,
in the assumption that one was basically acceptable
in the sight of God. This spirit could invade the
hermitage as much as the metropolis and certainly
did invade religious meetings. Constant watchfulness was needed to ensure that one did not fall
into worldliness even in the security of the
sanctuary.[69]
     The question of worldly conformity was
therefore much more complex than at first appeared
and consequently caused much heart-searching.
Sumner maintained that it was more invidious than
profitable to speak of a pronounced division
between church and world when the two could merge
so imperceptibly, a view increasingly difficult to
refute as evangelicalism gained in respectability.[70]
If he was less doctrinaire than many, few believed
that this life, preparation for death though it
might be, either could or should be spent
exclusively on spiritual exercises within the

evangelical fold. Most evangelicals had of
necessity to engage in secular employment in the
company of men of different convictions. 'Preserve
me' prayed Charles Wesley, 'from my calling's
snare', a statement which revealed both evangelicals'
fear that they might be led astray, and their
unshakeable conviction that their daily occupation,
however menial, should be regarded as a divine
calling.[71] However close they might come to it,
they regarded monastic seclusion, tarnished by its
Catholic associations, as unchristian.

A further reason for this was the tension
inherent in their faith between belief in the
rejection of the world as the stamping-ground of
the devil, renounced by the Christian when he
passed from its darkness into light, and belief in
its transformation into that which was well-pleasing
to God, a transformation to be consummated in the
second advent. The Christian Observer condemned
those who said that

> because a Christian is not to make the
> present world his final home and rest,
> he is to retire to the abstraction of his
> closet, or the indolence of a cell and to
> shun that share of responsibility in the
> great movements of the world for which his
> abilities fit him, or which his station
> requires of him ... in this respect some
> good men have betrayed a culpable degree of
> moral cowardice.[72]

Sumner argued along similar lines. St. Paul's
comments on shunning the world could no more be
interpreted literally than his remarks on the
avoidance of marriage could be applied universally.[73]
To withdraw from politics allowing the world to be
run by those beyond the pale of God's favour would
be to fail in Christian responsibility and to
invite God's judgment as did the favoured but ever-
sinning Israelites of old. The reiterated comparison with Israel was all-important for even the most
pietistic of evangelicals believed that the actions
of God in relation to the nations of Old Testament
times provided a model for interpretation of his
actions in subsequent eras. If the nation failed
to accord to the religious and moral standards
believed to be acceptable in the sight of God, it
would suffer the outpouring of his wrath. The
world might be the devil's stronghold but Christians
were still to seek to run it as God's vicegerents in

his chosen land.

The Old Testament concept of the godly nation thus encouraged evangelicals to engage in political and philanthropic activity. The latter was reinforced by the example of Christ who went about doing good, temporal as well as spiritual. Missionary activity also threw evangelicals back into the life of the world: the future life might be all-important but men were to be saved in this. The danger of contamination, so pronounced in political involvement, was less marked here for evangelicals were mixing with unbelievers only on their own terms.[74] Nevertheless the fact remains that they were mixing with them: the Biblical imperative would not allow them to hide in safe seclusion, however desirable, 'till the storm of life be past'.

Forced by the demands of subsistence, social responsibility and evangelism to associate with those they condemned as irreligious, many evangelicals were all the more concerned to avoid such contact during their times of leisure. While their disparagement of this world in comparison with that to come, their belief that only religion mattered, and their almost paranoiac concern for the proper use of time, disinclined some from engaging in any non-religious activity, the recreations which evangelicals did approve were invariably those which could be pursued in the security of the evangelical home. Believing that the stark division between the 'godly' and the 'worldly' would be reflected in their respective pleasures, many evangelicals not only avoided activities which involved them in promiscuous company but also anathematized such pursuits as the prerogative of the unregenerate. And so the opprobrious theological concept of 'the world' came to be equated with particular recreations, most notably those favoured by the fashionable who seemed in their frivolity singularly insensible of man's eternal destiny. The tastes and pastimes of these 'children of the world' were assumed to be incompatible with those of the 'people of God'.

NOTES

1. Willmer, op. cit.
2. EM i series xi (1803), p. 494 'this excellent work'; CO ii (1803), pp. 162-66, 240-44, 369-74. Cf. p. 151 where a delight in natural theology is cited as one of the characteristics of

The Theology of Evangelicalism

the model character, Eusebia.
3. E.g. MM xxvii (1804), pp. 29ff.
4. D. Wilson, The Evidences of Christianity (1828-30); T. Gisborne, The Testimony of Natural Theology to Christianity (1818); O. Gregory, Letters to a Friend on the evidences ... of the Christian Religion (1811); J.J. Gurney, Essays on ... Evidences (1825).
5. CO xvi (1817), pp. 101-02.
6. R.I. and S. Wilberforce, The Correspondence of William Wilberforce (1840) i, pp. 285f.
7. EM i series xii (1804), p. 321.
8. MM xxxv (1812), p. 665.
9. CO ii (1803), p. 371.
10. CO xvii (1818), p. 550.
11. MM xlviii (1825), p. 242 in an article entitled 'Depravity of man illustrated by the present system of nature'.
12. Quarterly Review xxi (1819), p. 57.
13. CO xvii (1818), pp. 533-51.
14. W. Cowper, The Task (1785), bk. v, 753-54.
15. W. Roberts, op. cit., iv, p. 139.
16. J. Foster, Critical Essays (1888-95) ii, p. 359 reprinted from ER ii series viii (1817).
17. Edinburgh Review xxviii (1817), pp. 339-40.
18. Hennell and Pollard (eds.), op. cit., p. 95; CO xi (1812), p. 665.
19. H. Corp, A Sequel to the Antidote to the Miseries of Human Life (1809), p. 87.
20. The Record, 24 March 1831.
21. C. Simeon, Horae Homileticae (1819-20), i, no. 1.
22. Cf. ER ii series i (1814), p. 442 where a reviewer criticised the belief that 'in the infancy of the world, there prevailed, in the human race, a simplicity, a peacefulness of character, analogous to that of childhood', and argued that on the contrary the Scriptural picture was 'of outrageous wickedness'.
23. CO xxix (1829), p. 682.
24. E.g. R. Hill, Village Dialogues ii (1802), pp. 135ff. where rationalistic belief and argument facilitate seduction.
25. R. Cecil, Ms Diary of Reflections and Prayers, p. 10: 'The great difference between us and the Socinians is that we apply Reason to the evidence of Revelation and not to the Doctrines, but they apply Reason both to the evidence and doctrines too'.
26. J. Butler, The Analogy of Religion, Natural and Revealed to the Constitution and Course of

64

Nature (1736).
    27. CO xxvi (1826), pp. 65-71, 129-35; MM
xxxvi (1813), p. 867.
    28. EM i series xxi (1813), p. 331; J.
Satchell, Thornton Abbey (2nd edn. 1814), i, p. 177,
ii, p. 100.
    29. CO xxviii (1828), pp. 773-74.
    30. J.J. Gurney, Substance of an Address on
the Right Use and Application of Knowledge lately
delivered to the mechanics of Manchester ... (1832),
p. 4.
    31. J. Foster, An Essay on the Evils of
Popular Ignorance (1820), p. 294.
    32. CO xvi (1817), pp. 573-74; xx (1821),
p. 776. Cf. xiii (1814), pp. 133-43 'On the
Connection betwixt the intellectual and moral
powers'.
    33. J. Styles, The Temptations of a Watering
Place and the Best Means of Counteracting their
Influence (1815), p. 26.
    34. G. Burder, Village Sermons (1843 edn.),
p. 224.
    35. See for example James Edmeston's poem
'Reason and the Passions', quoted with approbation
in ER ii series xv (1821), pp. 547-48:
        ... SATAN came, and whispered treason
        All against her gentle sway;
        Then the PASSIONS spurned at REASON,
        And they wandered each their way.
    36. W. Roberts, op. cit., i, p. 330.
    37. H. More, Florio: a tale for fine
gentlemen and fine ladies (1780), Works (1834 edn.),
v, pp. 279-311.
    38. H. More, Coelebs in Search of a Wife
(1808, 1809 edn.), ii, p. 32.
    39. EM i series ii (1794), pp. 480-81.
    40. CO xx (1821), p. 136. Cf. xxv (1825),
p. iii which speaks of 'the absolute obligation ...
not to be conformed to this world'.
    41. J.B. Sumner, Apostolical Preaching ...
(2nd edn. 1817), ch. viii; G. Burder, op. cit.,
no. li.
    42. Satchell, op. cit., i, pp. 34-35, 145.
Satchell (1757-1829) was a member of Andrew Fuller's
church at Kettering 1795-1817, and BM editor 1819-
23 (BM xxi, 1829, pp. 317-23).
    43. J. Venn, Sermons (1814-18), i, no. xxi
'The Christian's State of Pilgrimage on Earth'.
    44. M. Foot (ed.), Gladstone Diaries i (1968),
p. 97. Cf. A.M. Wilberforce (ed.), The Private
Papers of William Wilberforce (1897), p. 208;

G. Burder, op. cit., no. lvii; T.P. Bunting, op. cit., i, pp. 140, 189, ii, p. 277.

45. C. Buxton, Memoirs of Sir Thomas Fowell Buxton (3rd edn. 1851), p. 286.

46. H. Willmer, '"Holy Worldliness" in Nineteenth Century England', in D. Baker (ed.), Sanctity and Secularity: Studies in Church History x (1973), p. 197. Dr. Willmer seeks to explain why 'the possibility of worldliness ... long ... present in the Christian tradition ... was always seriously inhibited'.

47. H.F. Burder, Memoir of the Rev. George Burder (1833), pp. 208-09.

48. Newman Hall (ed.), The Author of 'The Sinner's Friend' An Autobiography (2nd 1000, 1865), p. 133.

49. J. Newton, Works (2nd edn. 1816), iii, Olney Hymns, bk. i, no. lx.

50. Venn, op. cit., iii, p. 193. Cf. ii, p. 137.

51. C. Simeon, Horae Homileticae (1831-32), vii, no. dcccxxvii.

52. A.W. Brown, Recollections of the Conversation Parties of Rev. Charles Simeon (1863), pp. 251-52.

53. Satchell, op..cit., i, p. 35; CO xxvi (1826), pp. 8-12, a sermon on the verse significantly largely concerned with religious pursuits.

54. A.R. Vidler, 'Holy Worldliness' in Essays in Liberality (1957), p. 99. See also A.M. Ramsey, Sacred and Secular (1965).

55. T. Gisborne, An Enquiry into the Duties of the Female Sex (9th edn. 1813), pp. 114ff.; EM i series xxiv (1816), p. 7.

56. W. Roberts, op. cit., iii, p. 62. While continuing to regard herself as a highly accountable being, Miss More adopted a more relaxed attitude to life as she grew older and resumed activities which she had dropped such as her literary correspondence with Sir William Weller Pepys.

57. Birks, op. cit., i, pp. 9-10. Cf. T.S. Grimshawe, A Memoir of the Rev. Legh Richmond (1828), p. 287: 'For all the sermons you have heard you will have to render an account on the last day'.

58. T.P. Bunting, op. cit., i, p. 190; J. Bateman, The Life of the Right Rev. Daniel Wilson, DD ... (1860), i, p. 229; J.B.B. Clarke (ed.), An Account of the Infancy, Religious and Literary Life of Adam Clarke, LLD, FAS (1833), i, p. 191.

59. Quoted Meacham, op. cit., p. 27. Cf.
'Advice to a new married couple', EM i series xiii
(1805), p. 256.
60. T. Babington, A Practical View of Christian Education ... to which is added A Letter to a
Son soon after the close of his education on the
subject of not conforming to the world (7th edn.
1826), pp. 251-52, reprinted from CO xvi (1817),
pp. 277-88.
61. A practice noted by T.B. Macaulay,
Edinburgh Review liv (1831), p. 456.
62. G. Burder, op. cit., pp. 395, 473.
63. J.H. Pratt, op. cit., p. 379.
64. J. MacDonald, Memoirs of the Rev. Joseph
Benson (1822), p. 476.
65. Babington, op. cit., p. 266.
66. E.g. BM xiii (1821), p. 156.
67. Styles, op. cit., p. 19. While assumptions concerning the vulnerability of the Holy Spirit
are implicit in much evangelical writing, the BM
criticised Styles' statement as improper (vii,
1815, p. 472).
68. Edinburgh Review xi (1808), pp. 341-62.
Smith's allegations were met by John Styles, whose
Strictures on two Critiques in the Edinburgh Review
on the subject of Methodism and Missions (1809) he
also condemned (xiv, 1809, pp. 40-50).
69. CO xvi (1817), p. 499.
70. Sumner, op. cit., pp. 287-88.
71. The opening line of the 3rd verse of
Wesley's hymn 'Forth in thy name, O Lord, I go'
Hymns and Sacred Poems (1749). Verse 3 was
omitted, perhaps on aesthetic grounds, from A
Collection of Hymns for the use of the people called
Methodists (1780), but the sentiment remained
common. See for example CO xxxi (1831), p. 173.
72. CO xxxii (1832), pp. 60, 555ff.;
xxxi (1831), Preface; xxxiii (1833), p. 437.
73. Sumner, op. cit., pp. 263-64.
74. Charlotte Elizabeth, The Museum (1832),
pp. 52ff. where a fictional father tells his
children 'as for those who are not religious the
less you have to do with them the better, except
in the way of instructing those who are willing to
let you speak to them of Christ'.

Chapter Three

FAITH AND FASHION

A. PUBLIC AMUSEMENTS.

It followed that when Rowland Hill issued <u>A Warning</u>
<u>to Professors containing aphoristic observations</u>
<u>on the nature and tendency of public amusements</u>,
he was primarily concerned to attack the communal
leisure activities of the more affluent sectors
of society. Admittedly evangelical periodicals
sometimes warned against the dangers inherent in
the pleasures of the poor, attendance at fairs
and prize fights, while·in open letter and fictional
tract Hill drew attention to the temptations of
public houses and sought to prevent performances
of strolling players.[1] Nevertheless the weight
of complaint in these and similar sources was
always directed against the frolics of the fashionable, an emphasis which does much to qualify
Sydney Smith's view that evangelicals were anxious
only to curtail the recreation of those earning
less than £500 a year.[2]
      Smith's complaint related to the activities
of the Society for the Suppression of Vice. That
this society focused its attention upon the
behaviour of the poor is only to be expected:
a parliament strongly antagonistic to state inter-
ference was loath to legislate even against the
cruellest sports of the lower orders, let alone
against those in which Lords, Commons, and Prince
Regent were more intimately involved; any attempt
to effect the prosecution of gentry or aristocracy by magistrates of their own class would have
been doomed to failure. But lack of legislative
activity does not denote disinterest in the
misdemeanours of the rich: while evangelicals
shared the common view that popular disorder was
immediately conducive to revolution, they condemned

fashionable vice too as indirectly subversive of
the social order. In A Practical View aimed
explicitly at 'the higher and middle classes',
Wilberforce attributed the sufferings of the French
to the corruption of their manners and morals,
the dissipation and irreligion of their society.[3]
His writings and those of Hannah More testify to
Evangelicals' anxiety to reform the rich as well
as the poor.[4] Their belief that God judged erring
nations was too firmly fixed for casual disregard
of upper class behaviour.

Wilberforce and Miss More were however unusual
in possessing the literary expertise, and more
significantly the social respect, which alone made
feasible a direct appeal to the non-evangelical
upper classes. Whether realistically or evasively
most evangelicals tended to assume that at this
level of society example was the best form of
persuasion. Most writings on public amusements
were therefore addressed to those already within
the household of faith.

The primary aim of such works was the safe-
guarding of the purity of the flock. In view of
this the concentration upon 'fashionable'
amusements is indicative of an unspoken assumption
that the pastimes of the affluent were more
tempting and more dangerous to evangelical well-
being than those traditionally practised by the
lower classes. With the advent of industrialism
the latter were already coming under attack, and
had from the beginning been anathematized by those
converted in the revival. In areas where evangelicals were in a minority, the pietistic tradition
of old dissent and the stringent discipline of
Methodism made improbable any participation in
the dissipation and drunkenness of working class
recreation. On the other hand, as John Rule has
shown with reference to Cornwall, in areas where
Methodism was strong and socially coherent,
traditional festivities were translated into
religious forms, which replaced and rendered
obsolete the original practices.[5] In either case
involvement in church or society provided
alternative leisure pursuits with which dissenters
could amply fill their scant non-working hours.

These differences in lifestyle were but a
reflection of a more fundamental distinction, for
membership of a dissenting community of itself
served to differentiate a dissenter from his
social equals. In contrast Evangelicals could
often only be distinguished from non-evangelicals

of similar status by their behavioural shibboleths,
of which anathematization of common pastimes was
the most obvious and hence the most significant.
As the movement became more respectable, attracting
adherents accustomed to the leisure pursuits of
the affluent, both the threat to and the need for
this one symbol of separation became ever more
acute.

The consequent concern was not restricted to
Anglicans, for dissenting leaders too, delighted by
the growing respectability of their congregations,
watched apprehensively for the first erosions of
nonconformist peculiarities. Thus the increasing
propensity of dissenters to attend spas in the
second and third decades of the century was cause
of some consternation: on 13 August 1815 John
Styles preached at Union Street, Brighton, on
The Temptations of a Watering Place and the Best
Means of Counteracting their Influence, while the
Evangelical Magazine warned that Christians who
frequented such resorts tended to conform to the
world, neglect their religious duties, and attend
worship only once each Sunday.[6] But dissenters
were not deterred: by 1827 a critical Baptist
writer had reconciled himself to the fact that
many Christians attended watering places for
health and recreation, and noted the provision
of piers, promenades and libraries, which facilities
might safely be enjoyed - save on the Sabbath.
Nevertheless he regretted that church members and
even ministers were to be found in public gardens,
the haunts of the frivolous, in culpable conformity
to the world and worldly ways.[7]

It is impossible to determine the extent of
such assumed laxity. Some biographies suggest
that evangelicals responded to greater respectability by adopting more rigid behavioural codes,
a process which in the case of certain Anglican
families has been convincingly traced by Michael
Hennell.[8] Among dissenters Ann Taylor later
excused her attendance at the theatre in 1799 on
the grounds that 'at the time the line had not
been so strictly drawn in the case of amusements
as it came afterwards to be in many Christian
families'.[9] But the periodical and pulpit
exhortations which caused families like the
Taylors, firmly established in the faith, to shun
the theatre and other such dens of vice, can be
interpreted as a response to the tendency of
fellow-travellers to frequent them. The young
Etonian, W.E. Gladstone, who recorded a game of

cards and visits to the theatre in his diary for 1826/27, may well be representative of other churchmen who, influenced in varying degrees by Evangelicalism, did not necessarily follow its behavioural precepts.[10]   Indeed it must not be assumed that these were universally obeyed even by those clearly aligned with the party.

The difficulty of determining evangelicals' practice from their polemic is further exacerbated by the, admittedly slight, range of opinion expressed in their written remains. While they were in greater agreement over fashionable amusements than any other form of leisure activity, even in this sphere consensus was not complete. The recurrent and often acrimonious periodical correspondence on the legitimacy of particular pursuits is testimony to the very real problems involved in translating theological anathemas into action, problems openly admitted by some, but by no means all, evangelicals. H.F. Burder argued that Christians could not expect to think alike on the application of principles.[11]   The tendency of The Record to condemn those who attended balls and races, without further consideration of their character and circumstances, was criticised by a correspondent of that paper, while a contributor to the Christian Observer objected to the 'excessive scrupulousness indulged by many religious persons...Straining at gnats is the very best preparation for swallowing camels'.[12]   Thus, although some evangelicals tended towards a blanket condemnation of worldly amusements, others sought to differentiate between more and less heinous activities, between circumstances in which certain pursuits might be legitimate and those in which they were not.

To men such as Simeon and Gisborne card-playing was one of the less profligate pursuits: both maintained that there was nothing wrong in playing cards with an elderly sick relative.[13] That they needed to make such statements is evidence of the strictness of others: Rowland Hill cited instances of 'innocent' games which nevertheless led to quarrelling, while the Methodist Magazine asked its readers if they could really envisage Paul and Silas playing cards.[14] The Evangelical Magazine masked as an obituary the dreadful case of the Rev. Mr. Porter who, warned by intestinal pains, nevertheless continued with his game, collapsed and died, hurried from the amusements of a card table to the bar of the

righteous God'.[15]   Some evangelicals objected even
to the possession of a pack of cards. They however
in their turn were rebuked by Isaac Milner,
Evangelical President of Queen's College, Cambridge,
who dismissed such objections as cant and warned
an acquaintance 'Never be afraid of bugbears'.[16]
But even Milner, who was fascinated by card tricks,
had long given up games of cards because of the
time thus wasted. Neither Simeon nor Gisborne
suggested that cards should be a regular part of
evangelical living for it was widely agreed that
they were suited only to empty minds, to be used
by those who had nothing better to do.   It seems
probable therefore that Benjamin Jowett was
describing an experience common to many when he
wrote in mock seriousness of his evangelical childhood:

> No day passes in which I don't feel the
> defects of early education. I was never
> taught how to play at cards, or even at
> billiards, and it seems too late to repair
> the error now. Do you think I could
> learn to waltz?[17]

In some families he might have been taught
to do so for there was a slightly more diverse range
of opinion about the legitimacy of dancing than
card-playing and correspondingly greater variations
in practice. Opposition to balls, scenes of mixed
company, was widespread, but Wilberforce and other
Evangelicals believed that there was no harm in
'domestic dances'.[18]   Elizabeth Fry's daughter,
Katharine, recalled that after the strict Quakers
had left a family wedding, the young people danced
quadrilles.[19]   The common complaint that even
dances in such select company encouraged undue
intimacy between young gentlemen and young ladies
was met by Mrs.Ely Bates, an Anglican with Moravian
associations, who approved of single sex dances:
these she maintained, improved a girl's health
far more effectively than attendance at a watering
place.[20]   That dancing aided deportment was
argued by one Christian Observer contributor while
another sought to justify the activity by reference
to Biblical precedent.[21]
This apparent blurring of the sacrosanct
division between church and world was vehemently
opposed by other correspondents who denied that the
religious act of dancing before the Lord could be
compared with fashionable cavorting.[22]   Their

horror was widely shared by dissenters, who
condemned the teaching of dancing at 'religious
seminaries of education', pointed out that grace
and health could otherwise be attained, and argued,
irrefutably, that if children of Christians were
taught to dance they could join in balls, a
circumstance which would be avoided if they were
happily ignorant of the requisite skills.[23] Even
Adam Clarke, in many respects the most liberal
of dissenters, employed what was for him unusually
strong language against dances.[24]

The response of the Christian Observer
suggests that attitudes to dancing may have been
to some extent denominationally defined, for it
accused Clarke of overstating his case, of
ignorantly associating 'ale-house hops' with the
more decorous eurhythmics of the refined.[25] Its
criticism was just for few dissenters can have
experienced the 'domestic dances' of the Anglican
and Quaker elite. While the complaints against
dancing in the dissenting press may well have been
levelled against their own number as well as against
Anglicans, dissenting publications were uniform
in their condemnation. In contrast, dancing in
carefully defined contexts was defended by some,
although not all, Evangelicals.

A similar denominational division can perhaps
be detected in reference to field-sports: the
Methodist Magazine complained that shooting was both
cruel and dangerous, considerations which do not
seem to have deterred the Anglican brothers-in-law,
Samuel Hoare and Fowell Buxton.[26] Their shooting
records have been analysed by Viscount Templewood
who draws attention to the remarkably high level
of the bags and the almost unbroken series of
shooting days, interrupted only for a religious
meeting (and not always then) or on account of bad
weather or illness; 'today' commented one of Buxton's
sons in 1828 'for the first time for above twenty
years which my Father has been the companion of
Uncle Hoare, Uncle Hoare staid at home when it has
been a shooting day'.[27] But if some Evangelicals
were happy to shoot there was widespread condemnation of hunting, a pursuit which, according to
the Christian Observer, caused exhaustion and
incapacitated participants for serious reflection.[28]
Since this argument was not applied to other forms
of physical exercise, it seems probable that the
more serious objection to hunting was the regularly
deplored company that was kept.[29] 'I too should
like to hunt', a mid-century Vicar was reputedly

to remark, 'if I could hunt with a field of
saints'.30 It was the possibility of playing cards,
dancing, and shooting with the elect which made
these pursuits less dangerous and hence more
acceptable in the eyes of some Evangelicals than
those in which mixed company was unavoidable.

In the opinion of many evangelicals however
the innocence of the company did nothing to
eradicate the taint of worldliness with which the
favour of the fashionable invested activities
such as shooting. The Methodist Magazine argued
that it was inconsistent for a Christian to enjoy
a sport which was followed by wicked and licentious
men.31 The argument had particular potency when
applied to the clergy for it was maintained that
the minister's 'spirit not being secular, his
amusements will not be such'.32 Evangelical
Anglicans could not but be aware of the challenge
of such statements for as W.R. Ward has pointed
out the Methodist justification for separate
communion 'was expressed overwhelmingly in terms
of hostility to the fashionable habits of the
clergy'.33 It is significant that the Christian
Observer's discussions on field sports were
invariably linked with clerical practice: in
one of many articles the periodical maintained
that it was undignified for ministers to hunt,
unbecoming that they should value themselves
primarily on their skill with a gun.34 Fox-
hunting parsons, the Record proclaimed, aided
dissent; for ministers to attend hunts, balls,
plays, or races was a prostitution of the clerical
character.35 While these statements reflect
the respect in which evangelicals held the
ministry, their primary significance lies in the
fact that ministers were expected to set an
example to their congregations. If a minister
took one step, Richard Cecil suggested, his hearers
would take two. If a man of the world expressed
surprise at meeting a clergyman in a particular
venue that was a sure sign that he should not have
been there.36 Notwithstanding some slight
variations in practice, Anglicans like dissenters
believed that evangelical faith combined uneasily
with the amusements enjoyed by the worldly, upon
whom they imposed their own expectations concerning
the incompatibility of the two. The participation
in worldly amusements of a man set aside for the
service of God merely highlighted this essential
incongruity.

Nowhere are evangelical assumptions about the

illegitimacy of most public recreations more
clearly exposed than in the rhetorical questions
with which writers attempted to shock recalcitrant
readers. The Methodist Magazine asked whether they
would really like to die on the hunting field, a
query regularly repeated with reference to other
locations.[37] The mock prayer which assumed what
it supposedly proved was regarded as a useful test
of legitimacy. No Christian, George Burder
maintained, could pray before going to the theatre:

> Lord! Go with me to Covent Garden. Bless
> the actors, strengthen the dancers, assist
> the musicians, let us have a merry evening,
> and render the whole performance useful to
> my religious interest.[38]

When Rowland Hill asked his readers whether they
would be prepared to allow plays in church he was
similarly confident that an instinctive gut
reaction would provide the horrified rejection he
expected, thus 'proving'the illegitimacy of plays,
in any circumstances.[39]
The extent to which evangelicals thus reacted
instinctively against worldly amusements must be
stressed. Many of the arguments they presented
against them sound like ex post facto justifications
of an essentially emotive and conscience-derived
certainty that such activities were beyond the pale
of evangelical living. Second and third generation
evangelicals inherited the shibboleths first and
were only subsequently called upon to find reasons
to explain their peculiarities. In the case of
the mildly evangelical descendants of Clapham this
appears to have led to less vigorous opinions but
no less decided behaviour. Leslie Stephen recorded
that his father taught him that there was nothing
intrinsically wrong with plays and balls, although
their abuse was to be condemned. But James Stephen
adhered to the ways of his Clapham youth in
eschewing both, categorising them as 'not convenient'.
His son commented 'We no more condemned people
who frequented them than we blamed people in
Hindostan for riding elephants. A theatre was
as remote from us as an elephant'.[40]
Evangelicals' aversion to the theatre must be
distinguished from their dislike of other worldly
amusements for two reasons. In the first place
their complaints against card-playing, dancing and
field sports were directed against pastimes
regularly enjoyed by the fashionable. By the early

nineteenth century, however, theatres were losing
their popularity among the more affluent classes.
The Select Committee on Dramatic Literature which
reported in 1832 attributed this change not only
to 'the supposed indisposition of some religious
sects to countenance Theatrical Exhibitions', but
also to 'the prevailing fashion of late dinner
hours', and the lack of royal encouragement.[41]
An historian of the theatre stresses that in
competition with opera and ballet, plays may simply
have become unfashionable in the highest circles,
while the raucous presence of the crowd in the
new large theatres of Regency London served to
deter the more respectable.[42]   Whatever the
reason for non-attendance evangelicals' disparagement of the theatre to some extent mirrored that
of their contemporaries.

Of evangelical disapproval there can be no
doubt.   T.B. Shepherd points out that in 1799 the
denominational magazine saw fit to presume that
'no Methodist attends a theatre'.[43]   A year later
the Anglican Eclectic Society adopted as its
topic for discussion the question 'On what grounds
should a Christian discountenance theatrical
amusements?', a form of words which precluded any
defence of the theatre.   In the opinion of one
contributor to the debate 'Frequenting plays
affords a proof of the depravity of human nature
beyond most other things'.[44]   The ubiquity of
this opinion provides the second reason for
differentiating between theatrical attendance and
other worldly amusements.   The Christian Observer
of 1805 noted that the Christian world was divided
over the legitimacy of balls, concerts, and other
such activities, but united in condemnation of
the theatre, a conclusion condoned by even the least
doctrinaire of evangelicals.[45]   Attendance at
plays was one of the first pursuits which
Wilberforce felt called to drop in his quest for
evangelical assurance, and while he prevaricated
in 1787 when asked whether parental injunctions
to attend the theatre should be obeyed, forty years
later he had little doubt that in this one instance
disobedience was a duty.[46]   A lady who in 1817
asked Simeon for guidance on the same issue was
similarly advised to disobey even the husband to
whom she had vowed her obedience, for Simeon was
inclined to believe that evil was integral to the
theatre and not merely circumstantial.[47]

Attendance at 'the devil's temple', providentially the subject of frequent gutting by fire, was

therefore assumed to be incompatible with Christian
profession for reasons more specific than its
popularity with the ungodly.[48] Evangelicals had
no doubt that plays inculcated values antagonistic
to religion and all too often masked evil in the
garb of good. Dashing young heroes, ambitious
and revengeful, attracted the audience's uncritical
admiration. Pride was presented as greatness of
mind, honour and romance as the all-important
determinants of action. Blasphemy, adultery,
duelling, murder, and suicide, were depicted without
censure, and, when associated with the hero, with
implicit approbation. Pageantry and spectacle,
tableaux, interludes, dancing and music intoxicated
those who watched, distracting them from moral
judgment. Theatregoers were thus familiarised
with sin, and, enjoying its exhibition, lost that
'holy indignation' over immorality which the
Evangelical Magazine believed should be a Christian
characteristic.[49]
          Such protest was not peculiar to evangelicals.
George Colman, the strict and, in the opinion
of many, capricious examiner of plays in the Lord
Chancellor's office, showed a sensitivity to
impious ejaculation, to Biblical and sexual
allusion, that surpassed that of many evangelicals.
The latters' dislike of theatrical display was
echoed by a playwright who regretted the tendency
of the new large theatres to concentrate on
spectacle rather than literary masterpieces, while
their fear that immorality portrayed on stage
was particularly potent was shared by J. Payne
Collier, who drew the Select Committee's attention
to the visual appeal and attractive presentation
of plays.[50]
          Evangelicals however extended their criticism
beyond the admittedly dubious productions of
Regency England, condemning even those plays
which they acknowledged to be morally irreproach-
able. Many appealed to past practice in an
attempt to show that the wise and pious of all
ages had discountenanced the theatre, however
'pure' the plays of their day might have been.[51]
Acting was believed to be morally harmful in
itself for it encouraged a thirst for admiration
and destroyed female diffidence by facilitating
too intimate a connection between the sexes;
Thomas Gisborne therefore refused to allow his
children to perform plays together at home.[52]
Hannah More, who as a young teacher had condoned
this and written plays for the purpose, in later

life condemned even the performance of the least
objectionable on the grounds that 'love being the
grand business of plays' young ladies who attended
them would conclude that 'love is the grand
business of life also...'[53]

Herein lay evangelicals' fundamental objection
to the theatre: it portrayed life as they did not
wish to see it. Plays depicted styles of living
which they daily sought to avoid and emphasised
experiences which they devalued. By displaying
the passions and appealing to the senses, the
theatre nurtured just those facets of the
personality which evangelicals believed it was
the task of religion to suppress. Works which,
by appealing to the mind, were more congruent with
the religious lifestyle as evangelically conceived,
were, as evangelicals never tired of pointing out,
better appreciated in the quietness of the closet.

Evangelicals therefore responded with
derision to suggestions that the stage might be
capable of reform: who would go to the theatre,
the Evangelical Magazine demanded, to see virtue
and religion? According to John Foster of the
more cultured and liberal Eclectic, successful
theatre catered for the tastes of people devoted
to amusement; these would not attend plays
mirroring Christian viewpoints.[54] 'If the
sentiments and passions exhibited were no longer
accommodated to the sentiments and passions of
the audience' wrote Hannah More, 'corrupt nature
would soon withdraw itself from the vapid and
inappropriate amusement, and thin, I will not say
empty, benches would too probably be the reward
of the conscientious reformer'.[55]

The common and unembarrassed assumption that
pure or religious amusement, the latter in
evangelicals' opinion a contradiction in terms,
would be vapid and uninteresting is indicative
of a significant desideratum within evangelicalism.
Lacking confidence in their own product when
confronted with the glittering ware of the world,
evangelicals readily admitted that values could
more effectively be communicated from the stage
than from the pulpit. On Sundays, Hannah More
explained, Christian doctrines were presented in
the forms of axioms, principles, and precepts;
every other night of the week beliefs diametrically
opposed to them were

    realised, embodied, made alive, furnished with
    organs, clothed, decorated, brought into

> sprightly discourse, into interesting action;
> enforced with all the energy of passion,
> adorned with all the graces of language, and
> exhibited with every aid of emphatical
> delivery, every attraction of appropriate
> gesture. To such a complicated temptation
> is it wise voluntarily, studiously,
> unnecessarily to expose frail and erring
> creatures? Is not the conflict too
> severe? Is not the competition too unequal?[56]

Her opinion was shared by the CMS secretary, Josiah
Pratt, who admitted that a sermon was 'the essence
of dullness' after a play, but the only conclusion
he drew was that this illustrated the evil of the
latter which should therefore be eschewed. [57]
The possibility of fighting the world with its own
weapons was not in this context seriously considered
for many evangelicals were properly critical of
preachers who sought to impress congregations with
their oratorical prowess and cultural competence
and, maybe more superstitiously, antagonistic to
liturgical pageantry, which was invariably associated with the Catholic appeal to the senses rather
than the intellect. Others shared their suspicions
but non-evangelical Christians, however austere
their churchmanship, were less fearful of the
world and less constrained by the need self-
consciously to examine every action; they could
therefore satisfy the emotional and aesthetic
demands of their nature with secular provision.
The tragedy of evangelicalism was that it rightly
stressed the importance of applying faith to the
whole of life while lacking a theology capable of
being so applied in any but the most negative
fashion. Evangelical faith was therefore liable
to appear unattractive when challenged by anything
appealing to the totality of the personality.
Hannah More was clearly aware of the danger but
was inevitably unable to produce a satisfactory
solution within the context of a theology which
slighted certain facets of human existence:
the house might have been cleansed of devils,
but evangelicals who could only subjugate and not
sanctify the senses had no option but flight
from new and worse invaders.
      These regularly took religious form. Expelled
from mainstream evangelicalism the senses took up
residence with a vengeance on the peripheries of
the movement, in 'enthusiastic' preaching and the
excitement and drama of Irvingism. More generally,

condemned within the church they found expression
in extra-ecclesiastical activity, in the multiplicity of May meetings and other such jamborees.
The growing worldliness of evangelicalism can thus
be explained in psychological as well as sociol-
ogical terms, for if, as evangelicals argued,
religious practices amply replaced the frivolity
and exhibitionism of worldly pursuits, this was
in part because they increasingly conformed to
their nature. Evangelical children, forbidden to
show off accomplishments in traditional fashion
to the admiring guests of their parents, displayed
their fine clothes and musical abilities at annual
Sunday school celebrations, to the disgust of the
Evangelical Magazine which feared for their
modesty.58   The prevalence of such complaint
shows that evangelicals were far from blind to
what was happening. Few, however, possessed either
the insight or the detachment of Marianne Thornton
who recognised that the ever-escalating May meetings
provided unparalleled opportunities for 'religious
dissipation', dazzling displays of oratory by the
greatest preachers of the day, histrionic disputes
and cordial reconciliations, 'very amusing to
we good people who do not go to plays but seriously
speaking it is sad to see such tricks played
before High Heaven'.59
     The common phrase 'the religious world' was
therefore potentially very ironic. While
expressing unease about many fashionable pursuits,
evangelicals conformed more closely than all cared
to admit to the ways and spirit of those they
despised even in 'public amusements'.

B.   GOD AND MAMMON

     According to later novelists, they conformed
to the standards of the world too in their concern
for social status and material comfort. At his
Clapham home, significantly 'separated from the
outside world by a thick hedge of tall trees',
Thackeray's Tommy Newcome was required to repeat
the horrific hymns of evangelical childhood 'to
his step-mother after dinner, before a great,
shining, mahogany table, covered with grapes,
pineapples, plum-cake, port-wine, and Madeira',
while in Middlemarch George Eliot's more
sympathetically portrayed Mrs. Bulstrode happily
combined 'the nothingness of this life and the
desirability of cut glass, the consciousness at

once of filthy rags and the best damask...'[60] In
the eyes of their contemporaries this easy juxtaposition of religion and good living was a sign of,
at best, extreme equivocation, at worst, sheer
hypocrisy. For all their religious talk Evangelicals seemed to be motivated by just the same
considerations as everyone else. Claiming otherworldly interests and a distinctive lifestyle they
appeared in no way to curtail the domestic comforts
common to their class. Similarly, though scorning
the world, they apparently sought after its riches
and the respect of the great. Thus Hazlitt, while
acknowledging Wilberforce's religious sincerity,
argued that he was nonetheless anxious to preserve
his reputation and maintain good relations with
those in high places: 'He acts from mixed motives.
He would willingly serve two masters, God and
Mammon'.[61] William Empson, future editor of the
Edinburgh Review, hinted that a similar desire to
make the best of both worlds was characteristic
of Evangelical clergy 'whose success in marrying
fortunes has become a proverb'. [62]

One who was undoubtedly successful in this
respect was the Rev. John William Cunningham,
curate to John Venn at Clapham from 1809 to 1811,
and Vicar of Harrow from 1811 until his death in
1861.[63] Cunningham's first wife, Sophia, who
died in 1821, was the daughter of Robert Williams
of Moor Park, Hertfordshire, M.P. for Dorchester
and partner in a successful banking firm. In 1827
Cunningham remarried. His bride, Mary Calvert,
was twenty-one years his junior, the daughter
of General Sir Harry Calvert, Bart. An urbane but
zealous man Cunningham was perhaps second only
to Wilberforce in attracting abuse. Attacked
in The Times, The Examiner, and Cobbett's Political
Register for supporting the government in the
Queen Caroline affair, he was depicted by
cartoonists as a time-server, 'the Cunning Man of
Harrow', who hated Catholicism yet supported
emancipation.[64]

The most vituperative attack upon Cunningham
came from one of his parishioners, Frances
Trollope, mother of the Victorian novelist. The
title character of her scurrilous novel, The
Vicar of Wrexhill, William Jacob Cartwright,
insinuates himself into the affections of a
wealthy widow whom he eventually marries, provides
an opportunity for his accomplice cousin to abduct
his step-daughter, and, incidentally, turns out
to have fathered an illegitimate child. Ever

justifying his plans for his own worldly advancement
on religious grounds, he tells his erstwhile
mistress

> To a man like myself, whose soul is altogether
> given to things above, the idea of making
> a marriage of love, as it is called, would be
> equally absurd and profane. My object in the
> connection I have formed, was to increase
> my sphere of influence and utility; and
> nothing, I assure you, can be more opportune
> and fortunate than my having found this
> very worthy and richly endowed person.[65]

According to his daughter, in whose spiritual well-
being he has no interest, evangelicals 'value
pleasure fully as much as other men...they struggle
for riches with anxiety as acute and hold it (sic)
with a grasp as tight, as any human beings can
do'.[66]   Cartwright's prime desire however is
for power: 'To touch, to influence, to lead, to
rule, to tyrannise over the hearts and souls of all
he approaches, is the great object of his life...'[67]
Emulating the authority of the God whom he
professes to serve the Vicar domineers over the
life of his family and the village alike, imposing
his will upon them, until, with the thwarting of
his plans, he exchanges livings and 'the pretty
village of Wrexhill once more became happy and
gay'.[68]
     Many of Mrs. Trollope's charges can be
immediately dismissed.   One of her son's biographers, a man by no means sympathetic to
Cunningham, maintains that she became obsessive
about baiting the Vicar and, in company with
the 'high and dry' Drury family, masters at the
school, conducted a 'crude and foolish vendetta'
against him.[69]   Her pique can in part be
attributed to the fact that having lived beyond
their means the Trollopes sought to solve their
financial problems by letting to Cunningham the
house which they had leased, while themselves
renting a smaller and shabbier abode.   Others
held Cunningham in far greater regard: the
account of his ministry provided by J.W. in
Harrow on the Hill, a narrative founded on facts
(1821) is as eulogistic as Mrs. Trollope's is
vindictive.   Moreover Cunningham was revered far
outside Harrow: a life-governor of the BFBS and
CMS, he was invited to become secretary of the
former society, a post he declined, and was the

most regular anniversary speaker of the latter.[70]
There may however be some germs of truth
behind Mrs Trollope's gross misrepresentations.
Cunningham's refusal to speak in distant towns on
account of the needs of his family and parish
points to a commendable rejection both of the
Jellyby syndrome and of any temptation to further
his own reputation in a wider sphere; nevertheless
his belief that there were few men to whom he
could safely entrust his pulpit suggests that he
was perhaps over-conscientiously possessive about
his parish, over-conscious of his own role as
evangelical Vicar.[71] There is some hint of this
in his later opposition to the construction of a
school chapel on the grounds that this would
weaken the traditional association of church
and school.[72] Sincere keepers of the faith
evangelicals could all too easily, maybe without
realising it, gratify the perennial human desire
for power. That Cunningham moved with marked
ease among the affluent can more confidently be
asserted for his 1825 diary reveals that he
regularly entertained and was entertained by the
titled. This was no indiscriminate mixing with
the rich, for all were firm supporters of
evangelical societies. Nevertheless Cunningham
clearly possessed the bearing requisite for high
society, what Trollope called 'suavity', what
evangelical obituarists more cordially labelled
'courtesy' and 'geniality'.[73]
Geniality is the chief characteristic of
the elderly Vicar who is the central character
in Cunningham's most successful religious novel,
The Velvet Cushion (1814).[74] Inside the venerable
pulpit cushion of his church the Vicar finds a
roll of paper, 'My own history', an account of
the cushion's experiences in, and opinion of, the
various churches and meeting houses in which it
has passed its long and checkered career. Out
of this rather unpromising material, Cunningham
produced a deservedly popular tale. Its strength
lies in the characterisation of the Vicar and his
wife: by investing his characters with a delicate
touch of humour Cunningham succeeded in the
difficult task of making goodness attractive, a
task which other evangelical novelists frequently
evaded, merely informing their readers of the
merits of the virtuous. Moreover, while evoking
the ire of some critics by portraying Anglicanism
as the ecclesiastical ideal, Cunningham was far
from censorious of other groups.[75] Neither he nor

his fictional spokesman set themselves up as
mentors: the latter is shown to be genuinely
humble, a tolerant man who frequently qualifies the
asperities of the cushion; the writer's style is,
with only a rare lapse, urbanely descriptive
rather than didactic.[76]
    While Cunningham's literary technique was more
sophisticated than that of some of his fellow
evangelicals, the difference in his style of
writing can also be attributed to a different
clientele and a different philosophy. Aiming at
an upper/middle class readership, he neither put
pressure upon his readers, nor talked down to
them, as did many authors of works for the
lower classes: the more oblique approach was,
perhaps, not only more congenial to his temperament,
but also more appropriate to an educated audience
unlikely subserviently to accept the dictates of
presbyteral authority. But those who like
Cunningham and Wilberforce thus sought to be 'all
things to all men' in order to reach the upper
classes inevitably ran the risk of being charged
with hypocrisy, compromise and equivocation.
    The assumption that evangelicals were
hypocrites owes much to the stereotyped evangelical
ministers of Victorian fiction about whom in
dissenting form Valentine Cunningham has written

> The stereotypes are sufficiently in touch
> with reality, sometimes more and sometimes
> less, to convince the unknowing reader
> that he has truly met a Dissenter. But
> novelists who only employ this signal system,
> and never go beyond its limited resources
> in their fictional treatment of Dissent,
> are really evading extensive contact with,
> or new thought about, Nonconformity.[77]

The charge is particularly well-brought against
Mrs. Trollope who presented in William Cartwright
not the, perhaps excusable, thumbnail sketch of
evangelical hypocrisy, but a sustained image,
unqualified, extending through three volumes.
The strength of her satire, like that of Thackeray,
lies in the exaggeration of recognisable
evangelical traits, its weakness in their
continued isolation from equally important
balancing characteristics. Thus she quite rightly
drew attention to evangelicals' practice of
identifying the religious utility of everything
they did, a practice which could easily have led

to widespread antinomianism had it not been
balanced by that equally typical sensitivity of
conscience, which Cartwright so signally lacked.
   If the charge of hypocrisy can be dismissed,
that of equivocation must at least be qualified.
Hazlitt who explicitly absolved Wilberforce from
the former, suggested that his tendency towards
the latter could be seen in the selection of
causes likely to win him the approbation of the
high and mighty, an argument hardly concordant
with the abolitionists' twenty year struggle to
persuade Lords and Commons to end the slave trade.[78]
The scarcity of Evangelical Bishops points to an
equal unwillingness on the part of Evangelical
clergy to compromise in order to gain place for
themselves: they were, according to their
contemporary James Bean, 'fully aware that
inferiority of rank and straitness of income are
the certain consequences of their fidelity'.[79]
That evangelicals deliberately - and astutely -
cultivated the patronage of the influential for
their societies and sought entrees among them
for religious ends cannot be doubted: in A
Practical View Wilberforce suggested that
'Christians ought to have a due respect and regard
to the approbation and favour of men' in so far
as these could be used 'as furnishing means and
instruments of influence'.[80] Yet the very
ingenuousness of such statements and the cautions
with which they were hedged militate against the
charge of equivocation. Evangelicals were far
more self-aware than Hazlitt was prepared to
admit, hence the reiterated fear that simplicity
might be lost as a result of royal patronage and
the warnings against reliance upon the approval
of the affluent. 'What doest thou here, Elijah?'
Hannah More asked herself, ill at ease in the
society in which she had once held such sway, and
added the confessional plea 'Felt too much
pleasure at the pleasure expressed by so many
accomplished friends on seeing me again. Keep me
from contagion'.[81]
   But if many of the charges against evangelicals
can thus largely be refuted, the question remains:
were they unduly concerned with material well-
being? In the eyes of some evangelicals worldly
possessions could symbolise conformity to the
world. Dissenting periodicals criticised those
who in furnishing their homes vied with the worldly
and, in particular, objected when Christians
followed 'vain fashions in dress', the inordinate

love of which, a Methodist feared, was becoming
increasingly common among them. Those who dressed
as the world dressed did so in order to be seen
of men; they therefore ran the risk of pride and
tended to mix with those who would appreciate their
finery, itself a sign that they were not taking
their religion seriously, and a stumbling block to
others who might think that the way to heaven was
wide.[82] Jabez Bunting hesitated before proposing
to his future wife because (among other short-
comings) her dress was 'by far too gay and costly
and worldly', and later wrote to her 'I cannot but
be pleased to hear that you have disposed of your
gaudy cloak'.[83] Similar pressure was put on
other preachers' wives, denounced in a private
memorandum at the Conference of 1802 for sporting
'double,triple, rows of buttons', a criticism
which suggests that Methodist ladies did not
altogether support the sobriety of appearance
favoured by the men of their society.[84]

Anglican women of the Clapham school seem
to have enjoyed a more liberal regime for the
Christian Observer rarely laid down the law as to
dress: a correspondent of 1832 complained that
the periodical spoke out against many tyrannies, but
not against that of fashion, discussion of which,
the editors tamely protested, would do more harm
than good.[85] The difference can be attributed to
social status: acknowledging the propriety of
dressing according to station, the dissenting
periodicals were primarily concerned to dissuade
their lower and middle class readers from aping
fashions which for them were synonymous with upper
class worldliness; in contrast, maybe in reaction
to the dissenting assumption that a Quakerish
simplicity was the Christian norm, Anglican
evangelicals found it necessary to urge that
Christians dressed up to their class. In 1806
'a lover of that which is proper' argued that the
gospel forbade not ornamentation but its excess.
On the one hand the dress of Christian women should
reflect the virtues of modesty, simplicity, and
economy; the female form 'which is particularly
pleasing' should be properly concealed but not
disfigured. On the other hand, while Christians
should not be in the van of sartorial change nor
dress in such a way as to associate themselves with
the excessively worldly, a reasonable degree of
regard to fashion was perfectly acceptable,
particularly when new styles were more feminine,
convenient, and cheap than old. Providing neither

modesty nor decorum were thereby infringed, a woman should adopt the style of dress appropriate to her class. It was no part of Christian humility to be taken for the maid.[86]

To dress below one's station was believed to be both an affectation and evangelistically counter-productive. It was wrong, Wilberforce maintained, to be singular, a complaint perhaps against his eccentric sister, Mrs. James Stephen, who wandered round Clapham in rags and tatters refusing to buy new clothes; in manners and appearance Christians should be like the rest of the world.[87] Henry Thornton recognised that either austerity or ostentation might prevent evangelicals from influencing their fellows and therefore required his wife to dress modestly but fashionably and elegantly.[88] Piety, Hannah More proclaimed, was not at war with elegance. The fashions which were not hostile to virtue could most certainly be pursued providing only that they were kept in their proper (subordinate) position.[89]

The same mode of thought extended beyond dress to the comforts of life generally. Dissenters and Recordites might inveigh against what they regarded as extravagance, but Simeon questioned the assumption that Christians should necessarily deprive themselves of the luxuries common to their class. He wrote to the Duchess of Beaufort in 1823:

> If a person in my situation were to affect the pomp and grandeur of a Duke, I should not hesitate to denounce him as violating his baptismal engagements. But does a person of your Grace's rank come under that anathema, because of the elegances that are around you? or if the King were to become truly alive to the best things, must he dismiss all that adorns his palaces? [90]

In her novel, Coelebs in Search of a Wife, Hannah More admitted that Christians might properly enjoy wealth and grandeur but stressed that they should not set too much store by them.[91] Paradoxically by enabling Evangelicals to assume that they, as true Christians, did not overvalue their possessions she perhaps facilitated that complacent and uncritical acceptance of material well-being against which her exemplary characters were arguing. These showed no real awareness that they might themselves fall into this particular sin; on the contrary they were more concerned to oppose undue asceticism, maintaining that 'at a mansion where an affluent family actually live (sic), all reasonable indulgences should be allowed'.[92]

There seems good reason to believe that 'all reasonable indulgences' were allowed in the homes of the Clapham sect and like-minded Evangelicals. 'Debarred from worldliness', G.W.E. Russell has suggested, 'the Evangelicals went in for comfort'.[93] In York the evangelical artist John Russell attended a meeting of 'religious people who drink tea and spend the time in religious exercises', and noted that the apartment in which they met was 'very elegant'.[94] Lord Teignmouth who left Clapham in 1808 described the house in Portland Square to which he had moved as

> airy, cheerful, and comfortable. I have perhaps paid about £2,500 more than I ought in prudence; but the difference of a comfortable or inconvenient house, of a bad and good situation, to such a family as ours, is so great, that I would save in any way for the accommodation. An inconvenient house is a perpetual temptation to discontent; and subject as I am to long bilious fits, it ought not to be risked.[95]

Charles Simeon was no less willing to pay out for the comforts of life: he was, as his latest biographer has shown, something of a dandy, decidedly partial to 'the pleasures of the table', and 'like many a bachelor don...extremely house-proud and very fussy about his carpets'. His horses too were a matter of pride and intense concern.[96]

Any criticism of evangelicals on these grounds must be carefully qualified. Their charities were so extensive as necessarily to reduce the standard of living that they might otherwise have enjoyed, a fact acknowledged by Wilberforce in a letter to his son; in their youth Thornton and Simeon regularly gave away about a third of their income.[97] The sheer number of evangelical charities as listed by Ford K. Brown and the recurrence of the same names on subscription list after subscription list reinforces the belief that Evangelicals were by the standards of almost any other group in any other period exceptionally generous. The willingness to give away large sums is of itself proof that they were not unduly possessive.

It is possible that contemporaries and those who later criticised Evangelicals for seeking the best of both worlds were not altogether aware of the extensiveness of their charity. The nature of their criticism however suggests that they were primarily concerned with the apparent discrepancy between what Evangelicals said and what they did. The real attack therefore was not so much against their enjoyment of worldly comforts as against their theological disparagement of that enjoyment. The charge cannot easily be refuted, for it can be questioned whether even Simeon's theology was sufficiently affirmative fully to embrace so whole-hearted an endorsement of the good things of life. At table and on horseback Simeon by his practice emphatically proclaimed that life was good in itself: his theology while not denying this failed to give it comparable importance. John Venn of Clapham like Simeon gained much enjoyment from life and urged his hearers against undue asceticism. Nevertheless when he attempted in the pulpit to define '...the value of human life', he only mentioned 'temporal enjoyments' in order to deny their importance. Life on earth was valuable because it provided opportunities to fulfil God's will, not just to eat and drink; it was infinitely important because it determined man's future well-being; and it was ennobled by the solicitude which God had expressed for it: 'Are men made in vain when the only begotten of the Father gave his life as a ransom for theirs?'[98] Whereas preachers in the period after Maurice would have elaborated this point by arguing that the Incarnation was itself an affirmation of human existence in all its fullness, Venn developed it into an evangelistic appeal: many by failing to avail themselves of that ransom gave every appearance of indeed being 'made in vain'. It would be anachronistic to suggest that Venn's contemporaries criticised evangelicals by reference to incarnational theology as such. Nevertheless they recognised that Evangelicals' theology was not altogether congruent with their lifestyle.

A more damning criticism is that Evangelicals appeared to condemn in 'the world' activities and attitudes which were acceptable within the household of faith. In particular they failed to recognise how closely their own social round mirrored that of the fashionable whose habit of passing from social engagement to social engagement they despised as a misuse of time. Yet Sophia

Cunningham's diary for 1808 can easily be construed
as a religious variant of the same theme, for
interspersed with the texts of all the sermons her
husband preached and accounts of his visits to the
poor are the details of the frequent journeys they
made from Moor Park to Surrey to Clapham, how they
travelled, whom they visited and dined with, and
who visited and dined with them...

The scene in <u>Coelebs in Search of a Wife</u> is
frequently set at a dinner table, at which
Evangelicals discuss the doctrine of substitutionary
atonement - and the merits and demerits of other
people, including previous guests, a practice
justified on religious grounds. The exemplary Mr.
Stanley, father of several daughters, tells his
family

> I would on no account speak so freely of a
> lady whom I receive at my house, were it
> not that, if I were quite silent, after
> Phoebe's expressed admiration, she might
> conclude that I saw nothing to condemn in
> Miss Sparkes, and might be copying her faults
> under the notion that being entertaining made
> amends for every thing.[99]

Similar double standards operate in Rowland Hill's
<u>Village Dialogues</u> in which on the one hand scandal -
and particularly scandal about the innocent - is
condemned, while at the same time exemplary
characters with no hint of authorial criticism
engage in an eight page discussion of the various
bad marriages which have recently taken place.[100]
The presumed justification, that the latter gossip
was capable of being 'improved' to religious
edification, only reinforces contemporary complaints
that evangelicals were self-satisfied and used
religion as a cover for sin: it is hard to believe
that prurient delight was totally absent from such
discussions.

The evidence of the novels cannot of course
unquestionably be assumed to reflect evangelical
practice. But there seems reason to believe that it
probably did. The authors need not have put
criticism of the irreligious into the mouths of
their exemplary characters, and had such gossipy
denunciations been generally disapproved presumably
would not have done so. The tendency of
evangelicals to gossip was noted by one of the
few who spoke out against the practice: 'You are
well aware' wrote Isaac Milner, 'that there are

few things which I dislike more in religious
people, than that spirit of gossiping which prevails
among them a great deal too much'. [101] Extant
letters supply some confirmation of his observation,
for when evangelicals could not talk to their
friends they wrote copiously to them. Mrs. Thornton
asked the Grants to give her all the latest gossip
and contributed her own quota: the Barclays
seemed to be enjoying Bath in a way incompatible
with their Quakerism - she wished they would drop
their profession; the Hoares had not yet dined
with her, an inevitable event to which she did not
look forward for it was not very convenient and
although 'she' was sweet 'he' was surly...[102]
    The Thornton letters are very refreshing for
they are chatty and frequently unguarded.
Religious reflections are juxtaposed with wry
accounts of their children's escapades and opinions.
And yet their very ease goes some way towards
confirming the charges levelled against evangelicals
for Mrs. Thornton appeared to have no qualm either
about criticising others or about the accuracy of
her own sometimes snide judgments. Her letters
suggest that Clapham Evangelicals conformed to the
standards of the world as much in conversation as
in clothing, comfort, and consumption.
    This apparent heedlessness of the worldly
conformity which they were generally so anxious
to avoid can be explained in two ways. Questions
concerning the use of time and the legitimacy of
recreation, so central to evangelical discussions
on 'lawful' and 'unlawful' pleasures were not so
immediately applicable to matters of comfort,
for clothing, furnishings, and food could all be
regarded as necessities of life. Evangelicals
therefore accepted with little qualm the common
practices of their fellows. More particularly,
within the security of their own homes, they were
on the whole protected from the contaminating
company which many regarded as the essence of
worldliness: they were therefore able to relax
and lapsed into gossip. If here, as at religious
meetings, they were only mildly aware of the
extent to which they resembled the world which
they professed to despise, they were for once
giving their over-taxed consciences a rest.

NOTES

    1. R. Hill, An Expostulatory Letter...in which
the bad tendency of stage amusements...is seriously

considered, (1795); Village Dialogues (1801-03),
passim; CO xviii (1819), pp. 510-12; xxii (1822),
pp. 418-20; EM i series xxx (1822), p. 349.
    2. Edinburgh Review xiii (1809), p. 342.
    3. W. Wilberforce op. cit., p. 388.
    4. H. More, Thoughts on the Manners of the
Great (1788); An Estimate of the Religion of the
Fashionable World (1790).
   • 5. Rule, loc. cit.
    6. EM i series xxiv (1816), p. 261.
    7. BM xix (1827), pp. 412-13. Biblical hints
were issued to those attending watering places as
early as 1809 (i, pp. 256-59) but the practice
was not then regarded as common.
    8. Hennell, 'Evangelicalism and Worldliness',
loc. cit.
    9. J. Gilbert (ed.), Autobiography of Mrs.
Gilbert (1874), i, p. 130.
   10. Foot (ed.), op. cit., i, pp. 38, 113-114,
144, 151-52. Cf. p. 28 where Gladstone recorded
his first visit to a ball by a series of exclama-
tion marks.
   11. EM ii series iii (1825), p. 65.
   12. The Record, 27 September 1830; CO xxxiii
(1833), p. 660.
   13. Hennell and Pollard (eds.), op. cit.,
p. 105; Gisborne, ...Female Sex..., p. 107.
   14. Hill, Village Dialogues ii (1802), p. 31;
MM xxxiv (1811), p. 389.
   15. EM i series i (1793), p. 32.
   16. M. Milner, The Life of Isaac Milner...
(1842), pp. 53f.
   17. E. Abbott and L. Campbell, The Life and
Letters of Benjamin Jowett (1897), i, p. 42.
   18. A.M. Wilberforce (ed.), op. cit., p. 231.
Cf. Gisborne, ...Female Sex..., p. 99; Hennell and
Pollard (eds.), op. cit., p. 105.
   19. J. Vansittart (ed.), Katharine Fry's Book
(1966), p. 122.
   20. T.G. Tyndale, Selections from the
Correspondence of Mrs. Ely Bates (1872),i,pp. 261ff.
   21. CO xxviii (1828), pp. 95-96, 380.
   22. Ibid.,pp. 245-46; xxii (1822), pp. 563-66.
   23. BM i (1809), pp. 357-58; iv (1812),
pp. 103-105; MM xli (1818), p. 940; xlii (1819),
p. 141.
   24. Clarke (ed.), op. cit., i, pp. 65-67.
   25. CO xxxiii (1833), pp. 677-78.
   26. MM xxxvi (1813), p. 704. Wilberforce
apparently disagreed with the MM for in an attempt
to show the greater heinousness of bull-baiting

Faith and Fashion

he argued that 'shooting afforded exercise to the
body, and the birds who fell by it were subjected
to no pain beyond the immediate deprivation of
life' (Parliamentary History of England, 1806-20,
xxxvi, p. 846). Hoare and Buxton married Louisa
and Hannah Gurney, sisters of Elizabeth Fry.
Both families moved from Quakerism to Anglicanism.
    27. Templewood, The Unbroken Thread (1949),
pp. 96ff.
    28. CO xxiv (1824), p. 552
    29. Ibid., p. 360-62.
    30. G.W.E. Russell, The Household of Faith
(1903), p. 234. The rebuke was addressed to
Russell's Evangelical father, an inveterate fox-
hunter, a salutary reminder of the risks of
generalising about evangelical practice from
polemic. Russell's claim that in the 1850s and
1860s no Evangelical condemned shooting although
some vehemently opposed hunting supports the
argument proffered above and challenges Ford
K. Brown's assumption that Buxton's love of game
placed him on the periphery of the Evangelical
party (op. cit., p. 406).
    31. MM xxxvi (1813), p. 704.
    32. MM xli (1818), p. 11.
    33. Ward, op. cit., p. 10.
    34. CO x (1811), pp. 556-57; xviii (1819),
pp. 288-95; xxv (1825), p. 488.
    35. The Record, 17 June, 27 September,
4 October 1830; 9 February, 30 August 1832.
    36. Josiah Pratt, Remains of the Rev. Richard
Cecil (1854 edn.), p. 44.
    37. MM xxxvi (1813), p. 704.
    38. G. Burder, Lawful Amusements (1805),
p. 29.
    39. R. Hill, An Expostulatory Letter...
pp. 15ff.
    40. L. Stephen, The Life of Sir James
Fitzjames Stephen (1895), pp. 61-62.
    41. Report from the Select Committee on
Dramatic Literature with the Minutes of Evidence
(IUPS edn. 1968), p. 3.
    42. M. R. Booth in Booth, Southern, Marker,
and Davies (eds.), The Revels History of Drama in
English vi, pp. 11-12.
    43. T.B. Shepherd, Methodism and the
Literature of the Eighteenth Century (1940), p. 203.
    44. J.H. Pratt, op. cit., pp. 157-62.
    45. CO iv (1805), p. 13.
    46. R.I. and S. Wilberforce, The Life of
William Wilberforce (1838), i, p. 88; Correspon-

93

dence... i, pp. 49ff; A.M. Wilberforce, op. cit.,
p. 234.
    47. Carus, op. cit., pp. 465ff.
    48. While believing that such fires were
'acts of God', the EM was concerned that victims
should be aided, and expressed pleasure at the
public response to an appeal for financial
assistance for those injured in the collapse of
the Brunswick theatre (i, series xvii, 1809,
p. 169; ii series vi, 1820, p. 158).
    49. EM i series xiii (1805), p. 171; CO
viii (1809), pp. 295-97; MM xlix (1826), pp. 153-
61; W. Wilberforce, op. cit., pp. 306-08;
R. Hill, A Warning to Professors... (1833 edn.),
pp. 9ff.
    50. Report...on Dramatic Literature pp. 21-36,
41-42, 59-70, 118-22, 160, 178. Collier was
critical both of 'persons who are usually considered
Methodists' and of Colman, who refused to resign
in his favour.
    51. J.H. Pratt, op. cit., pp. 157-58;
Burder, Lawful Amusements, p. 10; EM i series
xiii (1805), pp. 355ff; CO iv (1805), pp. 239-40;
MM xli (1818), pp. 300-01.
    52. Gisborne, ...Female Sex..., pp. 95-96.
    53. H. More, Preface to the Tragedies
(1801), Works (1818 edn.), iii, pp. 36-37. After
some deliberation Miss More decided to republish
her plays on the grounds that it was dangerous
to watch but permissible to read drama. See
pp.176f. below.
    54. EM i series xvii (1809), p. 426; ER i
series v (1809), pp. 1031-44; BM i (1809), pp.
464-66, reviews of Rev. James Plumptre, Four
Discourses on the Stage.
    55. More, Preface to the Tragedies...,
pp. 7-8.
    56. Ibid., pp. 24-25.
    57 J.H. Pratt, op. cit., p. 160.
    58. EM i series xviii (1810), p. 105;
xxvi (1818), p. 240.
    59. E.M. Forster, Marianne Thornton 1797-1887:
a domestic biography (1956), p. 133; Meacham,
op. cit., p. 135.
    60. W.M. Thackeray, The Newcomes (1853-55),
Works (1869 edn.), v, pp. 19-20; G. Eliot,
Middlemarch (1872, Penguin edn. 1965), p. 302.
    61. W. Hazlitt, The Spirit of the Age (1825),
Works (1930-34 edn.), xi, pp. 147-50.
    62. Edinburgh Review lii (1831), p. 448.
Cf. liv, p. 103.

63. The text of a lecture, 'Cunningham of Harrow' by Miss A.L. Wyatt, her research notes and correspondence are lodged in Lambeth Palace Library. A brief family history is provided in a biography of Cunningham's son, M.M. Verney, Sir Henry Stewart Cunningham K.C.I.E. (1923). I have also drawn upon the Cunningham diaries and other papers deposited in the Dorset County Record Office.

64. The Times, 18 September 1820; The Examiner, 24 September 1820; Political Register, 30 September 1820; M.D. George, Catalogue of Prints and Drawings in the British Museum: political and personal satires (1952), x, 13914, 13982, 15392.

65. F. Trollope, The Vicar of Wrexhill (1837), iii, p. 33.

66. Ibid., iii, p. 98.

67. Ibid., i, p. 286.

68. Ibid., iii, p. 343. Further discussion of Mrs.Trollope's novel, Cunningham's own work, and the conflict between them can be found in E. Jay, The Religion of the Heart (1979).

69. M. Sadleir, Trollope, a commentary (1927, new edn. 1945), pp. 58ff.

70. Letter dated 1 January 1823, BFBS archives; Canton, op. cit., i, p. 312; E. Stock, The History of the Church Missionary Society (1899), i, p. 277.

71. Many letters refusing invitations to speak are lodged in the BFBS and CMS archives.

72. W.W. Druett, Harrow through the Ages (1935, 3rd edn. 1956), p. 162; T.F. May, 'A Study of Harrow School in its relationship to its neighbourhood...' (London M.Phil.,1969), p. 129 points out that despite his reservations Cunningham eventually concurred in the school chapel scheme and subscribed to it.

73. T.D. Bernard, Departure into Rest, a sermon preached...on the occasion of the death of Rev. J.W. Cunningham (1861), p. 8; T.A. Trollope, What I remember (1887-89), i, pp. 72-89, an account of his mother's enmity more judicious than many but lacking any reference to her novel.

74. Cunningham's first novel, A World Without Souls (1805) was well-received by the evangelical press but neither it, De Rancé (1815) a narrative poem, nor Sancho or the Proverbialist (1816) were as polished or as popular as The Velvet Cushion which went through seven editions in two years.

75. EM i series xxii (1815), pp. 17ff, 64ff;

CO xiii (1814), pp. 585-96.
   76. Cunningham's style can be contrasted
favourably with that of the dissenters who
vituperatively replied in The Legend of the Velvet
Cushion (1815), published under the pseudonym
Jeremiah Ringletub, and A New Covering for the
Velvet Cushion (1815), attributed to John Styles.
   77. V. Cunningham, op. cit., p. 200.
   78. Hazlitt, op. cit.
   79. Quoted H. Hopkins, Charles Simeon of
Cambridge (1977), p. 215.
   80. W. Wilberforce, op. cit., p. 214.
   81. W. Roberts, op. cit., ii, p. 415.
   82. MM xl (1817), pp. 380-82; xli (1818),
p. 939; BM vii (1815), p. 103; xiii (1821),
pp. 154-56; xiv (1822), pp. 378-79; EM ii
series vii (1829), p. 445.
   83. T.P. Bunting, op. cit., i, pp. 155, 173.
   84. Ibid., p. 326.
   85. CO xxxii (1832), pp. 646-48.
   86. CO v (1806), pp. 472-76.
   87. A.M. Wilberforce, op. cit., p. 228;
Stephen, op. cit., pp. 17-18.
   88. Forster, op. cit., p. 27.
   89. H. More, Strictures on the Modern System
of Female Education (1799), Works (1834 edn.), iii,
p. 60.
   90. Carus, op. cit., p. 583.
   91. More, Coelebs..., i, p. 277.
   92. Ibid., ii, p. 344.
   93. Russell, op. cit., p. 234.
   94. G.C. Williamson, John Russell, R.A.
      (1894), p. 73.
   95. Teignmouth, op. cit., ii, p. 151.
   96. Hopkins, op. cit., pp. 12-13, 17-18, 153-
54, 157-58, 164, 211.
   97. Ibid., p. 60; Meacham, op. cit., pp. 137,
197-98; A.R. Ashwell, Life of the Right Reverend
Samuel Wilberforce (1880), i, p. 22.
   98. Venn, op. cit., i, p. 331.
   99. More, Coelebs..., ii, p. 98.
   100. Hill, Village Dialogues (1801-03), ii,
p. 126; iv, pp. 127ff.
   101. M. Milner, op. cit., p. 637.
   102. Letters dated November 1803, September
1807, Thornton papers, Cambridge University
Library.

Chapter Four

FAITH AND FAMILY LIFE

Suspicious of 'public amusements', wary of the
contamination of the outside world, evangelicals
felt most free to relax and have fun when they were
at home. It was within the confines of the home
that evangelical children had largely to seek their
recreation. And it was within the home that the
influence of evangelicalism was most signally felt
for 'the real strength of Evangelicalism lay not
in the pulpit or the platform, but in the home'.[1]
An analysis of evangelicals' leisure patterns must
therefore begin with a study of their family life.
    Notwithstanding their concern for the poor and
the oppressed, their anxiety to convert the un-
believer, evangelical parents believed that their
primary responsibility was towards their children,
for whose religious nurture they were accountable
to God. Superintendence of the family was a
fundamental duty, argued the younger William Goode,
and should not be neglected for more public
responsibilities.[2] 'My own soul should doubtless
be my first object', reflected Wilberforce, 'and
combined with it my children'.[3] Parenthood,
Standish Meacham has well said, was a mission.
Dickens' suggestion that philanthropically inclined
parents were forgetful of their own children is
singularly wide of the mark, for evangelicals
believed more firmly than most that mission began
at home: 'It is through the institution of
families' wrote Henry Thornton, 'that the knowledge
of God and of his laws is handed down from
generation to generation'.[4]
    It was imperative that such knowledge be
imparted to children from their earliest days, for
life was uncertain, child and adolescent deaths
were common, and few parents saw all their children
reach maturity. A child's eternal felicity

depended on the response he made to God in the few
years that remained to him once he reached the age
of accountability, the determining of which caused
evangelical parents much anxiety. The Methodist
Magazine of 1833 issued 'An earnest and affectionate
appeal to Christian parents' warning them that
unless their offspring were converted 'they cannot
possibly enter the Kingdom of heaven ... Their
precious souls are on the slippery verge of
destruction; and dying in their present state,
they will be eternally undone ...'[5] It followed
that evangelical children were exposed to intense
parental pressure well into maturity: 'You will
say there is no end of my recommendations',
Teignmouth wrote to a son about to take up a post
in India, 'but can I cease to be anxious for your
eternal welfare? If I were my profession of
Christianity would be a mere pretence.'[6]

Children were expected to respond to the
gospel in essentially the same way as adults.
'Except ye be converted and become as grown people',
E.E. Kellett has suggested, was a common evangelical
distortion of Scripture.[7] Religious precocity was
welcomed and encouraged. In 1818 the popular
writer Legh Richmond met a twelve year old
converted through reading one of his tracts and
commented:

> I never before, except in the case of
> 'little Jane' herself, saw so clear and
> so early an instance of decided grace,
> and of a truly enlightened mind: you
> would have thought her conversation
> equal to eighteen at least.[8]

Children's deathbed testimonies frequently mirrored
those of adults, a source of consolation to
bereaved parents, and a challenge to those whose
living children had not yet manifested any similar
signs of grace.[9] Typically over-anxious,
evangelical parents seized upon the slightest sign
of religious response with relief, one pair
convincing themselves that their thirteen month
child had listened attentively when addressed on
spiritual matters.[10] More harmfully they responded
to the slightest sign of declension with horror.
A father who was informed that his three year old
son had told a lie commented:

> I was thunderstruck and almost distracted;
> for the information seemed to blast my

most cherished hopes. This might, I
thought, be the commencement of a
series of evils for ever ruinous to our
peace. I am not - I never was - naturally
of a temper to augur the worst; but the
first grand moral delinquency even at such
an age, must commit a breach on the
noblest sensibilities of the heart, which
cannot but threaten a catastrophe at
which a parent may well shudder ... I am
not sure that my agony, on hearing of his
death, was much more intense than that
which I endured, from an apprehension of
his guilt.[11]

This nightmarish fear of the implication of any
departure from the evangelical norm derived from
the belief that early evil propensities, unchecked,
would develop and destroy: those who believed in
Scriptural denunciations, Hannah More argued, dared
not overlook the fault that might be the germ of
unspeakable miseries.[12] Furthermore many
evangelicals assumed that the irregularities of
children were inherently hateful as offences
against God, incurring divine punishment.[13] Hence
the tendency to judge childish misdemeanours with
a seriousness appropriate only to adult commission
of the same crime.

But if evangelicals expected their children to
act as little adults, they tried to keep them as
children. The world presented many snares to those
passing through the dangerous period of youth:
many evangelicals responded by being over-protective,
by exerting too overbearing a control, and by
failing to trust their children. They justified
their excessive watchfulness in terms of their
evangelistic mission, in fulfilment of which they
adopted a priestly role towards their children,
regarding themselves as divinely appointed spiritual
supervisors. It was their task to make upon their
children that continuing assessment of spiritual
development which they would constantly make upon
themselves when mature. Thus Richard Cecil wrote
to his son, Israel:

The truth is, my dear, that your mind
is greatly improved and we cannot but
notice it and rejoice in it; and you
may depend upon it we shall not fail to
encourage a right disposition to the
utmost of our power.[14]

In order so to monitor a child's development the
parents required detailed accounts from absentee
sons of their companions, of how they spent each
hour of the day, of their reading, of their use
of Sunday ...
Particular anxiety was felt when sons who had
previously been permitted to mix only with other
evangelicals went up to university. The Macaulay
and Thornton families went out of their way to
ensure that even the Cambridge laundress who served
their sons was exemplary.[15] Macaulay's parents
paid heed to the slightest rumour about his
behaviour and wrote to him in great concern about
his (supposed) democracy and (actual) novel-reading.
Convinced of the rectitude of his own conduct, able
to argue his case without resorting to over-
statement or emotionally charged language, Tom sent
reply after reply justifying his activities,
dispelling inaccurate rumours. Courteously but
firmly he put his parents in their place. 'My dear
Father', he wrote from Wales in 1821,

> I have just received your letter and
> cannot but feel concerned at the tone
> of it. I do not understand how I can
> be said to have written only two letters
> within the last five weeks, since not one
> week has elapsed during that time in
> which I have not sent a letter to Cadogan
> Place. Nor do I think it quite fair to
> attack me for filling my letters with
> remarks on the King's Irish expedition.
> It has been the great event of this
> part of the world.

Firm Macaulay might be but he was anxious for mutual
understanding. He continued:

> To me it is of little importance whether
> the King's conduct were right or wrong:
> but it is of great importance that those
> whom I love should not think me a
> precipitate, silly, shallow, sciolist in
> politics, and suppose that every frivolous
> word that falls from my pen is a dogma
> which I mean to advance as indisputable.[16]

Implicit in Macaulay's argument was the belief that
to demand carefully prepared scripts was to deny and
to stultify the spontaneity of love which felt free
to pass on to loved ones the most 'fleeting and

Faith and Family Life

unformulated thoughts'. Yet he could appreciate
that his parents' letters too were a product of
love: 'I value, most deeply value, that sollicit-
ude (sic) which arises from your affection for
me - but let it not debar me from justice and
candour'.[17]
    It is clear that in exercising their priestly
role evangelicals sometimes resorted to something
perilously close to religious terrorism. A Baptist
writer recommended that the story of Ananias and
Sapphira should be read to children who were not
strictly truthful.[18] The dire consequences of
disobedience were graphically described, for
evangelicals believed that parents were representatives of God and that undutifulness was therefore
akin to impiety.[19] Legh Richmond reminded his
children that parents

> watch over you for God, and are entitled
> to great deference and cheerful obedience.
> You may easily shorten the lives of
> affectionate and conscientious parents,
> by misconduct, bad tempers, and alienation
> from their injunctions. Let not this sin
> be laid to your charge.[20]

Believing that children would be held responsible
by God for any departure from the principles in
which they had been educated, evangelicals resorted
to the most underhand of methods to ensure that
such judgment was avoided. In a series of letters
a mother told her daughter that if she failed to
be converted she would break her parents' hearts.[21]
    But not all evangelicals approved of moral
blackmail of this type. John Foster opposed the
habit of threatening future judgment on children
for the slightest misdemeanour, while the elder
William Goode insisted that trifles should be
allowed to pass as trifles; both his letters and
his son's testimony reveal that as his children
grew up he, unlike the Macaulays, gradually yielded
his authority.[22] Thomas Gisborne opposed great
strictness which caused children to tremble before
their parents, maintaining that while 'pert
loquacity' should be discouraged, children should
feel free to join in parental conversations.[23]
Adam Clarke's children received long chatty letters
from their father of which only a small portion
was monitory, and even there the tone was neither
hysterical nor pressurising.[24] Thomas Fowell
Buxton's rare reprimands to his children took the

form of advice rather than rebuke and were very
tentatively given. He and his wife, Hannah Gurney,
unlike some evangelical parents, assumed that the
children whom they had committed to God would hold
to the faith and far from haranguing them encouraged
them accordingly.[25] Their confidence was shared by
Hannah's sister, Louisa Hoare, who possessed a
sympathetic understanding of childhood and wrote
manuals for parents that abound in common sense.[26]
She warned them of the danger of frightening
children and losing their affection, the risk of
making religion dull. She opposed the practice of
terrorising children into obedience by threatening
immediate divine retribution, and by incautiously
exposing them to funerals and corpses. She urged
her readers to let children be children and not to
punish them for being so. She emphasised that
children had rights.

While it is significant that Mrs. Hoare found
it necessary to criticise certain presumably
common practices, the popularity of her works
precludes the conclusion that her views were in
any way exceptional.[27] Moreover, it would be
wrong to divide evangelicals into those who were
according to twentieth century standards enlightened
and those who were not.. On the contrary the
evidence suggests that those who engaged in some
of the practices most abhorrent to twentieth century
thought, also showed what would now be regarded as
great insight. The Thornton family is a case in
point. Marianne Thornton recorded that her fear of
the dark was sympathetically soothed, indulged, and
gradually overcome. As a child she was with her
brothers and sisters free to engage in all the
idiosyncracies of childish play, bringing any
number of stones, flowers and other miscellaneous
playthings into the nursery. As she grew older
her father treated her as his intelligent equal,
discussed his political interests with her, and
allowed her to act as his amanuensis. Her biographer, E.M. Forster, certainly no sympathiser with
evangelicalism qua se, concluded that

> Battersea Rise was anything but a
> 'Victorian' establishment ... For an
> intelligent good-tempered child, life
> there must have been very pleasant, and in
> after days, with the nineteenth century
> cramping her, she looked back on it
> as golden.[28]

But Marianne's parents took her sister Lucy to see
the coffin of a child acquaintance and, no less
than other evangelicals, exposed their children to
a macabre glorification of death.

Death beds had an almost sacramental function
in evangelical experience. The questions of
onlookers were carefully designed to prompt dying
testimonies, for, while it was recognised that
assurance was sometimes lost under pressure of
illness, this was regarded as the supreme moment to
witness to the truth of the Christian gospel.
'You feel the power of those great truths you
have for so many years so fully declared to us',
Adam Clarke asked Joseph Benson, 'We have not
followed a cunningly devised fable'. 'He answered
"No, no; I have no hope of being saved but by
grace through faith"'.[29] To be present at such a
death bed was believed to be invariably edifying,
for the final power of the gospel was confirmed by
those who, in the words of a frequently repeated
refrain, showed that

> Jesus can make a dying bed
> Feel soft as downy pillows are.[30]

The occasion served, moreover, to challenge all
present to prepare for the transition to eternity,
and the obituaries, which dwelt in such loving
detail on the dying moments, enabled a far larger
congregation vicariously to hear both the comfort-
able words and the challenge to recommitment.

To twentieth century minds the practice of
recording for posterity every word and every
physical spasm was both morbid and sentimental. Yet
when, rarely, as with the unpublished account of
Mrs. Sophia Cunningham's death, the descriptions
rise above the stereotyping model, they suggest that
the prevalent sentiment was not so much morbidity
as wonder. Moreover, early nineteenth century
mourners were perhaps free to indulge in such an
excess of emotion over the physical separation
simply because they believed that this was the only
separation that was involved. When George Burder
wrote that his daughter was 'now a cold lifeless
corpse in a leaden coffin, much changed', he was
able to speak with such earthy realism because he
believed that his daughter's essence was no longer
encased in her body.[31]

But Burder was addressing a thirteen year old
son and there can be little doubt that he was trying
to scare him into deepened Christian commitment.

Yet even such abrasive methods may well have left
psychologically unscathed the child who was growing
up into a society which still practised the rituals
of birth and death, and, far from placing a taboo
upon the latter, accepted it as the fundamental
fact of life, its proper coda. This certainly
seems to have been the case with Lucy Thornton who
showed herself to be impervious both to the harmful
consequences predicted by modern psychology, and
to the inept moralising which her mother hoped
would be beneficial:

> Our Lucy stared rather than wept at
> the scene. 'Why Lucy', said Mama,
> 'perhaps the next burial may be yours.
> This little girl was just your age.'
> Lucy: 'It is a very pretty coffin,
> Mama. I had no idea that they made
> coffins so pretty.' 'Should you like
> to be in it?' 'Oh no, I should be very
> sorry to die and be shut up in a
> coffin.' 'Why, little Maria Venn is
> now an angel, she is happy with God.'
> 'But how do you know that, you cannot
> be sure for you have never been dead
> yourself?'[32]

Lucy's concluding comment could only have been
made by a child on very easy terms with her parents.
Indeed it was the easiness of the relationship
between parent and child which protected children
against the worst manifestations of evangelicalism.
Within the security of a loving relationship, a
child could face even a visit to a distressing
death scene with equanimity. Educational methods
might seem horrific but there was Father's hand
onto which to hold. The demands of God might
appear inexorable but Father loved and served God
and Father was not an ogre. If parental demands
were a foretaste of the demands of God, parental
love was a very real manifestation of that of the
Deity.

It is this context of love and security which
is the all-important qualification upon any
criticism of evangelical educational methods. For
evangelical children did not regard their homes as
prisons from which they longed to escape and their
parents as unwelcome task masters. Too much
attention has been paid to the few who left the
fold and inveighed against it. Others who moved
away from parental belief nevertheless spoke of

home and parents in tones of deep affection. Rev.
Brewin Grant wrote his autobiography when full of
bitterness towards nonconformity on account of his
expulsion from the Congregationalist ministry. Yet
his portrait of his dissenting childhood and
particularly of his father is sympathetic:

> I have no doubt I can say for my four
> brothers ... that if ever ... we were
> disposed to say with the Psalmist, 'all
> men are liars' ... the remembrance of this
> sterling example would silence our scepticism
> ... My father came home on the Saturday
> evening, and Sunday was a good day to us.
> The first thing for which we felt before
> quite awake was 'a plumb bun' by our
> pillows.[33]

The most striking example is Tom Macaulay,
who adored his home, suffered intense homesickness
at school, and lived for the holidays.[34] His
passion for domesticity, which a recent biographer
avers, was a passion aroused in an evangelical
home.[35] 'I am sure that it is well worth while
being sick to be nursed by a mother', he wrote to
Selina when as a student he had largely departed
from her beliefs, 'The sound of your voice, the
touch of your hand are present to me now, and will
be, I trust in God, to my last hour. The very
thought of these things invigorated me the other
day ...'[36] Macaulay's relationship with his mother
was admittedly easier than that with his father as
the greater spontaneity of his letters shows.
Constantly aware of the responsibility of directing
Tom's undoubted talents aright, anxious to curb in
his son the only too obvious manifestation of his
own worst faults, fearful of ministering to the
boy's conceit, Zachary only criticised, never
praised, thus depriving Tom of the paternal
approbation which his sensitivity may have
required.[37] But Tom's submission to his father's
conscience was not just the outworking of his need
for approval, nor simply a response to pressure
for he made plain to his parents even when obeying
that he disagreed with their demands. Rather his
acquiescence indicates the value he placed upon the
family tie. In 1823 he promised to discontinue his
contributions to Knight's Quarterly Magazine of
which his father disapproved, writing to the editor
'gratitude, duty, and prudence, alike compel me
to respect prejudices which I do not in the

slightest degree share'.[38] The closeness of the
bond was most obvious in 1833, a time of family
financial stringency in which Tom required the
emolument of office if he were to continue in
politics. His colleagues urged him to follow the
party line on the slavery bill rather than
suicidally offer his resignation. A loyal party
man Macaulay was loath to help defeat the ministry
at so crucial a time, but political affiliations
were subordinate to those of the family, and so he
insisted tersely 'I cannot go counter to my father.
He has devoted his whole life to this question, and
I cannot grieve him by giving way when he wishes
me to stand firm'.[39]

Further testimony to the respect and affection
in which evangelical children held their parents
comes in the plethora of filial biographies. These
are not always easy to use for loyalty and the
belief that biography should be edifying militated
against the depiction of 'warts and all'.
Biographers primarily interested in religious
experience and Christian activity frequently
described the former in terms of its theological
significance rather than in a more personalised
way, codifying a variety of experience into set
forms of words. Evangelicals therefore tended not
only to seek experience which conformed to the
established pattern but also to interpret that of
others in its light: 'he who has read the conversion and religious experience of one sensible man',
commented the Clarke biographers, 'has, in
substance, read that of ten thousand'.[40] But
biographies were not as stereotyped as this might
suggest. The general lack of discrimination of
compilers who thought nothing of producing weighty
tomes, containing many repetitive letters and
journal entries, enables the reader the more easily
to form his own picture of the original writer.
Moreover some biographers, anxious to delineate
every aspect of life, provide a wealth of
illustrative detail which throws light not only on
the personality of the subject but also upon the
pattern of family behaviour.

This is certainly the case with the Clarke
biography. When Clarke finally completed his eight-
volume commentary a family celebration was held,
at which his children presented him with a large
silver vase. His daughter described the occasion:

> His eldest son then filled the vessel with
> wine, which his Father raised first to his

own lips, then to those of his beloved
Wife's, and afterwards bore it to each
of the family present: he then put it
down, and in a strain of the most
heartfelt eloquent tenderness addressed
his children in the name of their
revered Mother and Himself in terms
which they will never forget.[41]

The stateliness and dignity of family relationships
are here communicated in the adjectives used, the
capitalisation, the religious aura of awe and
respect. These indicate too that acceptance of
symbol and ritual which enabled George Burder
formally to address his family on his seventieth
birthday and William Hey, an Anglican with Methodist
associations, to deliver a 'dying address' on the
last occasion when his children were likely to be
gathered together.[42] Later generations embarrassed
by such solemnity between those so intimately
acquainted have tended too easily to assume that
fathers who acted in this way must have been
distant and forbidding figures. But Clarke loved
to frolic with his children, 'carried them himself
up to bed, put, or playfully threw them in', and
'gained a game of marbles with as much delighted
satisfaction as any of the children with whom he
played'.[43] Thus in evangelical families, as
probably more generally, the stately patriarchalism
of the early nineteenth century coexisted with
close father/child affection. Clarke was both
paterfamilias and playmate.

If the biography of Adam Clarke is more wide-
ranging in its detail than many, it is but one of a
number of sources which point to the attractive and
winsome personalities of some evangelical fathers
and their friends. Touches of fun are evident even
in the letters of the most pensive and intense of
evangelicals, Henry Thornton, Zachary Macaulay, and
Richard Cecil, while gaiety and humour abound in the
correspondence between John Styles, critic of
watering places and the theatre, and Daniel Parken,
sometime editor of the Eclectic Review.[44] A similar
enjoyment of life and a delightful sense of humour
characterises the letters of Edward Hoare to his
father, who replied in like vein plotting with his
son to pacify Mrs. Hoare who was anxious lest
rowing injure his health.[45] Nephews and nieces
testified to the liveliness of Mrs. Hoare's child-
less sister, Richenda, whose vicarage home at
Lowestoft they frequently visited.[46] The characters

of other evangelical women are less easily
ascertained for they are often depicted in the
biographies of their husbands as shadowy and self-
effacing figures.   This is almost certainly a mis-
representation for unpublished papers show that
women like Mrs. Thornton and Mrs. Cunningham were
both vivacious and sociable.   So too was Hannah
More, one of the few to be accorded biographies in
her own right: the 'Bishop in petticoats' never
lost the animation which made her in her youth the
toast of London society.   Marianne Thornton
recollected that

> 'May is coming and then Hannah will be
> with us' was one of the earliest hopes
> of my childhood, and when she did arrive
> I always felt I had a fresh companion
> just my own age ... She was in many ways
> a charming companion for children, but
> she had very little power of resisting
> either persuasion or fun.[47]

Hannah More's home, Barley Wood, was for Marianne
'that Paradise of my childhood', a place where
children were welcome - and pandered - guests,
where they could enjoy the fascinating novelty of
village and kitchen tasks.   Tom Macaulay revisiting
the house in 1852 described it as 'the place where
I passed so many happy days in my childhood'.[48]
Macaulay was pleasantly surprised to enjoy the
company of another evangelical notable, Isaac Milner,
whom he had expected to be a severe and imperious
old man.   But Milner introduced him to the works
of Molière and Richardson, and made the 'gravest
sciences', to which Macaulay was not addicted, 'as
agreeable as an Arabian tale'.[49]   Insatiably
curious to know how contraptions worked, fascinated
by card-tricks and those of jugglers, he had an
inexhaustible fund of anecdotes about ventriloquism,
legerdemain, the performance of automatons, and
optical illusions.   Wilberforce was no less
entertaining: volatile and incorrigibly cheerful,
he delighted in the noisy exuberance of playing
children and was always ready to play with them
even in the midst of serious business, to their
delight and the frustration of his more orderly
friends.   Adults as well as children were infected
by his charisma, his popularity belying any
suggestion that evangelicals were necessarily
narrow-minded killjoys: 'Instead of having to think
what subjects will interest him, it is perfectly

impossible to hit one that does not', noted the politician and writer Sir James Mackintosh, 'I never saw anyone who touched life at so many points; and this is the more remarkable in a man who is supposed to live absorbed in the contemplation of a future state'.[50]

Any assessment of evangelical family life has to balance this weight of evidence against the more exclusively religious biographies, the sermons, improving books, and other polemical writings which are all too readily assumed to epitomise the tenor of evangelical living.[51] In particular it has to be balanced against the misleading picture of family life provided by evangelical novelists. These failed as dismally as writers of far greater merit in their attempt to depict vital goodness, which in Coelebs in Search of a Wife appears as pious insipidity, in Mrs. Sherwood's History of the Fairchild Family as sententious virtue. Mr. and Mrs. Fairchild show none of the vivacity, the humanity, or the human weakness evident in evangelical letters and diaries. They are portrayed as paragons who have already achieved the pedestal of perfection. There is no suggestion that they are themselves still battling against human frailty, still striving to live as they ought. Consequently descriptions of their effortless virtue fail to convince while their attempts from a position of vast superiority to force their offspring to be virtuous appear sadistic. That such a work was published (although not initially reviewed) is a disturbing indication of the ideal at which some evangelical parents were perhaps aiming: there was always the temptation to present to children a perfect persona. But there is evidence to suggest that at least some evangelicals resisted such temptation: when his daughter Fanny turned to him for help, Legh Richmond responded '... we will begin religion together. We will set out in the first step, for I have as much need as you to begin all again. We must go to Jesus Christ to be set right'.[52]

The occasion was memorable for Fanny, who had for long been the most recalcitrant of Richmond's children, recalled that her father had talked very little about religion to them, urging seriousness upon them primarily by letter.[53] Her comment shows how even the more personal writings of evangelicals can mislead if they are divorced from the personality of the writer which they do not always fully convey: the letters printed in Richmond's

biography give the impression that he like Mr.
Fairchild was for ever subjecting his children to
religious harangue. But letters are no guide to
conversation. When evangelicals chose to commit
themselves to paper they were often at their most
serious. Moreover the selectivity of the recipient
may well have led to the retention only of those
letters regarded as particularly helpful or
important. The more mundane letters and the day to
day conversations which might well have redressed
the balance tend by their very nature not to be
preserved for posterity.

Samuel Wilberforce, however, cherished over
600 of his father's letters.[54] His example is
informative for it confirms that evangelical
children did not receive the thick didactic screeds
with which their parents showered them with
expressions of unrelieved gloom, perusing them only
as in duty bound. For them as not for us the
personality of the parent would stand behind the
words. Moreover at least some evangelical children
seem readily to have accepted the religious concerns
of their parents, responding positively to the
reiterated plea to regard them as spiritual
advisers. Edward Hoare and Jane Taylor, like Fanny
Richmond, turned to their parents in times of
personal religious crisis, and Fanny implied that it
was her father's example which in the long term
caused his children to keep the faith: 'Religion
was unfolded to us in its most attractive form.
We saw that it was a happy thing to be a Christian',
a conclusion shared by many other children of
evangelical homes.[55]

That there was some kicking against the
religious pricks was only to be expected: 'I do
not want to go to heaven', protested three year old
James Fitzjames Stephen, 'I would rather stay on
earth ... I don't want to be as good and wise as
Tom Macaulay'.[56] Macaulay, paradoxically held up
as a paragon, was bored by the evangelical
'Sabbath' with its prohibitions on desired
activities.[57] Over Sunday observance which
evangelicals regarded as the bastion of godly
nationhood, children were given least leeway. Even
Louisa Hoare, generally so understanding, failed
here. Her husband read 'some good religious book'
to their children every Sunday but failed to
distinguish between adult and childish capabilities
with the result that his son later confessed

I fear sometimes one at least of his pupils

> greatly tired his patience by supineness
> and inattention but there was not then
> the same interesting books for young
> people that there are now, and such books
> as Wilberforce's Practical View and
> Doddridge's Rise and Progress were not
> calculated to attract the attention of
> a set of boys whose hearts were set
> on cricket.[58]

But complementary with this reaction of
healthy childhood was the equally normal acceptance
of family prayers and Sunday services as part of
the unquestioned fabric of family life, part of the
child's secure routine. Leslie Stephen, writing
after he had moved away from the family faith, told
how sermons and church services were in his childhood part, and a not unwelcome part, of the order of
nature.[59] The Sundays which were such 'good days'
for Brewin Grant would have contained a full quota
of chapel services. The child of another
evangelical home reminisced over childhood Sundays,
admittedly with much retrospective idealisation,
and on this subject alone achieved eloquence:

> The personal recollections of childhood
> now come to my aid, and recall the quiet
> Sundays which the mother and the little
> children spent together; the father,
> when at home, very grave and silent, during
> the short meal times; shut up, then, in
> his study except when in the pulpit ...
> then, after service, the only two hours
> leisure of the week; the children –
> other than those in arms – permitted to sit
> up and keep the festival; and the supper
> of cheap luxury as hard times allowed,
> and the friends who came in, and the
> hoarse but cheerful voice which spoke to
> us all, and the very short family prayers,
> and the softly creeping weariness, and the
> bed![60]

Evangelical religion provided not only security
but excitement. Adam Clarke's eldest sons sometimes
accompanied him on summer preaching appointments,
their imaginations stimulated by the stories of the
Old Testament, their experience of Methodist
persecution giving spice to their expectations of
an exciting life: '... each, a Goliah (sic) in his
own estimation, furnished himself with a stout

stick, in order to defend their father, should he
be attacked'.[61] By thus broadening children's
horizons, evangelicalism developed their imaginative
faculties. R.D. Altick comments

> The child's imagination ... was constantly
> stirred ... by the denominational
> magazines' tales of travel and lives of
> missionaries. Even in bleak Yorkshire
> there was no lack of exotic atmosphere
> and adventuresome narrative so long as
> Methodist periodicals kept arriving from
> City Road ...[62]

Even in bleak Yorkshire there was the additional
excitement of meetings of the auxiliaries of numerous evangelical societies, which gave to evangelicals of however lowly a background a sense of
participation in campaigns of cosmic moment. The
excitement was intensified for the children of the
evangelical patriciate who were able to attend
meetings which involved entertainment on the grand
scale: Hannah More invited 101 people to dinner
and nearly 200 to tea during an 1818 Bible Society
bonanza.[63] Freed from immediate parental supervis-
ion the children could engage in illicit activity
and shared caustic comment: Catherine Marsh
surreptitiously handed round to her friends a
packet of almond sugar plums to ameliorate the
tedium of a missionary meeting while the Thornton
girls were always ready to pass flippant and
penetrating comments on speeches and speakers.[64]
Small wonder that Anna Gurney should look forward
to the Bible Society meetings at Earlham as great
treats, regarding them as epochal events of her
childhood.[65]
    It was not only at such meetings that
evangelical children were able to congregate. The
Methodist Clarkes and Butterworths regularly had
supper together as did the Newtons and Buntings
when stationing permitted.[66] At Clapham the
children, like the parents, were constantly in and
out of each other's houses, with the Common as a
readymade playground. The Clapham families threw
large children's parties which boasted the
attractions of electrical contraptions, puppet
shows (written and performed by the parents),
magic lanterns, and that most ubiquitous of
childhood pleasures, 'dressing up'. New Year,
Christmas and birthdays were times of adult self-
examination, but they also provided opportunity for

childish festivity. If Wilberforce urged Samuel
'You must take pains to prove to me that you are
nine not in years only, but in head, heart, and
mind', he let his children celebrate Robert's ninth
birthday by dressing up in his court garb to play
at King and Queen.[67] Families went on holiday
together, and there were also visits to more
distant evangelical homes: each year Thomas
Babington kept open house for his nephews and nieces
with the result that Rothley Temple was in summer
the scene of noise, fun, youth, and gaiety.[68]
Similarly the Gurney clan - or parts of it -
holidayed together, sent children to stay with
various aunts and uncles, and congregated regularly
at each others' homes. Samuel Gurney 'used to
beam with joy as he saw the lads running wild over
the grounds, free from the restraints and discip-
lines of school-life, or joyfully rambling through
his parks and gardens'.[69] His brother-in-law,
Fowell Buxton, took pains to provide amusements for
young people, organising large parties to go on
excursions to beauty spots, masterminding charades
and Christmas games, and at one time starting a
family newspaper.[70] If evangelicals denied themselves and their children indiscriminate association
with their social equals their elitism by no means
led to loneliness and boredom.

But the large-scale conviviality of Anglican
Clapham and Quaker Earlham, the camaraderie of the
Methodist circuit and connexion, were not available
to all evangelicals. In the seclusion of Suffolk
the Taylors were deprived of evangelical company
for their father's Independent church verged on the
Socinian; some of their leisure was therefore
passed in more indiscriminate company than might
have otherwise been permitted.[71] Similarly removed
from more appropriate companionship, Branwell
Bronte, maybe - but not necessarily - more indulged
than other Evangelical sons, mixed with the village
lads. Most of his leisure, however, like that of
the Taylors, was focused within the family: Ann
and Jane Taylor spent hours together in imaginative
play, and were regularly entertained by their
father, who made them toys and took them for
picnics, sharing with them in the family festivities
which went in winter by name of 'the Parnassian
evening', in summer 'the Gipsy Ramble'.[72] As they
grew older the Taylors acquired a circle of
evangelical acquaintances with whom they inter-
changed letters and visits: during her first visit
to London Ann spent time at the home of the Rev.

Richard Cecil and later commented

> There was no family in which we were
> thenceforward more at home, or enjoyed
> ourselves with greater zest. Our friends,
> the Forbeses and the Conders, were already
> intimate there, with many other young
> people of about our own standing ... [73]

'... of about our own standing'. Evangelical
elitism was but a gloss upon that of a rigidly
divided society. The greater restrictions placed
upon the Bronte sisters than upon their brother
were probably as much socially as religiously
determined, for socially, if not always religiously,
evangelicals' contemporaries had a clearly circumscribed round of acquaintances. If England, as
H.J. Habakkuk and Harold Perkin have proposed, was a
federation of country houses, so too was English
Evangelicalism, while the movement as a whole
comprised at different social levels numerous,
sometimes interlocking, federations of godly
families. [74]
Measured against that of their contemporaries
the home life of these families does not merit
unduly harsh judgment. The tendency to treat
children as adults was a long established upper and
middle class habit. Patriarchalism was not
peculiar to evangelicalism but was equally characteristic of the upbringing of the young Charles
Darwin, whose father was religiously sceptical, and
of many others of like social status. [75] If, as Ivy
Pinchbeck and Margaret Hewitt suggest, evangelicals
helped perpetuate these practices, they also in
their anxiety to associate religion with 'domestic
tenderness' did much to encourage a more sympathetic
understanding of childhood, which, no less than
parental authoritarianism, is reflected in the
literature they produced. [76]
Children's literature was a comparatively new
genre and evangelicals played a significant part in
its development. F.J. Harvey Darton pays tribute
to Mrs. Sherwood's 'masterly prose', the economy
and vividness of her descriptions, while Gillian
Avery suggests that she came closer to describing
childish naughtiness than any previous writer. [77]
If her children sometimes request permission to
'say some verses, about mankind having bad hearts',
they also show more universal childish characteristics. [78] Full attention is paid to matters of
central juvenile concern. Acutely observant,

Mrs. Sherwood included in her stories an abundance
of homely minutiae, realising for her young readers
every detail of the family's surroundings, whetting
their appetites by describing what the children had
to eat, bringing vividly to life the animals that
properly formed part of the Fairchild entourage:
'Miss Puss stood with her head out at the door of
her house, mumping her parsley after the manner of
hares, and looking at Henry.'[79] After depriving
his son of food as a punishment for theft and lying,
'Mr. Fairchild cut a large piece of bread-and-
butter for Henry, which he was very glad of, for he
was very hungry'.[80] It is this ability to look at
life through a child's eyes and to communicate that
experience in language which is both simple and
evocative, that gives The History of the Fairchild
Family, and particularly its later less brazen
volumes, its peculiar charm. The book so often
taken to typify family life at its most terrifying,
testifies too, more subtly but no less surely, to
the underlying happiness of many evangelical homes.

NOTES

1. Smyth, 'The Evangelical Discipline', loc.
cit., pp. 103-04.
2. W. Goode, Memoir of the late Rev. William
Goode (1828), p. 85.
3. R.I. and S. Wilberforce, Life ..., iv,
p. 166.
4. Meacham, op. cit., p. 52; C. Dickens,
Bleak House (1853), ch. iv.
5. MM lvi (1833), p. 405.
6. Teignmouth, op. cit., ii, p. 339.
7. E.E. Kellett, Religion and Life in the
Early Victorian Age (1938), p. 73.
8. T.S. Grimshawe, A Memoir of the Rev. Legh
Richmond (1828), p. 380.
9. Jackson, Watson ..., p. 492; EM i series
xxii (1814), p. 100.
10. Ibid., ii (1794), p. 549.
11. ER ii series xviii (1822), p. 71.
12. More, Coelebs ..., ii, pp. 89-90.
13. MM xlvi (1823), p. 367.
14. Josiah Pratt, op. cit., p. 109.
15. Knutsford, The Life and Letters of Zachary
Macaulay (1900), p. 339.
16. T. Pinney (ed.), The Letters of Thomas
Babington Macaulay i (1974), pp. 160-61.
17. Ibid., p. 142.
18. BM ix (1817), p. 50.

19. Teignmouth, op. cit., ii, p. 163: 'Consider your duty to your parents, who are to you Gods on earth ...'.
20. Grimshawe, op. cit., p. 287.
21. EM i series xxvi (1818), p. 8.
22. Goode, op. cit., pp. 84-90; Foster, Critical Essays i, p. 382.
23. Gisborne, Female Sex ..., pp. 208-215.
24. Clarke (ed.), op. cit., ii, pp. 126-27, iii, p. 217 et passim.
25. Buxton, op. cit., passim.
26. L. Hoare, Hints for the Improvement of Early Education and Nursery Discipline (1819); Friendly Advice on the Management and Education of Children (1824).
27. Hints ... was highly praised in CO xviii (1819), pp. 518-30; ER ii series xiii (1820), pp. 185-89. The author of an essay on education in the MM of 1822/23 was greatly indebted to it.
28. Forster, op. cit., pp. 30-35.
29. Macdonald, op. cit., p. 507. For instances of loss of assurance see EM i series i (1793), pp. 124, 211.
30. E.g. EM i series xii (1804), p. 82.
31. H.F. Burder, op. cit., p. 201.
32. Quoted Meacham, op. cit., p. 23.
33. Brewin Grant, The Dissenting World: an Autobiography (2nd edn. 1869), pp. 12-13.
34. G.O. Trevelyan, Life and Letters of Lord Macaulay (1876), i, pp. 46ff.
35. J. Clive, Thomas Babington Macaulay (1973), pp. 39-40.
36. Pinney (ed.), op. cit., i, p. 155.
37. J. Millgate, Macaulay (1973), pp. 6-7; Clive, op. cit., pp. 34, 52-53. The likeness between father and son is clearly revealed in the early chapters of Knutsford, op. cit.
38. Pinney (ed.), op. cit., i, p. 189. Zachary later absolved Tom from his promise.
39. Trevelyan, op. cit., i, pp. 306ff.; Clive, op. cit., p. 235. The resignation was not accepted and since the abolitionists accepted a government compromise Macaulay had 'the singular good luck of having saved both my honour and my place'.
40. Clarke (ed.), op. cit., i, p. 79.
41. Ibid., iii, p. 117.
42. H.F. Burder, op. cit., pp. 266ff.; J. Pearson, The Life of William Hey (1822),ii, pp. 35ff., 297ff.
43. Clarke (ed.), op. cit., ii,p. 38; iii, p. 469.

44. Thornton papers; Knutsford, op. cit., p. 289; Josiah Pratt, op. cit., pp. 103-04; J. Styles, Early Blossoms (1819), pp. 153-262, a memoir of Parken including numerous letters.
45. J.H. Townsend (ed.), Edward Hoare (1896), pp. 22ff.
46. Ibid., pp. 55f.; A. Hare, The Gurneys of Earlham (1895), i, pp. 260-62; ii, pp. 129-30. Richenda Gurney married Francis Cunningham, brother of the Vicar of Harrow, whose children often stayed with her after the death of his first wife.
47. Forster, op. cit., p. 46.
48. Millgate, op. cit., p. 4; Knutsford, op. cit., pp. 278-79.
49. M. Milner, op. cit., pp. 561ff.
50. R. Coupland, Wilberforce (1945), p. 415.
51. The problem of relying on such written remains is discussed in D. Newsome, The Parting of Friends (1966), pp. 31ff., an outstanding account of evangelical family life, to which I am greatly indebted.
52. Grimshawe, op. cit., p. 607.
53. Ibid., pp. 599ff. I assume that the signature F.R. was Fanny's. Mrs. Ann Gilbert similarly exerted pressure in her letters but was hesitant about speaking to her children on spiritual matters (Gilbert, ed., op. cit., ii, pp. 156, 200).
54. Newsome, op. cit., p. 46.
55. Grimshawe, op. cit., pp. 598ff.; Townsend (ed.), op. cit., p. 31; I. Taylor (ed.), The Family Pen, Memorials, Biographical and Literary of the Taylor Family of Ongar (1867), i, p. 125. It is noteworthy that so many adhered to the faith of their fathers, and sought to pass it on to their own children. The regime of the Clayton family appears to have been strict and austere but all three sons followed their father into the Independent ministry (T.W. Aveling, Memorials of the Clayton Family, 1867).
56. Stephen, op. cit., p. 70.
57. Trevelyan, op. cit., i, p. 93. On the use of the Jewish term see T. Jackson, Recollections of My Own Life and Times (1873), p. 238: 'The French and Belgians have a Sunday, but they have no holy Sabbath'.
58. Townsend (ed.), op. cit., p. 5. Hoare, Hints ..., pp. 161-67; Friendly Advice ..., ch. xii. Mrs. Hoare was anxious that Sunday, although markedly different from other days, should be enjoyable. It can however be questioned whether Scriptural research along the lines she advocated would appeal

to any but the most intellectually able child.
59. Stephen, op. cit., p. 62.
60. T.P. Bunting, op. cit., ii, pp. 99-100.
The idealisation of Sunday was perhaps due to the fact that this was the one day when evangelicals were free of the tension arising from their attempt to be in the world but not of it.
61. Clarke (ed.), op. cit., ii, p. 34.
62. R.D. Altick, The English Common Reader (1957, 1963 edn.), p. 118.
63. A. Roberts (ed.), Letters of Hannah More to Zachary Macaulay (1860), p. 120.
64. L.E. O'Rorke, The Life and Friendships of Catherine Marsh (1917), p. 26; Forster, op. cit., passim.
65. Hare, op. cit., ii, pp. 21-22.
66. Clarke (ed.), op. cit., ii, p. 30; T.P. Bunting, op. cit., i, pp. 337ff.
67. A.M. Wilberforce (ed.), op. cit., p. 177; R.I. and S. Wilberforce, Life ..., iii, pp. 563-64; Coupland, op. cit., p. 306; Forster, op. cit., p. 58; Newsome, op. cit., p. 36.
68. Trevelyan, op. cit., i, p. 179.
69. Hare, op. cit., ii, p. 236 et passim.
70. Buxton, op. cit., p. 172.
71. I. Taylor (ed.), op. cit., i, pp. 122-23. Isaac Taylor sen. resigned his Colchester charge in 1810 because of the dominance of antinomian and Socinian factions.
72. Ibid., pp. 89-91; W. Gerin, Branwell Bronte (1961), pp. 22ff.
73. Gilbert (ed.), op. cit., i, pp. 39ff., 156-58.
74. Quoted H. Perkin, The Origins of Modern English Society (1969, 1972 edn.), p. 42.
75. G. Himmelfarb, Darwin and the Darwinian Revolution (1959), pp. 7-10.
76. R.I. and S. Wilberforce, Life ..., iv, p. 20; I. Pinchbeck and M. Hewitt, Children in English Society (1969), i, p. 305.
77. G. Avery, Nineteenth Century Children: heroes and heroines in English children's stories 1780-1900 (1965), pp. 84ff.; F.J.H. Darton, Children's Books in England (1932, 2nd edn. 1958), p. 175. Cf. pp. 187-92, a tribute to the Taylor sisters whose poems for children included 'Twinkle twinkle little star'.
78. M.M. Sherwood, The History of the Fairchild Family (1818-47, 1876 edn.), i, p. 13.
79. Ibid., p. 156.
80. Ibid., p. 43.

Chapter Five

FAITH AND FUN

While memoirs, biographies, and autobiographies,
reveal that evangelicals gained much pleasure from
what they described as 'domestic intercourse',
they yield only sparse information about their
enjoyment of more specific forms of recreation.
In many cases consideration of leisure pursuits
was irrelevant, or at best peripheral, to the
writer's main theme, the depiction of the inner
or public life of his subject. In other instances,
however, absence of description may well testify
to absence of activity for many evangelicals
accorded recreation a low priority.

Andrew Fuller is an archetype of an evangelical
whose religious interests caused him to despise
all else. Escorted round the principal buildings
of Oxford, he

> viewed them with little emotion; and on
> being requested to notice one object of
> peculiar interest, he said 'Brother I think
> there is one question, which, after all that
> has been written on it, has not yet been
> well answered...What is justification?'
> It was immediately proposed to return to
> the fireside and discuss the subject; to
> which Mr F. gladly acceded saying 'That
> inquiry is far more to me than all these fine
> buildings'.[1]

The tendency to depreciate non-religious matter
in order to emphasise the over-riding importance
of things spiritual, if more common among them, was
by no means peculiar to dissenters, for parallel
instances can be cited from within Evangelicalism.
'There is a beautiful Cathedral in this city'
Edward Bickersteth wrote from Lincoln, 'and a little

company that love our Saviour, far more beautiful
in Papa's eyes than all the beautiful cathedrals
and churches in the world'.[2] The most striking
example is Richard Cecil, concerning whom Daniel
Wilson commented 'Though his relish for the arts
was exquisite, he had such infinitely more sublime
interests before him, that they were forgotten in
the comparison...'[3] Notwithstanding his love
of art, music, and literature, Cecil eschewed
these and all other non-religious pursuits as
'vanity'.[4]

     Another, equally important, factor militating
against evangelical enjoyment of recreational
activities was the belief that 'serious Christians'
both could and should be identified by their
'gravity' and 'soberness', the antitheses of which
were not only 'levity' and 'frivolity' but even
'vivacity' and 'vitality'. John Satchell's
heroine, Miranda, had once been 'too vivacious',
but her growing 'sense of eternal things' had
given her 'a becoming gravity'.[5] According to
Hannah More Wilberforce had 'as much wit as if
he had no piety'.[6] Jabez Bunting was anxious lest
his wife's vitality should cause her to become
a 'trifler', and both his biographer and Isaac
Milner's took pains to show that in these rare
instances wit and light-heartedness in no way
impaired religious seriousness.[7]

     Suspicion of light-heartedness and trifling
was inevitably accompanied by suspicion of
amusement, which evangelicals tended to equate
with a hedonistic disregard for matters of eternal
moment. 'Whatever dreams the votaries of amusement
and pleasure may cherish', John Pearson commented,

>   It may be seasonable to remind them that...
>   nothing can be more stupid and senseless, than
>   to live and act as if the world were made
>   for intelligent beings as we are told the
>   sea was for the Leviathan, 'that he might take
>   his pastime therein'.[8]

According to the Christian Observer, which stressed
that the Christian would be divinely protected
in the course of duty but not of pleasure, 'The
good like the great man...will ever seek his
pleasures in the field of his duties, and though
he suffers mere amusement will seldom court it'.[9]

     The emphasis upon duty recurs in all
discussions on the place of leisure activities
in evangelical living. Some, finding full

satisfaction in family life and religious calling,
denied that Christians needed any more specific
forms of recreation.10   Others, however, believed
that 'innocent amusements' might properly be
followed - in order to equip evangelicals the
better to perform their various responsibilities:
'There can be no dispute' wrote Wilberforce
'concerning the true end of recreations. They are
intended to refresh our exhausted bodily or mental
powers, and restore us with renewed vigour, to
the more serious occupations of life'.11   But
even those who thus legitimised some leisure
pursuits were anxious lest they trespass upon time
which should be devoted to duty: 'How hard it is
for corrupt creatures to enjoy the most lawful
pleasures in a lawful degree' lamented Daniel
Wilson.12   Hannah More's exemplary heroine
delighted in gardening, that most innocent of
evangelical pleasures, supposedly sanctioned by
Milton's Eve, but Lucilla was nevertheless aware
that 'An enjoyment which assumes a sober shape may
deceive us, by making us believe we are practising
a duty when we are only gratifying a taste'.13
Her mother dissuaded her from giving up 'so pure
a pleasure', and elsewhere in the novel the
author inveighed against excessive asceticism, but
Lucilla's qualms of conscience were obviously
designed to endear her not only to Coelebs in
Search of a Wife but also to an evangelical readership. It was altogether in accordance with
evangelical priorities that she should compromise
by hanging her watch upon a tree, a constant
reminder to limit the time spent in the garden.14
     Unease about their use of time impinged even
upon the recreation of those evangelicals most
confident of the value of leisure. Fowell Buxton
both worked hard and played hard, but occasionally
wondered whether he was right to do so:

>   The world and the spirit of the world are
>   very insidious, and the older we grow the
>   more inclined we are to think as others
>   think, and act as others act;...I speak here
>   feelingly, for the world has worn away much
>   of the little zeal I ever had... I have more
>   game and better horses and dogs than other
>   people, but the same energy,disposed of in
>   a different way, might have spread Bible and
>   Missionary Societies over the Hundred of
>   North Erpingham...No man has a surplus of
>   power - time, talents, money, influence...

> It is therefore, arithmetically true, that
> so much as he devotes to the secular object
> he withdraws from the spiritual.15

Notwithstanding such qualms Buxton continued both
to support the Bible and Missionary Society
auxiliaries he had been influential in establishing
near his holiday home, and to shoot with immense
glee and exuberance. Moreover, within clearly
defined limits, he was prepared to justify his
activity:

> I feel about shooting that it is not time
> lost if it contributes to my health and
> cheerfulness. I have many burthens, and
> it is well to cast them off, lest they should
> so dispirit and oppress me that I become
> less capable of active exertion. But now
> my holiday is nearly ended; shooting
> may be my recreation, but it is not my
> business...16

Attitudes such as Buxton's were perhaps more
common within Anglicanism, natural home of the
more leisured classes, than within dissent. Any
meaningful comparison is however made impossible
by the shortage of biographies of dissenting laymen,
and the total absence of biographies of lay
Anglicans of similar social status to the average
dissenter. Whereas biographers of Evangelical
clergymen occasionally describe the hobbies of
their subjects, their dissenting counterparts
rarely refer to any 'recreational' pursuit
other than reading. The apparent difference
between Methodist and Evangelical practice can
be attributed to a difference in opportunity:
Anglican incumbents could if they wished make
time for leisure activity; the exigencies of the
preaching plan left some Methodist ministers
with little time even to read. The contrasting
workloads may reflect not only the demands which
Wesley made upon his followers but also the
secular work experience of the classes from which
the two ministries were respectively drawn.
Since old dissenters are depicted as deploying
their spare time in much the same way as Methodists,
it seems probable that the congregations for whom
dissenting biographers were writing, if not also
the ministers themselves, were less ready than
Evangelicals to grant recreation a place in
ministerial and hence in lay Christian living. This

impression is reinforced by the Christian Observer's
critique of a work by the editor of the Evangelical
Magazine: George Burder's Lawful Amusements, as
his Anglican critic rightly suggested, might more
appropriately have been entitled Unlawful Amusements,
for Burder always found it easier to condemn than
to recommend leisure pursuits. The reviewer criticised Burder for being too censorious and for
lacking discrimination, and warned his readers
against the dangers of over-seriousness: those
who opposed 'amusements' should be careful that they
did not also condemn cheerfulness and 'rational
enjoyment'.[17]
    While any denominational comparison remains
highly tentative, it is clear that Evangelicals
often shared the positive attitude towards
recreation practised by Buxton and recommended by
the Christian Observer's reviewer. Unpublished
papers reveal not only the liveliness of their
writers, but in some cases categoric approval of
'amusement': Mrs. Henry Thornton told Charemile
Grant that she 'took courage and told Mrs.R that
she and her friend would be more amiable if they
amused themselves a little, and I hope in time
to convince her of it'.[18] Her sentiments, if not
her tendency gratuitously to proffer advice, were
shared by Charles Hoare, Vicar of Blandford
Forum, who told J.W. Cunningham

> I think we want amusement. In fact every
> thing is so, that is not business; and all
> work and no play makes Jack etc. In fact
> Jack has been a dull boy many a day for
> wanting... a good game at chess. The mind
> covets occupation and is not always able
> to rouse itself. The Quakers admit their
> poetry, gardening etc. and even condescend
> as we know from Nancy to joke - and all these
> are but modes of amusement: and I cannot
> think that real bona fide amusement for
> amusements' sake would be often carried to
> excess, by those who have any rational
> pursuits besides. If they have not these
> we must not attack their amusements but their
> want of rational pursuits.[19]

If in their published writings Evangelicals were
less outspoken, there too they regularly stressed
the importance of 'rational' pursuits and enjoyments
It was widely acknowledged that those who chose
to indict the pernicious play of the world had to

provide some acceptable alternative; that other
forms of recreation, both innocent and rational,
were available was a powerful and valuable argument
against fashionable amusements. It was moreover
an argument employed by Anglicans and dissenters
alike: while there was clearly room for variation
in definition, the dissenting press was just as
anxious as the Evangelical to urge what it regarded
as rational recreations upon its readers.

Reading was universally regarded as the most
rational and enjoyable of leisure pursuits, while
other cultural activities, the practice of music
and the enjoyment of art, were also recommended.
The concern of this chapter is to outline those
recreations which cannot properly be classified as
either cultural or purely academic, but which a
number of evangelicals regarded as both innocent
and rational. Information that can be gleaned
from periodicals and biographies, largely Anglican
but occasionally dissenting, reveals that these
were not only widely approved as harmless alter-
natives to fashionable frivolity but also
thoroughly enjoyed.

'Bodily exercise' was one of the few Lawful
Amusements recommended by George Burder.[20] It
appears similarly to have been encouraged by some
Sunday Schools. The famous Whit Walks, which date
from the turn of the century, were designed to
distract scholars from the attractions of wakes,
fairs and races: Thomas Laqueur records how by
the 1830s and 1840s they had expanded into full-
scale excursions, incorporating boat trips and
sports days.[21] Upper class Anglicans were
equally concerned to promote appropriate amusement
for their children: thus Thomas Babington
organised long walks and excursions, and, according
to a mid-Victorian chronicler, sought to prevent
pusillanimity by encouraging sea and river swimming,
'manly sports', and 'active exercises'. [22] Charles
Simeon, mentor of so many young Evangelicals,
maintained that 'exercise, constant regular and
ample, is absolutely essential to a reading man's
success'; an enthusiastic horseman, he went
out for a ride every day 'unless my work or the
weather render it particularly inconvenient'. He
recommended tennis as well as riding to his
students, and a daily six mile walk, a practice
followed by Lord Teignmouth, independent of Simeon's
advice, as late as his eightieth year.[23] One
Simeonite who needed little encouragement was
Buxton's nephew Edward Hoare whose one complaint

about his school life under Henry Venn Elliott,
himself an enthusiastic athlete, was that 'as he
only took six pupils there was the same difficulty
that we found at home in getting good play, first
class cricket', a defect removed when he went to
Cambridge 'although I could not play much of it,
as it took too long a time'. Like John Venn
before him, whose passion afforded him the nickname
'the admiral of the Cam', Hoare had no difficulty
in finding time for boating...[24]
   A love of sport, if sometimes indulged more
excessively than was strictly necessary for bodily
health, could always be justified on those grounds.
Isaac Milner's scrupulously honest but highly
defensive biographer had a more difficult task when
she attempted to vindicate her uncle's enthusiasm
for scientific experiment. But Milner who adopted
a different 'hobby horse' each year, inventing a
lamp in 1808 and a waterclock in 1810, experienced
no such qualm about his activity nor apparently
did many other evangelicals who like him played
around with mechanical devices and were fascinated
to understand how things worked.[25]   The extent of
the interest is indicated by the periodicals, for
both the **Record** and the **Christian Observer** regularly
listed recent inventions while brief reports on
curious scientific happenings were common.
   One of the most enthusiastic was again John
Venn, whose early diaries refer to the machines
he assembled, and who combined his mechanical with
his sporting interests when he built a boat in his
student rooms, which he was sadly unable to get out
of the door. According to a descendant he lacked
'philosophical capacity' but 'had a decided taste
for trying practical experiments': both the taste
and, from time to time, the incapacity, were
reflected in the introduction of the latest domestic
equipment into Clapham rectory.[26]   Venn's student
notebooks contain details and diagrams about optics
and hydrostatics, mechanics and astronomy, about
which subject he later corresponded with his former
boating companion, the evangelical scientist Francis
Wollaston.[27]   Astronomy was also the hobby of John
Russell, who from 1785 spent time delineating a
lunar map, and in 1797 patented a selenographia
for exhibiting lunar phenomena.[28]   Daniel Wilson
developed an interest in chemistry during his final
year at Oxford, while the particular interest of
Legh Richmond and his son was mineralogy: when the
boy's lessons were over they would frequently
engage in scientific study and experiment.[29]

Richmond was one of a number of
evangelicals to take full advantage of the sight-
seeing opportunities provided on journeys of
evangelical duty. During a preaching tour in the
summer of 1814, he went to see his host's

> great iron-works, near Rotherham. Saw a
> cannon cast, and went through the whole
> manufactory. It is most ingenious and
> interesting. Saw the rolling mill and
> manufacture of tin plates. Observed on our
> return in the evening, the effect of the
> many surrounding blazing furnaces.

A week later he saw 'the ruins of Fountains Abbey;
it far exceeds everything I have seen or shall see;
imagination is filled, and more than filled...'[30]
Richmond's ecstasy and obvious enjoyment was
matched by that of the most constitutionally curious
of Methodists, Adam Clarke. The journals of his
tours show that he was fascinated by the history,
antiquities, monuments, geography, agriculture,
mode of life - indeed by everything relating to the
places he visited. He wrote to his wife after
a visit to Warwick Castle:

> I saw some bronze cups, from the ruins of
> Herculaneum, some of which I found cost 150
> guineas... We likewise got into the armoury,
> where...I was permitted to fit on some of
> the armour, and felt almost the spirit of a
> knight errant coming upon me. In short, we
> went through all this interesting and
> magnificent place; but I must reserve till
> I get home, to tell of Guy, Earl of Warwick's
> sword, which I endeavoured to wield, twenty
> pounds weight; also of his spear, his
> shield, his breast-plate, his tilting pole, &c.
> all enormously gigantic: nor can I wait to
> mention particularly the rib of the dun cow;
> the shoulder blade, and back-bone of the wild-
> boar, all of which I suspect are bones of
> large fish...[31]

Visiting Stonehenge some years later, he took pains
to ascertain its original formation and marvelled
over the ingenuity of our ancestors who transported
such huge stones of a rock that he identified as
not being local. On an Irish tour he visited the
Giant's Causeway 'one of the most celebrated
basaltic formations perhaps in the universe', and,

as ever, recounted the history of all the places
he visited, imaginatively reconstructing the events
at the battle of the Boyne. Intrigued by the Round
Towers he requested permission to visit one, made
deductions from it about their origins and purpose,
and sought to confirm his conclusions by inspections
of several more. Far from criticising historical
monuments and antiquities as the mere products of
fallen man, Clarke delighted in them and was
properly concerned for their preservation. Enraptured by the extensive collection of antiques at
Wilton House he was horrified

> at seeing many of these invaluable relics
> of antiquity injured...by the joiners,
> plasterers, &c. &c., who had even erected
> their benches against some of the finest
> productions of the sculptors of ancient
> Greece.[32]

The curiosity of most evangelicals had of
necessity to be restricted to the sights and
monuments of England, but some few had the
opportunity to visit Europe on holiday, Bible
Society or other philanthropic business. 'Cross
a river, or a mountain, or an arm of the ocean,
and a new and unexpected system of manners, - new
modes of life, - and a new series of conventional
usages burst upon you', wrote an Eclectic Review
contributor,

> All is surprise and delight, as soon as this
> new world reveals itself in its first gloss
> and freshness. It can hardly be conceived
> by those whom long and frequent wanderings
> over the continent have deadened to the
> excitements of curiosity...with what a
> restless, delighted eye and beating and en-
> livened heart, the untravelled stranger
> hails the objects that rush upon his senses
> when he first arrives in a foreign country.[33]

Exploration abroad often involved evangelicals in
more indiscriminate company than they might otherwise have chosen. Whereas those who holidayed
in England immediately sought out fellow evangelicals, there was, in the words of Henry Venn Elliott,
no place in continental travelling society for
a religious man as such.[34] That Elliott, John
Venn's nephew, was not thereby deterred from a
three year grand tour is testimony to the depth

of his interest in matters other than the purely
religious: he was an inveterate, and often
extravagant, collector of medals and rare coins.
Enamoured by the Venus de Medici, he was anxious
to view not only the arts and the antiquities but
also the people and customs of the countries he
visited, differing in this respect from some fellow
travellers who abstained in principle from society.
By involving himself in fashionable company

> I saw many things that I would not have seen,
> and heard much that I would have rejoiced not
> to hear. But if my intention in travelling
> was to see not merely things, but men and
> manners, there was no alternative. I must
> have done, as I did. Whether this speculation
> has been injurious to me, is a question as yet
> unsolved.[35]

As pragmatic in his attitude to the church as to
the world he attended mass and joined in the psalms
and the prayers though refusing to prostrate himself at the elevation of the host. He frequently
stayed in monasteries and developed an affection
and respect for his Catholic hosts: in no doubt
where he stood in a courteous dispute with a Roman
Catholic priest, he was far from exhibiting the
horror and hysteria of some Protestants at the
slightest sight or mention of anything Catholic.[36]
     By no means all Evangelicals, however wide
their interests, condoned such exposure to things
continental and Catholic. J.W. Cunningham believed
that it was detrimental for Englishmen to stay on
the continent long enough to be infected by foreign
manners and religion, while Hannah More was fearful
lest the habit of much travelling should cause
dissatisfaction with the plainer pleasures of
country living and encourage further absenteeism.[37]
While there was a clear political component to
their belief in the virtues of country life,
Evangelicals had no doubt that real religious
advantages were to be gained from regular rural
residence.[38] In the country a Christian was removed
from the worst temptations of fashionable life,
and was able to develop domestic predilections.[39]
Above all he had abundant opportunity to study the
works of God. His faith might curtail some
pleasures but evangelicals of all schools were
agreed that it enhanced a Christian's delight in
the natural world. Indeed it was repeatedly argued
that he enjoyed nature more than his unconverted

neighbour for it was his privilege to look 'through
nature up to nature's God'; in the lines from
The Task which evangelicals quoted most frequently,
the natural scenes around him were

> his to enjoy
> With a propriety which none can feel
> But who with filial confidence inspired,
> Can lift to heaven an unpresumptious eye,
> And smiling say - 'My Father made them all'.[40]

The appreciation of nature was thus the one pleasure
in whose innocence all evangelicals believed, and
which many happily indulged. Jane Taylor enraptured
by Devon wrote exuberantly to Josiah Conder

> I promise not to detain you with descriptions
> of the scenery around us...it is not the most
> agreeable thing to be told that 'you can form
> no idea - you can't imagine - you never saw
> anything like it' &c. So then to do the thing
> more politely, I must tell you that I had
> formed no idea of the kind of scenery with
> which we are surrounded; and that I had never
> before seen anything like it...Ilfracombe is
> situated in a deep valley, surrounded on one
> side by barren hills, and on the other by
> stupendous rocks which skirt the sea...Our
> rambles among the rocks I enjoy most; though
> at first they excited new sensations of awe
> and terror, rather than pleasure. But now we
> climb without fear amid a wilderness of rocks
> where nothing else can be seen, and nothing
> heard but the roar of the distant sea...[41]

Some evangelicals felt obliged to turn their
enjoyment of the world around them to religious
use, but many others were like Jane Taylor genuine
nature lovers, delighting in what they could
actually feel and smell, hear and see. While the
pleasure gained from the natural world, as from
sport, scientific experiment, and sight-seeing,
may well have been enhanced by the knowledge
that such recreations were conducive either to
health or to education, the enthusiasm with which
they were described suggests that they were in
practice thoroughly enjoyed not just as means to
ends but in their own right.
Thus while some evangelicals condemned all
pursuits but the purely religious, and while all
were liable to occasional qualms about their use

of time, a number - and certainly more than can
be listed - threw themselves wholeheartedly into
those recreations which could be labelled 'innocent'
and 'rational'. The regular use of the latter
term is significant for it associates evangelicals
with the early rational recreationists who
similarly opposed not recreation as such but only
those recreations which they deemed to be irration-
al, demoralising, and socially dangerous. Moreover,
parallels can be drawn between the pursuits of
which the two groups primarily approved. While
evangelicals provided Whit walks and Sunday school
sports days as counter-attractions to wakes, fairs,
and races, the 1833 Select Committee on Public
Walks, anxious to wean the working classes from
'low and debasing pleasures', recommended the
provision of open spaces and bathing facilities,
so that they could walk, play games and swim, and
thereby improve their health and their respectability.[42]   Brougham and others involved in
Mechanics' Institutes were concerned to provide
the poor with opportunities of understanding
the world about them and in particular of gaining
'useful knowledge', an appreciation of those
scientific and mechanical principles, which so
fascinated John Venn and his early industrial
contemporaries.[43] The provision of libraries at
such Institutes, and of Literary and Philosophical
Societies at which intellectual matters could be
discussed, is symbolic of the prevalent belief
in an increasingly literate society that reading
was the most rational of all recreations.
     Where evangelicals perhaps differed from
other early rational recreationists was in the
extent to which they sought to urge such pursuits
upon the upper as well as the lower classes.
Public walks and Mechanics' Institutes were in
time to become very much the preserve of the
increasingly significant middle classes, but they
were explicitly designed for the lower orders, to
deal with what J.F.C. Harrison has described as
'a new and unfamiliar problem', the imperative need
to fill the leisure hours of those who might
otherwise resort to idleness and dissipation.[44]
In the eyes of evangelicals' contemporaries this
was essentially a problem relating to the newly
emergent urban working class. Evangelicals by
condemning and eschewing the fashionable amusements
of the day, believed that it related to all levels
of society. While money, time, and opportunity
obviously influenced the choice of leisure

activities by evangelicals of different classes,
recreation was perhaps less influenced by class
within evangelicalism than without. The musical,
artistic, literary and intellectual pursuits to be
discussed in the following chapters were in varying
degrees recommended to and followed by rich and
poor alike.

NOTES

1. J. Ryland, The Work of Faith...in the
Life and Death of the Rev. Andrew Fuller (1816),
p. 574.
    2. Birks, op.cit., ii, pp. 52-53.
    3. D. Wilson, The Blessedness of the Christian
in Death... (1810), p. 28.
    4. Josiah Pratt, op. cit., pp. 28 145. Cf.
90-91.
    5. Satchell, op. cit., ii, p. 256; iii, p.11.
    6. W. Roberts, op. cit., ii, pp. 140-41.
    7. T.P. Bunting, op. cit., i, pp. 180, 340;
M. Milner, op. cit., p. 419.
    8. Pearson, op. cit., ii, pp. 241-42.
    9. CO vi (1807), p. 669; xii (1813),
p. 145.
    10. See for example EM i series xxii (1814),
p. 175 where students were advised to use any
intervals from study to instruct the ignorant, to
encourage those on the brink of Christian commitment
and to reclaim backsliders.
    11. W. Wilberforce, op. cit., p. 453.
    12. Bateman, Wilson..., i, p. 90.
    13. More, Coelebs, ii, pp. 49 ff, 109, 115.
    14. Ibid., i, pp. 215-22; ii, pp. 112-13.
    15. Buxton, op. cit., pp. 187-89.
    16. Ibid., p. 281.
    17. CO iv (1805), pp. 234, 306.
    18. Letter dated January 1807.
    19. Letter dated 16 January 1817.
    20. G. Burder, Lawful Amusements (1805), pp.
30 ff. Burder also cited intellectual exercise,
music (in moderation), occasional conversation with
the intelligent and pious, philanthropic activity.
The CO (iv 1805, p. 234) denied that the last was
an 'amusement', and expressed surprise at his
omission of drawing and gardening: the classes
for which Burder was primarily writing may not have
had the opportunity to garden, or to take drawing
lessons.
    21. T. Laqueur, Religion and Respectability:
Sunday Schools and working class culture 1780-1850

(1976), pp. 235-36.
    22. J.C. Colquhoun, <u>William Wilberforce: his friends and his times</u> (2nd edn. 1867), pp. 222ff.
    23. Hennell and Pollard (eds.),op. cit., pp. 105, 145; Teignmouth, op. cit., ii, p. 525.
    24, Townsend (ed.),op. cit., pp. 9-10, 19, 22-23; J. Bateman, <u>The Life of Rev. Henry Venn Elliott</u> (1868), pp. 109-10; J. Venn, <u>Annals of a Clerical Family</u> (1904), p. 122; M.M. Hennell, <u>John Venn and the Clapham Sect</u> (1958), pp. 42-43,52.
    25. M. Milner, op. cit., pp. 51-52, 325, 364-65, 416. Isaac Taylor junior like Milner provided himself with a workshop: I Taylor (ed.), op. cit., i, p. 72.
    26. Venn, <u>Annals...</u>,pp.121-24,where reference is also made to Venn's interest in heraldry and antiquarian research.
    27. Hennell, op. cit., pp. 42, 52. Venn's interests were inherited by his son Henry who introduced popular scientific lectures on subjects such as astronomy to St. John's Holloway (W. Knight, <u>Memoir of Henry Venn...</u>, 1882, p. 76).
    28. Williamson, op. cit., ch. xiii.
    29. Bateman, <u>Wilson...</u>, i, p. 62; Grimshawe, op. cit., p. 602.
    30, Ibid., pp. 235-36.
    31. Clarke (ed.), op. cit., ii, p. 28.
    32. Ibid., pp. 125-28, 132-33, 255-75.
    33. <u>ER</u> ii series xxiii (1825), p. 332.
    34. Clarke (ed.), op. cit., ii, p. 129 records how when the Clarkes and Butterworths went on holiday together in 1806 'almost our first enquiry was "are there any religious people here?"' They immediately went to find the evangelical baker who so pleased them as to be invited back to supper at the inn.
    35. Bateman, <u>Venn Elliott...</u>, p. 80.
    36. Ibid., pp. 53-54, 59, 61-62, 71-72, 88.
    37. J.W. Cunningham, <u>Cautions to Continental Travellers</u> (1823); H. More, <u>Moral Sketches</u> (1819), pp. viff.
    38. On Evangelicals' desire to preserve the old rural patriarchal society, the peace and well-being of which was dependent upon resident local gentry, see R.I. and S. Wilberforce, <u>Correspondence...</u>,i, p. 219.
    39. Gisborne, <u>...Female Sex...</u>, pp. 112-13.
    40. Cowper, op. cit., book v, 743-47.
    41. I Taylor (ed.), op. cit., i, pp. 260-61.
    42. <u>Report from the Select Committee on Public Walks with the Minutes of Evidence</u> (1833, IUPS edn.

1968), pp. 8-9, 52, 58.
    43. Altick, op. cit., pp. 188-204; J.F.C.
Harrison, Learning and Living 1790-1960 (1961),
pp. 62-74.
    44. Ibid., p. 76.

Chapter Six

FAITH AND HARMONY

The enjoyment and practice of music was widely
regarded as a most acceptable evangelical recreation. While the accuracy of claims such as that made
by Thomas Jackson concerning the musical taste and
knowledge of his fellow Methodist, Richard Watson,
cannot easily be assessed, it is significant that
such attributes were considered worthy of praise.[1]
Other biographers stressed that music was one of the
rare leisure activities in which their subjects
engaged, a declaration made in respect of the
Anglicans, William Goode and William Hey, and of the
Independents, Daniel Parken and Josiah Conder.[2]
According to Mrs. Grant of Laggan the evangelical
branch of the family who lived in Clapham excelled
in music, while their latest biographer affirms that
the Gurneys were an 'incurably musical family'.
Although Elizabeth renounced music along with most
other cultural activities when she became a 'Plain
Friend', her example was followed neither by her
husband, nor by her Anglican evangelical sister
Richenda who continued to gain great satisfaction
from her piano.[3]
    The family who most obviously and most notably
combined a love of music with evangelical faith was
the Jowett. The evangelical tradition dated back to
the conversion through Whitfield of Henry Jowett
(1719-1801), two of whose four sons were to become
famous evangelical teachers: Henry (1756-1830)
taught the children of many leading Evangelical
families at Little Dunham, while Joseph was
Professor of Civil Law at Cambridge. The eldest
son John, like his father a wool-stapler, was
involved in the foundation of the CMS; his son
William was the first graduate to be sent out by the
society, while his daughter Elizabeth married its
future secretary Josiah Pratt. Their brother

Joseph, Rector of Silk Willoughby, was for nearly
seventeen years editorial superintendent of the
BFBS. The least successful of old Henry Jowett's
four sons and possibly the least religiously
committed was Benjamin: accounts of the childhood
of his more famous grandson reveal that the
evangelical tradition, if somewhat vitiated, and a
love of music was passed down through his stock
too.[4]
    The musical tradition was as extensive as the
evangelical: in the second generation Joseph
organised concerts at Trinity Hall, while John's
home was a centre of musical culture. His Moravian
friend, Christian Latrobe, was astonished and
delighted 'to find here a choir of vocal performers,
the most perfect of its kind ... They sang all
Handel's Oratorios, or rather select portions of
them with great precision ...'[5] John and Henry of
Little Dunham sang tenor, the Cambridge professor
alto, John's two daughters treble and their brother
Henry bass. Two other brothers no doubt also
contributed for Joseph of Silk Willoughby was later
to write hymn tunes, while Joshua sought to forget
the business failures with which he, like his
cousin Benjamin, was afflicted by giving musical
parties.
    The Jowetts apparently felt no qualm about
their musical activity. Occasionally and characteristically other evangelicals wondered whether they
were right to devote their time even to this
'delightful recreation'.[6] Richard Cecil, unable to
restrict himself to the daily fifteen minutes which
he allowed for violin-playing, gave the instrument
up entirely, a decision which testifies as much to
the attractions of music as to evangelical strength
of will.[7] The status of music as a fashionable
accomplishment caused others to fear that it might
be one of the 'pomps and vanities of the world':
a Christian Observer contributor, ACG, warned that
'it would be ... inconsistent for the child of God
... to desire even the most elegant and refined of
the pleasures of sense'.[8] Nevertheless the vast
majority of evangelical writers (including ACG
himself) stressed that music was a gift of God, 'a
relaxation so beneficial ... that the time required
for attaining a competent knowledge of the science
would not be unprofitably employed'.[9]
    A knowledge of music was profitable because
music was an adjunct of worship and a means of
enhancing devotion. Whereas the fashionable associations of many recreations caused evangelicals to

dismiss them as essentially worldly, the overriding
example of the saints and angels in light enabled
them to regard music as peculiarly innocent, 'a
foretaste of that eternal bliss'.[10] Thus DWH,
another of the Christian Observer's correspondents,
argued that music was the most elevated of the arts:
'it is the only one which is to accompany us to
another world, and to be a part of the employment
of the blessed above ... it is the only one which
may be directly used in the worship of God'.[11]

Believing that music had a sacred function
evangelicals did much to foster its wider
appreciation in the community at large. Christian
Latrobe's Selection of Sacred Music, published in
six volumes between 1806 and 1826, has been
described as a 'pioneering work' which 'opened an
entirely new realm of music ... to English musicians': through it the British public was made aware
for the first time of the church music of composers
such as Pergolesi, Haydn and Mozart.[12] It is
possible that the larger Sunday Schools may have
played some part in the popularisation of classical
music for Thomas Laqueur points out that pieces by
Handel and Haydn were performed by Ashton New
Connexion School at its 1838 anniversary, and
suggests that knowledge of classical music as well
as the ability to read, write, and cipher was
instilled into Sunday school children in Stockport.[13]
More confidently, it can be argued that evangelicalism encouraged an awareness of music by enhancing
the importance and improving the quality of that
played in church services. If the impetus came
from dissenters, Evangelicals were quick to follow
suit, producing their own psalm and hymn collections
to replace the uncompetitive monotony of Sternhold
and Hopkins: 'the singing has been a great
instrument in the Dissenters' hands of drawing away
persons from the Church', wrote John Venn, 'and why
should we not take that instrument out of their
hands?'[14]

Any attempt to appeal to the masses by the use
of 'secular' hymn tunes was, however, vehemently
opposed by Evangelicals and dissenters alike:
according to the Evangelical and Methodist Magazines
the God of holiness should not be praised in the
same style as the gods of licentiousness and vice.[15]
In 1832 Methodist missionaries were urged to

> discourage entirely the use of light and
> especially song tunes, which, though a very
> bad taste, have we regret to learn, been not

> only permitted, but encouraged, by
> the brethren on some of our stations.
> 'Christian psalmody' says a great
> authority, and a man of the finest
> taste, ought to be 'simple, and noble
> withal'.[16]

In issuing such instructions the missionary secretaries were acting in accordance with established
Methodist views: Wesley himself, as John Lawson
has shown, favoured simple and stately measures,
encouraged thoughtful rather than over-lusty singing
and was utterly opposed to fugues since the words
could not be heard.[17] Similar considerations
presumably moved Conference of 1805 when it forbad
the singing of different words at the same time,
the use of recitatives and solos, and the introduction of any instruments other than the 'bass
viol' into services.[18]
   The passing of this legislation is but one
indication of the extent to which public worship
served as an encouragement to musical virtuosity.
Fear that players would improperly seize the
opportunity for display lay behind much of the
debate on the use of instruments in worship.[19]   The
need for some instrument to lead the singing,
particularly that of larger congregations, was
widely recognised; the growing preference for the
organ can be related not only to its more stately
tones, but also to the greater ease of controlling
one rather than a multiplicity of instruments.[20]
This was certainly the impression given by Thomas
Jackson when he recollected Conference's by no means
unanimous decisions to permit the construction of
organs in certain chapels:

> Into several of the Methodist chapels the
> choirs had introduced almost every variety
> of musical instrument, destroying the
> simplicity and devotional character of the
> singing, to the great annoyance of the
> preachers, and of the more sober part of
> the congregations; and they often
> threatened to withdraw their services
> altogether, unless they might be allowed to
> have their own way. In many places
> organs have corrected this evil; and
> when they are so used as not to overpower
> and supersede the singing of the
> congregation, but to guide and aid it,
> especially in large chapels, they are a

real benefit; incomparably better than
the 'flute, harp, sackbut, dulcimer, and
all kinds of music', with which men of
perverted taste used to stun the ears
of our congregations when they stood up
to sing the praises of God.[21]

Jackson was able to support his case that choirs
and preachers were at odds by citing the example of
Samuel Bradburn who locked his Wakefield choir out
of their singing gallery in protest against their
use of unsuitable tunes, and their practice of co-
opting 'persons of lax morals'.[22] The case at
Wakefield was not unique: in 1816 the Leaders'
meeting of the Canterbury society determined that
'No person shall be admitted into the Orchestra as
a singer, who lives in open habitual sin', and
further that 'No person shall be permitted to
retain his seat in the Orchestra whose behaviour
is irreverent during Divine service'. Concerned to
safeguard against every eventuality, the meeting
also decided that choir members who subsequently
fell into 'acts of immorality' should be subject to
expulsion.[23]

The significance of these regulations, and of
the more generalised complaints about the behaviour
of choirs published in the periodicals, lies in the
implication that Methodism, and indeed evangelicalism
in all its forms, provided musical opportunities
for the community at large and not just for its own
membership.[24] Those tempted to irreverence during
divine service presumably attended more to perform
than to pray. Choral and instrumental classes
were admittedly provided at the larger Mechanics'
Institutes, but in view of the limited response to
these organisations and the more numerous attendance at Methodist chapels, it seems reasonable to
conclude that the latter were major centres for
the dissemination of musical culture well into the
nineteenth century.[25]

But how far did evangelicals encourage the
enjoyment of music in general as opposed to purely
sacred pieces? Revealing the inadequacy of his
doctrine of creation an _Eclectic_ reviewer argued
that were it not for its religious utility

we should not ... have been made
susceptible of the pleasures of music.
He who created us what we are, as regards
our physical capacities, has made us what
we are for his own glory; and, in

> endowing us with this extraordinary faculty
> of giving melodious expression to our
> feelings, and in making us capable of the
> physical emotions produced by harmony,
> the Almighty doubtless had in view some
> end connected with that only worthy
> purpose of our being.[26]

Some evangelicals therefore assumed that all music
should have 'a sacred end and design': the
dissipations of Fribble, a character in Rowland
Hill's Village Dialogues, included violin-playing
and the exemplary Lovegood censured him for skipping
and fiddling about the room like a monkey.[27] Those
who like Hill attempted to list innocent recreations
often specified 'sacred' music ...
    The context within which they were writing
must however be noted. Much of the music available
for family performance was vocal and evangelicals
of all schools were agreed that Christians should
not give voice to impure, immoral or impious ideas.
Their unease about romance, evident in their attitudes to the threatre, may well have caused them to
exclude many of the more popular songs from their
repertoire: Hill was horrified that music should
be used to celebrate 'the worst of passions'.[28]
Their concentration upon religious works was in
part a reflection of a lack of acceptable alternat-
ives: according to the (probably hypercritical)
Evangelical Magazine it was very difficult to find
suitable songs to fill the vacuum between 'devotional psalmody' and 'light and trifling' airs.[29] More
positively evangelicals assumed a responsibility
to further the cause of religious as opposed to
fashionable music, a responsibility which derived
from their belief in the essential purity of the
pursuit. Anxious to change the opinion of pious
parents who indicted music as a fashionable
accomplishment, they recognised the possibility of
worldly corruption and therefore called upon
Christians to effect 'The Rescue of Music':

> Listed into the cause of sin,
> Why should a good be evil?
> Music, alas, too long has been
> Prest to obey the devil.
> Drunken, or lewd, or light, the lay
> Flow'd to the soul's undoing,
> Widen'd and strew'd with flowers, the way
> Down to eternal ruin.

Who, on the part of God will rise,
And innocent sounds recover;
Fly on the prey, and take the prize,
Plunder the carnal lover;
Strip him of every melting strain,
Of ev'ry melting measure;
Music in Virtue's cause retain;
Rescue the holy pleasure?[30]

While sacred works were the most obviously
'innocent sounds', evangelicals did not necessarily
equate the two. Far from restricting themselves to
religious themes, many appear to have excluded from
their repertoire only that which they regarded as
'exceptionable'. In so doing they may well have
allowed themselves considerable latitude. While
the Brontes were less constrained than some
evangelical children, it is not without significance
that their albums of extant music contain 'not only
the "Sacred Oratorios" but the "profane music" of
the period, the fashionable arias and overtures from
the romantic operas of Bellini, Donizetti and
Auber'.[31] William Wilberforce, a more typical
representative of the movement if only because
others appealed to him for advice, told one such
inquirer that 'the songs to be sung should be
selected with some caution', but admitted
hesitantly that there was

nothing criminal in singing songs the
words of which contain no sentiments
improper for a Christian to utter.
It must undoubtedly be our wish that they
whom we most dearly love, should always
have it in their view to please their
God and Saviour, but this does not require
us to be always speaking the sentiments
or language of religion ...[32]

That others shared this viewpoint can be seen in
one of the few debates about music in the Christian
Observer. In 1821 the editors published a selection
of five letters, which represented a cross-section
of the viewpoints expressed in the substantial
correspondence they had received in response to a
query concerning the legitimacy of concert attendance. None of the five condemned 'miscellaneous
music' qua se: on the contrary even ACG, who was
critical of concert-going, stressed the value of
family performance and condemned any tendency to
restrict children to sacred music alone.[33] For DWH

the belief that music was religiously sanctioned
justified attendance not only at oratorios but also
at symphony concerts. The assumption that men had
been endowed with musical ability for specifically
religious purposes was explicitly repudiated by
another contributor to the debate, on the grounds
that beautiful scenery, architecture, sculpture,
and painting, could all be innocently and lawfully
admired without any religious feeling. Asked
whether a Christian might legitimately attend a
concert of secular music, he therefore responded

> I cannot help thinking it might rather
> be asked, 'Why should it not be lawful
> for Christians?' as, surely, unless every
> kind of amusement unconnected with some
> positively religious duty be deemed unlawful,
> music cannot be so ...[34]

His conclusion, reiterated, if less confidently, by other contributors, constitutes yet another
instance of the freedom of some evangelicals from
the religious constraints which so circumscribed
others. It indicates too the extent to which some
were influenced by cultural as well as religio-
moral considerations in determining the legitimacy
of recreations. Card-playing, balls, and the like
were condemned as frivolities: in these instances
there was no benefit to be gained to compensate
for the risk of worldly contamination. The risk at
musical concerts was perhaps less acute. That it
was run at all is proof of evangelicals' greater
sympathy for cultural than for courtly pursuits:
in the pre-Victorian age the one was markedly more
concordant with seriousness and rationality than the
other. The obvious comparison however must be
with the theatre. Evangelical suspicion of the
senses, so prevalent in discussion of plays, was
rarely voiced in reference to instrumental music,
a fact which suggests that it was closely related to
fear of moral dissipation. Theatrical performances
were conducive to immorality in a way that symphony
concerts were not. Paradoxically the fact that
music was in general a non-didactic art may have
facilitated its acceptance by some evangelicals,
who tended all too frequently to justify cultural
activities because of the lessons that could be
learned from them. But arts which could communicate
acceptable ideas could also be used to disseminate
views of which evangelicals disapproved. The
innocence of music perhaps lay in part in its

inability to communicate harm.

It would be wrong however to suggest that
fears of worldliness and sensuality were completely
absent from evangelical discussions on the public
performance of music. But such fears were generally
expressed in relation to performances of sacred
rather than secular music, maybe because these
were the concerts most likely to appeal to the
majority of evangelicals. From the beginning some
evangelicals had been happy to support them
believing that they were conducive to seriousness
and a devotional frame of mind. Characteristically
pragmatic, Wesley doubted whether an audience at a
1758 production of The Messiah 'was ever so serious
at a sermon, as they were during the performance',
and his approbation was shared by other patriarchs,
Martin Madan, Thomas Haweis, and Henry Venn of
Yelling.[35] Hey and Wilberforce attended oratorios
as presumably did many of their evangelical
contemporaries for the Record complained that 'many
pious people' did not discern the evil in musical
festivals, at which they were frequently performed.[36]
The Record was no less in accord with a patriarchal
tradition than Wilberforce. In a laboured but often
quoted analogy John Newton was scathing about the
behaviour of 'prisoners' who chose to sing about
their plight and the offer of pardon, rather than
availing themselves of it.[37] His close friend
Cowper complained that 'ten thousand sit ... content
to hear ... Messiah's eulogy for Handel's sake':

>   Remember Handel? Who, that was not born
>   Deaf as the dead to harmony, forgets,
>   Or can, the more than Homer of his age?
>   Yes - we remember him; and while we praise
>   A talent so divine, remember too
>   That his most holy book from whence it came
>   Was never meant, was never us'd before,
>   To buckram out the mem'ry of a man.[38]

Their view was shared not only by the Record, the
most vocal and persistent antagonist of musical
festivals and oratorios, but also by the Evangelical
Magazine: while appreciating the work of Handel
because of the 'pleasing and instructive narratives
it contains, all of which are taken from the Bible',
contributors opposed the theatricality of public
performances.[39] And even the more cultured
Eclectic Review was uneasy about 'the profanation
of sacred music to mercenary purposes, as in
oratorios'.[40] That four of the five Christian

Observer correspondents were not opposed to
oratorios scarcely balances out this weight of
periodical complaint.
     Part of the objection to oratorios lay in the
belief that they were not effective vehicles for
worship. Evangelicals' tendency to despise the
senses was clearly revealed in the Record's refusal
to accept that aesthetic appreciation could enhance
devotion: if the plain majesty of the Word of God
read silently and alone did not kindle fervour
equal to that excited by songs and instruments, then
the latter was nothing but the ebullition of a
natural feeling in no way religious.[41] The paper's
belief that those who attended oratorios did not do
so with a desire to worship was reinforced by the
observation that afternoon performances at musical
festivals were frequently followed by fancy dress
balls which attracted the same clientele. Here at
least 'the world' appeared 'in its own proper
livery'.[42] In this respect balls were less
insidious than oratorios for it was the inter-
mingling of sacred and secular in the latter which
so horrified many evangelicals. For a hired singer
to mouth words in which he did not believe, or to
mimic the tones of the Almighty was blasphemy;
for an audience to listen to the language of
adoration for mere entertainment was profanity;
devotion was being debased into an elegant pastime.[43]
And so in 1809 the Baptist Magazine pointed out that
Christ did not undergo his sufferings that men
might be amused by them.[44] Two decades later
Richard Watson, notwithstanding his love of music,
warned his Methodist congregation that a forthcoming
'sacred music festival' was but a reconciliation of
Christ and Belial, an attempt to disguise the
pleasures of sin under the garb of religion:
'Forsooth, these men are pledged to mime the
sacrificial wailings of my blessed Lord; and to
sound on catgut the groans which redeemed the
world!'[45]
     Statements such as Watson's reveal how substan-
tially some evangelicals' religious presuppositions
inhibited their enjoyment of culture. Religion was
for them not just a serious but a solemn matter,
and as such could not easily be combined with
anything that conformed to mere amusement. That
cultural pleasures could be truly serious, albeit
not necessarily in a narrowly religious sense, was
not readily conceded. Thus the cultural exploration
of a religious theme as in oratorios was discouraged
save within the context of devotion. While

evangelicals believed that the practice of music was Biblically sanctioned, some appear largely to have restricted its use to those purposes to which it was apparently devoted in Scripture. When they elevated music above the other arts they were invariably concerned with religious utility not with cultural quality.

On the other hand the utilisation of music for religious purposes undoubtedly had cultural consequences. By emphasising the role of music in worship, evangelicals did much to extend the musical education and aesthetic experience of the communities in which they were involved. While most of the music which evangelicals enjoyed at church and at home was sacred, the door into the wider musical world had been opened for them. The belief that music was a peculiarly innocent recreation was one factor enabling some to disregard the constraints surrounding most fashionable pleasures and attend concerts of both sacred and secular music. Thus if evangelical faith sometimes curtailed the enjoyment of any but the most obviously devotional pieces (a criterion which excluded oratorios), it also served to introduce many to music in its ecclesiastical forms, and was compatible with and conducive to the development of wider musical interests.

NOTES

1. Jackson, <u>Watson ...</u>, p. 172.
2. Goode, op. cit., p. 17; Pearson, op. cit., i, p. 111; Conder, op. cit., p. 343; <u>EM</u> i series xx (1812), p. 377.
3. D. Swift, <u>Joseph John Gurney, Banker, Reformer and Quaker</u> (1962), p. 29; Vansittart (ed.), op. cit., pp. 18, 30; Hare, op. cit., ii, pp. 6, 288; J.P. Grant (ed.), <u>Memoir and Correspondence of Mrs. Grant of Laggan</u> (1844), pp. 159, 271. I have been unable to establish the exact relationship between Mrs. Grant, author of the best-selling <u>Letters from the Mountains</u> (1806), and the Grants of Clapham whose refinement and culture she regularly praised.
4. Abbott and Campbell, op. cit., i, pp. 1-14; G. Faber, <u>Jowett</u> (1957), pp. 47-61.
5. C. Latrobe, <u>Letters to my Children</u> (1851), p. 7.
6. J.H. Pratt, op. cit., p. 335; Teignmouth, op. cit., ii, pp. 327-28. Goode and Hey both curtailed the amount of time they spent on music.

7. Josiah Pratt, op. cit., p. 136.
8. CO xx (1821), p. 352.
9. ER ii series xx (1823), p. 222.
10. Latrobe, op. cit., p. 44.
11. CO xx (1821), p. 552.
12. S. Sadie (ed.), The New Grove Dictionary of Music and Musicians (1980).
13. Laqueur, op. cit., pp. xii, 86; D. Martin, 'To School on Sunday', Times Literary Supplement, 29 April 1977.
14. Quoted Hennell, op. cit., p. 267. Bickersteth, Cecil, and Goode were among those to publish hymn collections.
15. EM ii series viii (1830), pp. 53ff.; MM liii (1830), pp. 96-99. Cf. ER ii series xxiv (1825), pp. 122-23.
16. Jackson, Watson ..., p. 577.
17. Davies and Rupp (eds.), op. cit., i, pp. 188-89, 201; MM xxxviii (1815), p. 866; xlvi (1823), p. 809.
18. MM xxviii (1805), p. 524.
19. CO iv (1805), pp. 212-14; EM i series xiii (1805), p. 467; ER i series ii (1806), p. 234; MM xli (1818), p. 696.
20. T.P. Bunting, op. cit., ii, pp. 230ff. Disputes over organs may thus throw light upon battles for power between clergy and laity in individual churches as well as, in the case of the Leeds organ debate, in the connexion at large.
21. T. Jackson, Recollections of my own Life and Times (1873), pp. 133-34.
22. Ibid., p. 148. Bradburn, President of Conference 1799, was stationed at Wakefield in 1806.
23. J.A. Vickers, The Story of Canterbury Methodism (1961, 2nd edn. 1970), pp. 20-21.
24. Criticism of choirs can be found in CO xxvi (1826), pp. 19, 214-15, 340-41; ER iii series vi (1831), pp. 478ff.
25. E.D. Mackerness, A Social History of English Music (1964), pp. 147-51 discusses the musical role of Mechanics' Institutes.
26. ER ii series xx (1823), p. 217, an article reprinted in BM xvi (1824), p. 108.
27. R. Hill, Village Dialogues iii (1803), p. 83.
28. Hill, A Warning to Professors ..., pp. 34ff.
29. EM i series xxix (1821), p. 383, a review of Legh Richmond's 'The Gypsy's Petition' and 'The Negro Servant'; being the first Numbers of a Series of Songs of Sacred Character, with an accompaniment for the Piano Forte.

30. BM xiv (1822), p. 528.
31. W. Gerin, Charlotte Bronte (1967), p. 52.
32. Quoted Newsome, op. cit., pp. 51-52.
33. CO xx (1821), p. 352: ACG was concerned that sacred music should not be thoughtlessly used for recreative purposes.
34. Ibid., pp. 349, 552.
35. L.E. Elliott-Binns, The Early Evangelicals (1953), p. 81; A. Skevington Wood, Thomas Haweis 1734-1820 (1957), p. 89.
36. The Record, 1 October 1830; Pearson, op. cit., i, p. 111; R.I. and S. Wilberforce, Correspondence ..., ii, p. 490, in which Wilberforce regretted the 'attendant circumstances' which were 'so sadly calculated to damp and dissipate those spiritual affections, which the music of itself is fitted to call forth'.
37. EM i series xiii (1805), p. 173; The Record, 11 November 1829.
38. Cowper, op. cit., book vi, 633, 635, 637, 645-52.
39. EM i series vii (1799), p. 163; ii series x (1832), p. 64.
40. ER i series ii (1806), p. 234; ii series ii (1814), p. 69; xx (1823), p. 223.
41. The Record, 1 October 1832.
42. Ibid., 11 November 1828; 20 September 1830; 24, 28 October 1833.
43. Ibid., 8, 12 October 1829; 14 March, 18 November 1833.
44. BM i (1809), pp. 367-69 'The nature of the evil of attending oratorios'.
45. Jackson, Watson ..., p. 459.

Chapter Seven

FAITH AND THE FINE ARTS

A. EVANGELICALS AND ART

Evangelicals who approved of musical concerts sometimes sought to convince those uncertain of their
legitimacy by arguing that there was no more reason
to condemn public performances of music than public
exhibitions of art.[1] Similarly those who discussed
innocent and rational recreations frequently
bracketed drawing and music together as amusements
appropriate for evangelical enjoyment. The parallel
between evangelical attitudes to art and to music
must not however be overstressed, for the fine arts
lacked the Biblical sanction which was the motive
force behind much evangelical appreciation of music.
Whereas music played an important part in evangelical worship, it has traditionally been asserted that
visual aids to devotion were eschewed, both on
account of the priority which evangelicals accorded
to verbal communication and as a residual reaction
against Catholic 'idolatry': like the Puritans,
Horton Davies suggests, evangelicals 'exalted the
ear-gate at the expense of the eye-gate of the
soul'.[2] A vehemently anti-Catholic Eclectic reviewer appealed 'to fact' - 'what devotion is produced
by the works of art in churches in Italy?' - while
John Russell, a practising artist, denied that the
pictures in Burleigh House Chapel did much to
enhance worship.[3] While some evangelicals expressed
appreciation of Gothic architecture, this may well
have been for associational rather than aesthetic
reasons: Richard Cecil regretted the use of any
other style for he believed that Gothic was most
suggestive of the praise which had echoed within
such walls for generations.[4] Dissenters, making a
virtue of necessity, refused to allow the arts even
this limited value and denied that architecture had

147

any useful religious function. On the contrary one
spokesman argued:

> Any attempt to connect the arts with
> religion, and to blend the emotions
> which they inspire with the feelings of
> devotion, has been one of the great causes
> of destroying the simplicity and corrupt-
> ing the purity of the gospel. The arts
> undoubtedly ought to be encouraged, they
> refine the pleasures of society and impart
> lustre and dignity to the national
> character: but the sanctuary of God is not
> the place for their display ...[5]

A study of evangelical attitudes to the arts
exposes many curious ironies. Evangelicals opposed
any attempt to 'connect the arts with religion',
but were apparently happy to connect religion with
the arts. Religious paintings might not be acceptable in church, but they were among the artifices
which 'refined the pleasures of society'. Objections to the use of religious themes in art are
rare. On the contrary when annuals flooded the
market in the late 1820s, the Methodist Magazine
urged its readers to pay particular attention to
The Iris because its illustrations were exclusively
concerned with Scriptural subjects.[6] While evidence
is necessarily scant, it is clear that some
evangelicals displayed religious pictures in their
own homes. The Brontes owned engravings of at least
four of John Martin's highly dramatic paintings on
Biblical themes.[7] J.W. Cunningham listed in his
will not only numerous family portraits, which the
more affluent evangelicals like their contemporaries
appear to have favoured, but also prints of St. John
and of Raphael's Virgin, and two 'of our blessed
Lord', one after de Vinci.[8]
     Evangelicals' apparent willingness to accept
religious art in non-ecclesiastical contexts was
confirmed by the Edinburgh Review, which condemned
the cant and casuistry of those who objected to the
introduction of sacred subjects and expressions
onto the stage but not onto canvas, condemning
the one but not the other as 'a blasphemous
representation': 'Amusement is the object of both.
And the instruments of communicating it, the artist
and the actor, may be equally strangers to any
serious impression'.[9] The reviewer's criticism was
not entirely just. Evangelicals who looked at
pictures in the quietness of their own homes, or

even perhaps at public exhibitions, were not exposed
to those 'attendant circumstances' which rendered
public performances so objectionable to them. More
significantly there was a profound difference in
nature between a picture which existed in its own
right distinct from its creator, and a play or
oratorio which in one sense only existed when given
life by the performers. It was this distinction
which the Edinburgh Review failed to consider when
it complained that evangelicals approved of pictures
of praying women, but disapproved of women praying
on stage. But the one was a representation of a
religious act, the other in evangelical eyes an
imitation. Those who pretended to pray or who in
oratorios aped the words of adoration were therefore
regarded as impiously insincere, while the singer
who took upon himself the role of God, impersonating
the Almighty, was adjudged guilty of blasphemy. In
contrast the artist stood outside his work in a way
not dissimilar to that of others who viewed it.
Since the painting was not to be used in worship,
there was no question of idolatry. On the contrary
the artist who imaginatively reconstructed a religious
scene merely enabled avid readers of the Bible more
clearly to envisage events over which they had long
exercised their imaginations. This was the
justification of religious art implicit in a brief
discussion in an Eclectic Review article of 1821.
The reviewer maintained that some Biblical events
such as the act of Creation were beyond human
representation and even the greatest artists
consequently failed to depict 'so impalpable and
inconceivable an energy'. The attempt 'transcended
the legitimate boundaries of art'. Other Scriptural
scenes, however, such as the Flood and the Last
Judgment were 'capable of being elevated and
expanded by the sublime delineation of poetry or
painting', as the ceiling of the Sistine Chapel,
one of the 'proudest monuments of human genius',
so supremely proved.[10]
    The classical argument that it was the role of
art to elevate and expand subjects of the highest
order and hence to elevate and expand the human
mind was regularly employed by Eclectic reviewers.
The existence of a long established theory of art
was perhaps one of the factors enabling evangelicals
the more readily to accept the cultural exploration
of a religious theme in that medium than in music.
The models for western art were primarily classical.
Western music in contrast was more immediately the
product of the churches. Believing on both histor-

ical and Biblical grounds that music was an
essentially religious pursuit, evangelicals tended
to judge it by devotional criteria. Lacking any
such rationale for art, they were more prepared to
appraise it according to traditionally established
aesthetic canons. Thus while oratorios, a
comparatively novel form of culture, were sometimes
condemned as religious pursuits perverted to the
purposes of amusement, religious paintings were
praised as works of art which properly selected
for their subjects themes which evangelicals regarded as the most important, sublime and interesting.

Evangelicals' interest in art was by no means
confined to purely religious matter. Paradoxically,
the fact that the fine arts lacked religious
sanction of the sort accorded to music may have
facilitated their wider acceptance. Since they
were assumed to make no contribution to worship
there could be no question of confining them to
devotional purposes. In view of this some evangelicals rejected them as they rejected everything that
served no immediate religious function.[11] But the
tendency of some to judge all pursuits at the bar of
moral and religious utility, and to depreciate
anything that could not be so tested, was explicitly
repudiated by John Foster in an article on the
Elgin Marbles published in the Eclectic Review of
1812:

> Put things in their right gradation,
> from the highest extreme to the lowest,
> and the man that gratefully exults in
> our having received so long from Judea,
> and indeed partly from Greece, the grand
> rectifier of our intellectual and moral
> faculties, in their most important
> relations - the Bible - will not
> therefore fail to acknowledge the value
> (though certainly small according to his
> scale) of these latest contributions of
> Greece to discipline our faculties to a
> more correct perception of beauty in
> forms.[12]

Other Eclectic reviewers shared Foster's belief
that the fine arts, albeit of lesser value than
religion, nevertheless enhanced life: a genuine
delight in painting, architecture and sculpture was
regularly revealed in the periodical's artistic
reviews.[13] No attempt was made to provide a
justification for the study of art; on the contrary

reviewers assumed that their readers would like them
regard the fine arts as inherently valuable. They
were therefore vehemently opposed to iconoclasm.
While appreciating that the Early Church had strong
religious reasons for destroying pagan images,
Foster, unlike Wesley, denied that Greek statues
still evoked idolatrous sentiments, and criticised
some of the early Christians for destroying them
out of mere barbarism.[14] Another reviewer was
similarly disgusted by the philistinism of the
Protectorate, and showed no awareness that this
might have been religiously inspired:

> The stern warriors and statesmen of the
> Commonwealth, had neither relish nor
> leisure for the pursuits of virtu;
> and we could have forgiven them their
> want of taste, had they not with mere
> sordid, money-making calculation, chosen
> to disperse those inestimable treasures,
> and dismiss to foreign countries
> productions of value too great to leave
> any hope of their re-acquisition.

Far from aligning himself with the English Puritans,
the reviewer attacked the present administration
for similar short-sightedness and spoke out in
favour of government spending on the arts:

> The same absurd economy prevented the
> acquisition of the marbles of Egina (sic),
> of which the skill and enterprise of an
> Englishman had procured the right of
> refusal. We trust that the time of
> ill-judged parsimony, the constrained
> result of thoughtless extravagance, is
> gone by; and that a judicious application
> of the national resources will obtain for
> us those advantages, available on the
> spot, which our students have hitherto
> been compelled to seek in foreign capitals.[15]

The other evangelical periodicals were perhaps
more loyal to the established authorities than the
Eclectic, but they too quietly echoed its concern to
further the cause of the fine arts in Britain.[16]
The production of annuals, which owed their main
attraction to the embellishments with which they
were liberally bestrewed, was on the whole welcomed,
in the words of the Evangelical Magazine, as a
'noble effort to improve the taste and to encourage

151

the fine arts too much depressed in this great
mercantile community'.[17] The Record especially in
later years was predictably more critical, condemning annuals as frivolous, devoid of right principle,
and sometimes indecent.[18] It also objected to the
exhibition of Titian's Venus.[19] But the paper was
by no means totally opposed to works of art: from
time to time it communicated information about them,
and a correspondent of 1833 who complained about
the indelicacy of some of the pictures on display at
the Dulwich Picture Gallery, argued that these
should be kept in one room for those who wished to
see them so that others could satisfy their love of
the arts without blushing.[20]

   While the Eclectic Review was in general less
moralistic in its outlook, some of its reviewers
shared the Record's qualms. One questioned whether
the publication of pictures of naked Greek gods was
compatible with 'purity of mind and genuine
delicacy', and criticised the Royal Academy practice
of drawing from life, 'flattering the passion for
nudity', as 'needless and pernicious'.[21] Another
complained about the display in church of 'heathen
deities' and naked statues such as that of a
renowned sea-captain, a sin 'against naval order,
correct taste, national decorum, and Christian
morality'. Nevertheless even he was not opposed to
the exhibition of such works in the National Gallery
where visitors knew what to expect: 'We are no
fanatics; we can tolerate a little heathenism
here'.[22]

   It is within this context of a substantial
divorce between religion and art, the exclusion of
the latter from churches but its ready acceptance
often on its own terms in non-ecclesiastical
contexts, that evangelical attitudes to art must
ultimately be assessed. If the inconsistencies in
those attitudes can to some extent be explained,
they cannot entirely be dismissed. It was perhaps
an attempt to impose consistency that led to the
traditional assumption that evangelicals were
aesthetically insensitive. It is probably true as
their biographers have claimed that their tastes
were in many cases literary and intellectual rather
than artistic. It is more certainly true that their
appreciation of the written and spoken word and
their dislike of Catholicism caused them sometimes
indiscriminately to devalue non-verbal modes of
communication in church. But it does not therefore
follow that they emulated puritan philistinism by
condemning the arts in every walk of life. On the

contrary the evidence seems to suggest that save
within the context of worship evangelicals welcomed
the fine arts, regarding them as pleasurable and
civilizing facts of life.

B. THE ARTISTS OF EVANGELICALISM

In accordance with this belief many evangelicals
were happy to practise the arts. Moreover,
whereas evangelical musicians were famed if at all
for producing editions of sacred music, evangelical
artists explored a far wider range of subject
matter. Thomas Gisborne might recommend landscape
drawing on the grounds that this enhanced awareness
of the works of God, but neither Richenda Cunningham
nor Edward Edwards, Rector of St. Edmund's North
Lynn, confined themselves to such obviously
devotional material.[23] Mrs. Cunningham's Nine Views
of the Continent, the profits of which were to be
devoted to charity, are mainly of objects of
architectural interest. Edwards favoured similar
subjects: over one third of the drawings displayed
in a 1973 exhibition 'The Town Scene' at the King's
Lynn Museum came from his hand.[24] That his work was
thus exhibited is some indication of its merit.
To lay eyes Mrs. Cunningham's work too is remarkably
competent: the buildings at which she was most
skilled are intricately detailed while the tiny
figures are lively and natural. She had no doubt
benefited from good teaching for the Gurney girls
had enjoyed the instruction of John Crome, one of
the founders of the Norwich School.[25]
     The competence of other evangelical practit-
ioners of the fine arts can be more confidently
determined, for there were many professionals
among them, who achieved royal or aristocratic
patronage, and in some cases exhibited at the Royal
Academy. Undoubtedly the evangelical whose
reputation was to prove most lasting was Thomas
Sheraton (1751-1806), a Baptist. The editor of a
study of Sheraton Furniture notes that very little
is known about him, and virtually nothing about his
first forty years, during which his name was
established. He published religious tracts as well
as his famous Cabinet Directory, and was ordained
in 1800 to assist in the ministry of a religious
community in Stockton. By 1804, Ralph Fastnedge
suggests, his mind had given way ...[26]
     A study of evangelical artists is beset by
similar tantalising silences. Thus little more is

known about Sheraton's fellow Baptist, Thomas
Holloway (1748-1827) who, born into a dissenting
family, examined the doctrines and practices of
various denominations before being baptised on
profession of faith along with Joseph Hughes.[27]
According to one of his executors, who published a
brief memoir, lucrative business opportunities were
open to him as the eldest son, but he chose instead
to be apprenticed to an engraver. His increasing
reputation brought him into acquaintance with the
leading artists of the day, one of whom, Benjamin
West, gained him access to Windsor. Appointed
Royal engraver, he was given the sole right to make
a new engraving of the Raphael cartoons. His
biographer paid tribute to his charity, noted that
he sometimes acted as supply preacher, and promoted
the dissenting interest wherever he went. His
Christian zeal was however 'well-regulated'.[28]
Even less information is immediately available on
the Huguenot Rigaud family. John Francis (1742-
1810) and his less renowned son Stephen Francis
Dutilh (1777-1861) exhibited at the Royal Academy:
the father, an academician and historical painter to
Gustavus IV of Sweden, numbered among other
commissions ceiling decoration at Windsor, and the
restoration of ceiling and staircase paintings at
the old British Museum ...[29]
     In view of the shortage of biographical
remains, the analysis that follows can be no more
than a prologomenon towards a more substantial
study of evangelical artists, based on any unpublished papers that can be unearthed. It is
possible, even assuming the availability of material,
that such a study would prove disappointing: the
family biography of the Taylors of Ongar, engravers
for several generations, yields little information
about the attitude of evangelical artists to their
work, and this may well reflect the extent to which
art was automatically accepted as an appropriate
profession for a Christian.[30] Nevertheless there
were bound to be some clashes between religious
and professional demands, and discovery of the way
in which evangelical artists responded to these is
crucial to a full understanding of evangelical
attitudes to art. Tentative suggestions only can
be proffered on the basis of a brief preliminary
examination of three of the evangelical academicians
who were in their own day most renowned outside
evangelical circles.
     Relationships with fellow artists, with
aristocratic patrons, generally essential for

professional advance, and with clients invariably
brought evangelicals into close contact with 'the
world'. When John Jackson (1778-1831), future
portrait painter to the Wesleyan Conference, moved
to London seriously to commence his studies he
informed his parents that he had made 'a serious
acquaintance ... which I am sorry to say I think is
almost the only example amongst the great number of
artists in London'.[31] The Methodist Magazine gives
the impression that Jackson continued to feel this
want, lamenting that the company which he was
obliged to keep sometimes robbed him of his peace.[32]
But the pious obituarist, who certainly exaggerated
Jackson's artistic ability, probably also over-
estimated the extent to which he conformed to the
expected evangelical pattern. The testimonies of
his fellow artists give no indication that he was
either ill-at-ease in mixed company or made non-
evangelicals uncomfortable by his religious
scrupulosity. On the contrary he appears to have
maintained cordial relations both with his artistic
colleagues and with the world at large. Benjamin
Haydon, a fellow student, recorded

> It was impossible not to like Jackson.
> His very indolent and lazy habits engaged
> one. His eternal desire to gossip was
> wonderful. Sooner than not gossip, he
> would sit down and talk to servants and
> valets, drink brandy and water with them,
> and perhaps sing a song. He would stand
> for hours together with one hand in his
> trowser's pocket, chatting about Sir
> Joshua and Vandyke, then tell a story
> in his Yorkshire way, full of nature
> and tact, racy and beautiful, and then
> start off anywhere, to Vauxhall or
> Covent Garden, 'to study expression and
> effect'.[33]

Francis Chantrey, who was Jackson's companion on a
visit to Rome, regarded him as 'easy and
accommodating to a fault' and apparently remained
ignorant to the last of his friend's religious
persuasion:

> Since his death I have heard that latterly
> he spent much of his time with the
> Methodists - consequently some if not much
> of his money must have been swallowed by
> those holy sinners. So close was he on

> this subject that I never discovered
> his inclination either by his conversation
> or manner.[34]

Such statements inevitably raise questions
about the nature and extent of Jackson's evangelicalism. Clearly he suffered neither from the
tortured anxiety to spend every moment aright, so
characteristic of many evangelicals, nor from a
pressing evangelistic impulse. Yet it would be
wrong to cast doubt on his commitment for these
reasons alone. Converted, according to the
Methodist Magazine, in a 1793 revival, he remained
a loyal Methodist, meeting in class, for the rest of
his life, writing in 1826 to a brother

> this world with all that it can offer is a
> mere bauble, and few persons of my age have
> experienced more of its frowns, its
> flattery, its goods, and its ills; we
> are well acquainted I can assure you and
> the more we are so, the less I feel
> disposed to court or to fear it.[35]

The letter may provide a hint towards understanding
Jackson. Unlike some evangelicals who jibbed even
at the mention of Covent Garden or Vauxhall, he
was not afraid of the world. While he retained a
belief in its ultimate vanity, he accepted both
'its goods and its ills' rather than fleeing fear-
fully from them. He was perhaps typical of the many
evangelicals, lambasted by their leaders and
frequently neglected in a study of this kind, who,
as the movement became more respectable, combined
personal piety with a ready acceptance of 'the
world'. Their faith if less fervent than that of
others was also less fraught. For them there need
be no conflict between religion and art.

If John Jackson showed some of the traits
common to a certain form of second generation
evangelicalism, characteristics associated with the
first were well represented in another portrait
painter, John Russell (1745-1806), who recorded
that he was converted at about 7.30 p.m. on 30
September 1764.[36] Russell's patrons, clients, and
colleagues could not but be aware of his faith, for
he recorded in his diary for 1767 'Lord Montague
said my manner was hateful so like a Methodist,
and would frighten anyone from religion', and
three months later, 'We talked religion over tea.
I perceived that he (Lord Aylesford) wanted me

gone, but I thought fit to break through good
manners rather than withhold any blessing from a
child of God, and so staid four hours'.[37] This
cannot simply be dismissed as the brashness of a
new convert which would mellow as he matured, for
in later life Russell still tended to take advantage of his subjects' captive position: on 25
November 1801 he 'endeavoured to speak a few words
of instruction to an old lady sitting to me but
could make no impression'.

Russell might try to turn his profession to
religious use but he nevertheless believed that it
was hazardous to his own spiritual well-being:
'in much business all day' he noted earlier the
same month 'but kept watchful being without
temptation'.[38] Social gatherings of fellow artists,
such as the Royal Academy dinners, could to some
extent be avoided: whenever he attended them
Russell left early and noted in 1773 that he was
'nearly choked by a fishbone, because of going to
the R.A.'.[39] But the company of potential clients
could not so easily be eschewed. Russell's diary
entry for 4 December 1801, if more extended than
some, is typical:

> Was exposed to temptation at the house
> of Dr. -----, a great, rich and highly
> related clergyman, but a proud man of
> the world, who had invited some
> distinguished men to meet me, but I
> escaped without injury tho (sic) I was
> in great fear - tried to avoid their
> company but could not. I thank God I
> received no harm praying for deliverance.
> Oh what a snare is the world to a
> Christian man.

But Russell never assumed that it presented
greater snares to artists than to other Christians
whose professions similarly necessitated involvement in worldly company. Throughout his writings
his fears related to those with whom he was obliged
to mix not to the nature of the work itself.
Indeed whereas evangelicals tended to disapprove of
biographies which commemorated the irreligious,
unless moral lessons could be clearly drawn from
them, they did not extend the same complaint to
portraiture. It can safely be assumed that Russell,
an enthusiastic supporter of the Evangelical
Magazine, for which he supplied portraits, shared
that periodical's antipathy to the stage: in 1768

he took Miss Hannah Faden, to whom he was later to propose, 'to hear Romaine. I conclude her to be a converted person now, and I delivered her a letter concerning the stage'.[40] Yet by the end of his career Russell, like Jackson, had acquired an extensive theatrical clientele, painting among others the actress Mrs. Scott Waring who, his biographer records, 'possessed a somewhat battered reputation'.[41]

There is no indication that Russell, whose sensitivity of conscience cannot be doubted, was aware of any inconsistency in his behaviour.[42] While he seized every opportunity to further the cause of religion he does not appear specifically to have justified his portraits of the ungodly on the grounds that he might be 'useful' to them. Materially they were frequently of use to him and Russell was happy to accept any profferred assistance for his growing family. Colonel Grove was

> a Deist, a man of very depraved morals,
> but has been raised up to serve me,
> when (sic) it shall not be accounted
> for but from Providence, who will feed
> his people by ravens as well as men.[43]

It was clearly impracticable for an artist to pick and choose his clients, and it seems probable that Russell accepted the obligation to paint according to order as an integral part of a job which was the divinely sanctioned means of feeding his family. If the profession itself was legitimate then no further thought need be given to the particularities of the exercise.

This attitude to artistic employment was made explicit by the sculptor John Bacon (1740-99) who formed a triumvirate with Russell and Francis Rigaud, living like them and Jackson after them in the artists' quarter of London, Newman Street. A close friend of John Newton, a member of the original CMS committee, and one of the few lay members of the Eclectic Society, Bacon was one of the most eminent sculptors of his day: 'to many of the educated public', Ann Cox-Johnson has written, 'his name would have been considered almost synonymous with the word sculpture. The demand for his work came not only from the capital but from all over the country and from abroad'.[44] A brief memoir was written by Richard Cecil who asked his friend to explain how he justified spending time and effort on the production of mere artefacts:

'Upon what principle ... do you
continually labour to meet the taste
of such sickly wanderers?' ... 'I
consider' said he, 'that profession in
which I am providentially placed, and
prosperously and honourably succeeded,
to be as lawful as any other that is
not concerned in furnishing the
necessities of life; besides which,
part of it, especially the monumental,
may be employed to an important moral
purpose; but the truth is, if the work
itself be innocent, the workman I hope
is not accountable for the abuse made of
it; and as the world will have not only
its necessaries, but its <u>toys</u>, I may as
well be the toy-man as any other'.[45]

Bacon's claim that the construction of
monuments, in which he was primarily engaged, could
be turned to moral use, however sincerely believed,
has to be condemned as unduly naive. Even if, as
Cecil claimed, he refused to execute monuments of
which either the design or the inscription was
unchristian, he was no more free than Jackson or
Russell to refuse to commemorate individuals of
whose morals he disapproved. Indeed the first of
several commissions he received for Westminster
Abbey was for a bust of Lord Halifax, who loved
horse-racing and kept a mistress.[46] Moreover, it
is difficult to believe that the easily comprehensible symbols of charity and other virtues which
are the hallmarks of his monuments were so different
from those commonly employed as positively to
further the cause of morality.[47]
It is possible that Bacon was pushed into
defending his profession by the importunity of
Cecil, who having given up even the leisure pursuits
he dearly loved for the sake of religion, found it
hard to comprehend how Christians could engage in
any but the most utilitarian of non-religious
employment. Yet if Cecil is to be believed Bacon
himself was indifferent to his work maintaining
'that, if he worked on a thousand blocks, they
remained but dead forms - that a few sparks of even
natural life, which he could not produce, seemed to
exceed them all'.[48] Here once again is exemplified
the evangelical tendency unduly to depreciate human
artefacts, because they could not compete with the
work of God, a tendency all the more striking
because attributed to one who spent his life in

their production. The propriety of the attribution
is confirmed by the epitaph which Bacon composed
for his own grave, an epitaph which suggests that,
if he did not altogether disregard his artistic
achievements at the time, he was unable to grant
them any meaningful place in his religious schema:

> What I was as an artist, seemed to me of
> some importance while I lived: but what
> I really was as a believer in Christ
> Jesus, is the only thing of importance
> to me now.[49]

A brief consideration of the sons of Russell
and Bacon who perpetuated the family friendship
begun by their fathers forms a fitting postscript
to this chapter. Both John Bacon junior (1777-1859)
and William Russell (1780-1870) abandoned the
artistic professions to which they had been bred
and in which both had shown considerable facility,
exhibiting at the Royal Academy. Bacon's diaries
and letters reveal that he, like the sister whose
memoir he published, was highly introspective,
suffering from intense religious depression as a
result of his reliance upon the fluctuations of
feeling: 'a cold barren week' he recorded on 22
March 1817, 'though no actual sin'. A popular
speaker at CMS and BFBS meetings he was terrified
lest he gave the impression of being more godly
than he knew himself to be. If his apprehension
testifies to his deep-rooted honesty, his conviction
of his own sinfulness sometimes reached megalo-
maniac proportions:

> O Lord thou Son of David, I will now
> put thy grace and power to a far more
> severe test than it was ever subjected
> to whilst Thou wast upon earth. I bring
> Thee the most diseased victim ... I now
> put thy power and mercy to the greatest
> test it has known.[50]

For a man of this temperament inheriting both his
father's tendency towards miserliness and his
unpopularity in the artistic world, the financial
pressures of professional practice constituted a
serious spiritual trial.[51] Bacon could not
understand why God allowed him to be distracted
by business failures consequent upon his substantial
investment in property, and exposed his disquiet and
his perplexity in the pages of his diary:

> The mysterious dealings of God in
> providence is ... my grand difficulty.
> I do not desire great things in this
> world, but I desire such competency and
> such temporal circumstances as shall not
> oblige me to think or care about the
> things of this life. And as we are
> warned against being choked with the
> thorns and cares of this world, it is
> a difficulty with me to fathom the
> reason why worldly difficulties are
> conducive to the health of the soul;
> they cannot be experienced without more
> or less and of necessity engaging the
> mind and the attention.[52]

While the firm that bore his name continued to churn
out monuments at a great rate Bacon retired
prematurely from active involvement.

William Russell ceased to exhibit at the Royal
Academy after his ordination in 1809. According to
his father's biographer he 'took a vow never to
touch pencil or brush again, for fear that his love
for art might interfere with or displace his
spiritual duties'. He remained Rector of
Shepperton, Middlesex, for the rest of his life,
about which little is known.[53]

Absence of information precludes firm
conclusions. Evangelicals like Russell who gave up
cultural pursuits to follow what they regarded as a
greater calling have perhaps received an unduly
harsh press: those who praise Schweitzer, enamoured
of his exotic surroundings, cannot logically condemn
Russell. Moreover, if Williamson's report is
accurate, Russell's decision to renounce painting
even as a leisure pursuit was, like Cecil's
renunciation of music, the product not of
philistinism but of profound appreciation of an
engrossing activity. All the available evidence
suggests that evangelicals approved of art both as
an embellishment of society and as a profession
proper for Christian pursuit. Some evangelicals,
most notably Jackson, appear to have engaged in it
without qualm. The unease felt by others, John
Russell in the first generation and John Bacon in
the second, related not to artistic activity itself
but to its attendant worldly circumstances: John
Bacon could no more have coped with any other
profession, while his publications in the 1840s
reveal that he retained an interest in the arts to
the end of his life.[54] Nevertheless some slight

caveat has to be introduced. Art might be a desirable embellishment of society but it was no more
than an embellishment, in the disparaging language
of Richard Cecil and Bacon's father, a toy to be
contrasted with true religious treasure. Bacon
senior's epitaph remains sad testimony to the inability, even of an evangelical firmly committed to
art, theologically to reconcile 'what I was as an
artist' with 'the only thing of importance to me'.

NOTES

1. E.g. CO xx (1821), pp. 348, 553.
2. H. Davies, Worship and Theology in England:
from Watts and Wesley to Maurice (1961), p. 236.
3. ER i series ii (1806), pp. 389-90;
J. Russell, Ms Journal of Visit to Leeds, York,
Burleigh, Tedcaster, 27 August - 24 November 1799,
pp. 54-55.
4. C. Cecil, The Remains of the Rev. Richard
Cecil (1876 edn.), p. 50: 'the very damp that
trickles down the walls, and the unsightly green
that moulders upon the pillars are more pleasing to
me from their associations, than the trim, finished,
classic, heathen piles of the present fashion'.
5. Ringletub, op. cit., pp. 25ff. Cf.
Satchell, op. cit., iii, p. 195.
6. MM lii (1829), p. 835; liii (1830), p. 833.
7. W. Gerin, Charlotte Bronte (1967), pp. 42-
45, includes a brief discussion of annuals and of
Martin's prolific contributions to them. The son
of pious parents, Martin did not apparently share
their faith, although his childhood familiarity
with the Old Testament is reflected in his art.
8. Will dated 4 May 1861.
9. Edinburgh Review liv (1831), pp. 107-08.
10. ER ii series xvi (1821), pp. 220-21.
11. E.g. J. Hughes, A Tribute of Friendship
(1829), p. 3 where it is affirmed that Mrs. Rebecca
Wilkinson of Clapham Common, a Baptist, might have
acquired a reputation as an artist 'had she not in
the midst of a promising career, laid aside the
pencil, and under a strong sense of duty, determined
to occupy the leisure of a single life in a way most
contributory to human happiness and the manifestation of the Divine glory'.
12. ER i series viii (1812), p. 357, reprinted
Foster, Critical Essays ..., ii. Contrast the
determination to turn all to religious use in a two-
year EM series 'Of terms of art used by the apostle
Paul derived from existing antiquities in the

British Museum': 'My wish is ... to explain certain
of his allusions hitherto imperfectly understood.
It is true, they are but dead stones; yet with a
little attention, we hear them speak, and bear a
living testimony to the Gospel ...' (i series xxvi,
1818, p. 13).
13. ER i series i (1805), pp. 783-86; iii
(1807), pp. 52-65; ii series vii (1817), pp. 442-
48; viii (1817), pp. 539-47; xxi (1824), pp. 216-
24, 448-63; xxiv (1825), pp. 519-27; iii series
ii (1829), pp. 233-40, 333-43, 'Publications of
this kind (Flaxman's Lectures on Sculpture) are
exceedingly to our taste'; iii (1830), pp. 58-64;
v (1831), pp. 369-70.
14. ER i series viii (1812), pp. 357-60;
Lecky, op. cit.,iii,pp. 87-88.
15. ER ii series xxiii (1825), pp. 278-80.
The discovery of statues on Aegina 'not inferior to
the celebrated sculptures of the Elgin collection'
was noted with interest in CO x (1811), p. 722.
16. Dissenting insistence on the right to
criticise both the civil and ecclesiastical
establishment was a major factor causing Anglican
withdrawal from the Eclectic Review (J.E. Ryland,
ed., The Life and Correspondence of John Foster,
1846, i,pp. 374ff.).
17. EM ii series vii (1829), p. 495. Cf.
MM li (1828), p. 834.
18. The Record, 8 December 1831; 30 December
1833.
19. Ibid., 20 November 1828.
20. Ibid., 5 September 1833. Cf. 4 June,
24 August 1829.
21. ER i series vi (1810), pp. 626-27.
22. Ibid. ii (1806), p. 390.
23. Gisborne, ... Female Sex ..., p. 44. The
friendship between Edwards and the Gurney family
whom he influenced towards evangelical faith is
discussed by Hare, op. cit., i,pp. 190-92.
24. The Town Scene, selected topographical
material from the King's Lynn borough collections
(1973).
25. Swift, op. cit., pp. 8-9.
26. R. Fastnedge, Sheraton Furniture (1962)
is prefaced by a short account of Sheraton's life.
27. J. Leifchild, Memoir of the late Rev.
Joseph Hughes A.M. (1835), p. 33.
28. Memoir of the late Mr. Thomas Holloway by
one of his executors (1827).
29. A manuscript memoir was available to the
compiler of the DNB entries.

30. I. Taylor (ed.), op. cit. In 1791 Isaac Taylor sen. won a Society of Arts award; he continued to engrave, exercising a tent-maker ministry, after ordination, and trained his six children in the art. His father, also an engraver, had numbered the young George Burder among his apprentices (H.F. Burder, op. cit., pp. 10ff.) while his son continued the family tradition of book illustration, his drawings enumerated in H. Taylor, City Scenes 1806 (1913).

31. Quoted H.C. Morgan, 'The Life and Works of John Jackson R.A. 1778-1831' (Leeds M.A. 1956), p. 24, a work to which I am indebted for its lengthy extracts from Jackson's unpublished letters.

32. MM liv (1831), p. 511.

33. T. Taylor (ed.), Life of Benjamin Robert Haydon from his Autobiography and Journals (2nd edn. 1853), i p. 45.

34. Quoted Morgan, op. cit., p. 193; A. Cunningham, The Lives of the Most Eminent British Painters, Sculptors and Architects vi (1833), p. 282. Cunningham's suggestion (p. 291) that at the end of his life Jackson suffered from religious despondency 'frequenting prayer meetings' probably derives from Chantrey's inaccurate use of the word 'latterly'.

35. Quoted Morgan, op. cit., p. 143; MM liv (1831), p. 511. A letter in Methodist Archives confirms that Jackson was in Joseph Butterworth's class.

36. Williamson, op. cit., p. 9.

37. Ibid., pp. 13, 16.

38. J. Russell, Ms Diary, 5 November 1801.

39. Williamson, op. cit., pp. 33-34.

40. Ibid., pp. 20-21.

41. Ibid., pp. 80-81; Morgan, op. cit., pp. 95, 101, 109, 115, 125-26.

42. Russell's diaries and journals are largely written in Byrom's shorthand. No sense of inconsistency can be detected in the few volumes of which transcriptions are available, nor does Williamson, who had access to a wider range of material, refer to any such unease.

43. Williamson, op. cit., p. 81.

44. A. Cox-Johnson, John Bacon R.A. 1740-99 (1961), p. 43; B. Martin, John Newton (1950), p. 322; Stock, op. cit., i, p. 69; J.H. Pratt, op. cit., pp. 97-98, 130-31.

45. R. Cecil, Memoir of John Bacon esq. R.A. with reflections drawn from his Moral and Religious Character (1801), pp. 93-94. The CO's unease about

the last statement constitutes yet one more
instance of evangelicals' inability theologically
to accommodate activity that was not obviously
religious (i, 1802, p. 521).

46. R. Cecil, op. cit., pp. 37-38; Cox-
Johnson, op. cit., p. 15. Bacon's most notable
commission was for a monument of Lord Chatham
erected in the Abbey. Subsequently the nation's
heroes were commemorated in St. Paul's Cathedral;
Bacon's monuments of John Howard, Dr. Johnson and
Sir William Jones were among the first to be
erected there.

47. Bacon invariably employed a pelican as a
symbol of charity, Cox-Johnson, op. cit., p. 16.
A. Cunningham, op. cit., iii (1830), p. 243 provides
a cruel and possibly apocryphal anecdote on its use,
and reprints from Cecil three of the hundreds of
epitaphs which Bacon composed in an attempt at
graveyard edification (p. 226). He was a better
sculptor than poet.

48. R. Cecil, op. cit., p. 94.

49. Ibid., p. 21.

50. Ms Diary, 27 (or 29) May 1817. Bacon's
Memoir of Miss Ann Bacon ... (1813) is a useful
illustration of experience-centred evangelical
religion.

51. Bacon senior's reputed closeness with
money and the hostility of other artists as he
became ever more successful are discussed in Cox-
Johnson, op. cit., pp. 11-12, 19-20.

52. Ms Diary, 9 May 1822.

53. Williamson, op. cit., p. 99.

54. J. Bacon, 'Remarks on Monumental
Architecture', Transactions of the Exeter Diocesan
Architectural Society i (1843), part ii, pp. 117-26;
A Letter to the Right Honourable Sir Robert Peel ...
on the Appointment of a Commission for Promoting the
Cultivation and Improvement of the Fine Arts with
some Suggestions respecting a former Commission,
denominated 'The Committee of Taste' (1843). Bacon
revealed not only his continuing interest in the
arts and approval of government sponsorship but
also a forty-year grievance against the Committee
of Taste, an amateur body which had sought to alter
some of his designs and those of his father.

Chapter Eight

FAITH AND FANCY

Richard Cecil renounced not only art and music but
also imaginative literature. His library and
written remains testify to his widespread
familiarity with secular authors. Nevertheless
he determined while seriously ill that, if he
recovered, he would read nothing but the Bible.[1]
Few evangelicals were prepared so to limit
themselves. On the contrary biographies reveal
that many read and enjoyed a wide range of secular
authors, albeit with some qualm about their moral
and religious teaching. Secular literature was
favourably reviewed in both the Christian Observer
and the Eclectic Review. Indeed the latter
regarded itself as the counterpart of the contemporary literary reviews, differing from them in that
its values and criteria of judgment were specifically Christian: it aimed 'to blend with impartial
criticism an invariable regard to moral and
religious principle', to effect the reconciliation
of 'those long divorced parties, Religion and
Literature'.[2] The content of the popular press
was, predictably, more exclusively religious, but
reviewers stressed that poetry which was neither
licentious nor effeminate was welcomed into
evangelical homes, and did much to foster the
reading of imaginative literature on religious
themes. Devotional poetry and religious novels
were immensely popular. Thus while Miss Ann Price,
whose obituary appeared in the Baptist Magazine,
discarded even Thornton Abbey through which she had
been converted and Watts' poems in which she
delighted 'lest reading Poetry should produce
spurious enjoyments and improper feelings', her
reaction, like that of Cecil, appears to be more
idiosyncratic than typical.[3]
        This chapter has four main concerns. Granted

that evangelicals read imaginative literature, how competent were they as critics in comparison with their contemporaries? What sort of literature did they enjoy? Why did their views on the legitimacy of novel-reading change? And finally how did they relate a love of literature to their theology?

A. THE QUALITY OF EVANGELICAL CRITICISM

According to evangelicals' assessment the best polite literature was that which was also pious, the work of Milton and Cowper, James Montgomery and Robert Pollok.[4] There was perhaps some slight preference for devotional writing as against works descriptive of Biblical events, for whereas Biblical paintings were readily accepted, some, but by no means all, evangelicals doubted the propriety of emulating the Bible in its own medium. A Methodist reviewer, who praised Scriptural art, criticised 'fictitious narratives, founded upon Scripture facts, in which the divine simplicity of the inspired volume is lost'.[5] Others however were far from convinced that the fictionalisation of Scripture was wrong. Thus the <u>Christian Observer</u> praised an author who 'without venturing on any flagrant departure from the simple history of Scripture ... has filled up the short outline of the account of Jephthah with genius and dexterity'.[6] What was important, all were agreed, was that a work should uphold a Christian world view and writers who failed to do so were severely criticised.

Herein lay the seeds of some inadequate literary criticism: evangelicals were accustomed to read for edification; they had moreover a profound belief in the efficacy of the written word; when they moved from Scripture to secular literature they were unable - or unwilling - totally to change their reading habits and so tended to judge a work too readily on the ideas it inculcated. Pertinacious concern for content sometimes carried with it a disregard for form. Commenting on a volume of religious poems, the <u>Evangelical Magazine</u> maintained that 'the man of taste may read them for their poetic excellence; but the experienced Christian will be too much absorbed in the piety of the sentiment to think about the poetry'.[7] Similarly a <u>Baptist Magazine</u> contributor dismissed literary quality as unimportant: 'This poem is introduced by a very modest preface, in which the pious author contends, and we think successfully, that mediocrity is not to be despised. Whatever is useful is valuable ...'[8]. Their concern that literature should be useful led evangelicals to misread some non-evangelical works, the enjoyment of which they legitimised by discovering a moral. Homer, the Christian Observer noted approvingly, wrote to display the crime and consequences of adultery and the rewards of conjugal love.[9] An Eclectic reviewer stifling his intuitive response managed to persuade himself that there was no nobility in Cleopatra's suicide:

> Nothing more beautiful and bewitching than this voluptuous queen: yet with all this beauty and witchery, her utter worthlessness and falseheartedness are fairly brought out, and entirely deprive her before the end of the Tragedy, of esteem and admiration. Not that the poet seems to be reading such a lesson, but facts are given according to nature, and the reader cannot fail of drawing the right conclusion.[10]

This tendency to impose their own views on the literature which they read resulted in further hindrances to the task of criticism. Convinced of their own rectitude and the invalidity of other views of life, evangelicals did not easily 'suspend disbelief', accepting for the duration of their reading the standards and values of the author. The rigid simplicity of their moral code did not allow them fully to appreciate tragedies deriving from behaviour which they regarded as improper. Harriet Corp maintained that Juliet should have attempted to dissuade her father when he pressed her to marry Paris. She was foolish to trust Romeo's fidelity: he had already revealed his inconstancy of character by deserting Rosaline.[11] Similar limitations of sympathy precluded evangelical responsiveness to Catholic tragedies for 'nothing can be more ridiculous in fiction than a Roman Catholic saint ... It is Christianity alone which can render death sublime'.[12] Above all evangelicals found it impossible to empathise with atheistic literature. Totally convinced of the rationality of their own position, they could not conceive that others in all good faith might come to opposite conclusions. Writers who perpetrated an anti-Christian view of life must

be conscious blackguards motivated by the desire
for publicity and fame. Byron, John Styles implied,
was deliberately malicious:

> Why an unbeliever should delight to
> propagate his opinions, it is impossible
> to explain on any principle of benevolence
> and humanity. What good can any man
> propose to accomplish, by persuading his
> fellow-creatures - that there is no God -
> that they live in a fatherless world -
> that the infinite spirit is gone - that
> the only solid foundation of virtue is
> wanting ... O, it is impossible not to
> turn with abhorrence from the apostate
> spirit who would thus involve the whole
> creation in his own ruin and wretchedness
> ...[13]

Hypersensitive to the interests of religion,
evangelicals were utterly insensitive to the ideas
of others and all too often approached the
literary expression of them with closed minds.
  Underlying such attitudes is a failure to
distinguish between art and life, an unwillingness
to recognise that a poet can adopt a persona and
is not necessarily speaking in his own voice as
from a pulpit. Such distinctions would have
appeared casuistical to evangelicals fearful lest
the reading of impious literature proved to be the
first step on the road to damnation. The same
consideration made them suspicious of the portrayal
of vice. There was little point in protecting
the young from the evil of the world if they were
to meet it vicariously in print. Even the most
moral works might mislead in this respect. The
Methodist Magazine warned:

> In all compositions, particular delicacy
> should be studied in making mention of
> sinful actions ... A strict guard should
> be placed upon the fancy, lest the writer,
> while seeking to check the progress of
> vice, should become inadvertently the
> means of increasing it.[14]

Fear of thus putting a stumbling block in the way
of the young may have incapacitated evangelicals'
own literary efforts. An Eclectic reviewer
praised the author of a novel Self-Control because
she made 'her vicious character so far from

attractive, that he does not excite a moment's
interest'. On the other hand this very achievement
made the heroine's passion for the man unconvincing
and her struggle against his influence incomprehensible: 'Instead of sympathising with Laura in
her regrets, we are more disposed to wonder at her
having felt any'.[15] It was dangerous to make vice
appealing, but consequently the temptations to
which characters were exposed were unlikely to
appear convincing. Similar assumptions led
evangelicals almost universally to repudiate
satire: 'Wickedness' wrote a <u>Baptist Magazine</u>
reviewer 'is too serious a matter for ridicule'.[16]
So too was religion, hence evangelicals' horror
when satire was directed against the clergy: they
were too earnest and maybe too insecure to expose
their faith - or its recognised representatives -
to criticism.

Such evidence goes some way to substantiating
charges of evangelical philistinism, but it is by
no means conclusive. Evangelicals should not be
subjected to more stringent tests than others.
It was as hard for evangelicals to empathise with
a Catholic or an atheist as it would be, in Wayne
C. Booth's example, for a post-war Englishman to
admire a Nazi S.S. hero.[17] Moreover instances in
which evangelicals failed to suspend disbelief can
be paralleled by many others in which they had no
difficulty in doing so. One <u>Eclectic</u> reviewer
shuddered 'at the vengeance of Minerva', while
another recognised that admiration could be
awakened by that of which one disapproved:
'forgetting the wickedness of Lady Macbeth, or
Satan, ... we feel ourselves for the time fully
possest (sic) with the grandeur of their
sentiments'. Evangelicals were moved 'by the
strong delusion of sympathy' in medieval legendary
tales and were able totally to lose themselves in
the imaginative worlds created by Sir Walter
Scott.[18] Reviewers frequently praised works which
had no apparent moral.

At the same time many were highly critical of
authors who seemed to assume that 'if a song have
but a moral cast, the absence of every other
recommendation is sufficiently compensated'.[19]
Neither the <u>Eclectic Review</u> nor the <u>Christian
Observer</u> regarded religion as a cover for a
multitude of literary sins: 'a poem must, after
all, be criticised as a work of taste; and there
is one rule for the appreciation of moral, and
another for that of literary excellence'.[20] Examples

of disregard for matters of taste can be paralleled
by many more in which evangelicals engaged in
detailed criticism of prosody and expression. The
editor of the Christian Observer was sufficiently
interested in such matters to give considerable
space in his 1812 edition to two philosophical
works on the nature of taste.[21] Urbane and
courteous, the reviewers of both periodicals gave
praise to non-Christian works where praise was due.
Nor was the work of Christian writers accepted
uncritically: the Christian Observer constantly
complained about the poor standard of religious
verse, regarded Montgomery's The World before the
Flood as of variable merit, and, to the author's
intense chagrin, was not wholly complimentary about
Coelebs in Search of a Wife.[22] It would be wrong
to suggest that even the popular press was totally
insensitive to matters of literary merit for the
reviewers were only too aware of the stylistic
weakness of much religious poetry. The Evangelical
Magazine tended to be sympathetic towards the
publication of mediocre verse by ladies in
distressed circumstances who needed emolument, but
it constantly criticised others who foisted on
the public poetry fit only for circulation among
friends.[23] The Methodist Magazine made the point
yet more forcefully:

> ... had he consulted ... the credit of
> that religion which he seems anxious to
> recommend he would have been careful not
> to associate the sacred doctrines of
> evangelical truth with the most consummate
> doggerel that ever offended the good taste
> of the educated part of mankind.[24]

Evangelicals shared the taste of 'the educated
part of mankind' to a far greater extent than is
always recognised. Their literary values
frequently resembled those deriving from the thought
forms of the day of which their theology was but
the evangelical expression. Basil Willey has
suggested that from the late seventeenth century
the prevalent philosophy militated against poetry:
truth was ascertained not through the imagination
but through 'naked reason'; Pope did not convey
his beliefs through mythological and allegorical
machinery for the age of the Royal Society favoured
straightforward explanation and did not conceive
of the imaginative communication of a truth that
was conceptually inexpressible.[25] The theological

form of such thinking can be seen in the intellectual formulations of natural theology, in the anti-
sacramentalism of the latitudinarians, and in the
paucity of eighteenth century contributions to the
development of liturgy and ecclesiology: the only
'symbol' in many eighteenth century churches was
the three decker pulpit. Similarly evangelicals
felt no need of an imaginative approach to the
apprehension of religious truth: God had given not
a book full of stories (useful though these were
for children) but a book full of statements. Their
assumption that truth was conceptual, a matter of
doctrine and precept, and art an embellishment,
thus derived from a heritage wider than the purely
sectarian. The distaste of more cultured evangelicals for allegory was not just due to religious
scrupulosity, for Jabez Bunting's objection to
highly figurative oratory bears the insignia of the
eighteenth century as well as of evangelicalism:

> -----'s flights of fancy are truly
> ludicrous; and, indeed, I think that,
> in general, the fewer excursions we make
> into the regions of metaphor and
> allegory, the better it will be. Plain
> sense, expressed in plain words, without
> any show of learning, or affectation of
> rhetorical brilliancy, is most likely to
> be of ultimate use to our hearers. Other
> things may dazzle, but they seldom
> illuminate or sanctify ...[26]

The affinity between evangelical theology, at
least in its less enthusiastic forms, and eighteenth
century classicism has been briefly explored by
Donald Davie who suggests that the typical
characteristics of the Calvinist aesthetic were
simplicity, sobriety, measure, and an awareness of
the totality of any artistic scheme; thus Isaac
Watts, one of its greatest exponents, determined 'to
restrain my verse always within the bounds of my
design', an intention no less classical than
Calvinist.[27] The critical vocabulary of evangelical
reviewers testifies to their acceptance of neo-
classical canons of criticism, to which the Eclectic
Review and the Christian Observer like the Edinburgh
and Quarterly Reviews largely adhered. The
conventions of classicism combined easily with
evangelical seriousness when the Christian Observer
rejected puns as improper accompaniments of
Shakespearian death-scenes.[28] Similarly it refuted

in true eighteenth century style Irish-born Adam
Clarke's claim that fairy stories had predisposed
him to an awareness of the spiritual world; the
reviewer denied that God would employ 'ridiculous
fabrications' to aid his purpose.[29] Objections to
improbability abounded in evangelical as in non-
evangelical reviews, John Foster scorning the
'absurdity' and 'wretched barbarism and super-
stition' of Southey's poem The Curse of Kehama. As
an evangelical Foster was particularly shocked that
a Christian poet should in his own person invoke
members of the Hindu pantheon, but his basic
objection to polytheism was shared by many non-
evangelicals: the Quarterly Review, generally
sympathetic to Southey, who was one of its regular
contributors, complained about the 'tumid and
unimaginable absurdity of Hindu mythology', as,
more vituperatively, did Francis Jeffrey of the
Edinburgh Review.[30] Jeffrey's critique closely
resembled that which Foster wrote for the Eclectic.
    Concern about the moral and religious tenor
of works and the legitimacy of the literary
depiction of evil similarly extended far beyond
evangelical circles. In The Rambler of 31 March
1750 Samuel Johnson had examined the respective
claims of realism and morality, concluding that
'it is necessary to distinguish those parts of
nature which are most proper for imitation'. While
agreeing that credibility demanded the portrayal
of vice, Johnson was adamant that it should always
appear repugnant, never united with ameliorating
graces. Not only the evangelical press but also
the Quarterly Review condemned irreligion and
immorality in fiction; its critics and those of
the Christian Observer made very similar judgments
on Miss Edgeworth's Tales of Fashionable Life.[31]
The religion and morality demanded by evangelicals
was admittedly often more strict than that required
by their contemporaries, but the principle was the
same.
    Set within the context of their own day
evangelicals' criticism was neither as idiosyncratic
nor as contemptible as has sometimes been implied.
Twentieth century editors, collating reviews of
various leading authors, regularly see fit to
include those from the Eclectic and, less
frequently, those from the Christian Observer as
part of a Critical Heritage. Describing the early
nineteenth century response to Coleridge, J.R. de
J. Jackson pays tribute to the insight of the
Eclectic Review which alone recognised his stature:

> During these years appreciative
> comments were rare. One of the few was
> a long, detailed, and enthusiastic review
> of The Friend, which appeared in the
> Eclectic Review ... The review deserves
> a careful reading as the first description
> of Coleridge's thought and prose style,
> and for its anticipation of later
> apologists ... More than ten years were
> to pass before Coleridge was to be served
> as well by a reviewer.[32]

This later appreciation of the Eclectic was shared
by some contemporaries. The poet laureate Robert
Southey frequently endorsed the literary judgments
of its editor, Josiah Conder, writing in 1814,
'I wish my coadjutors in the Quarterly had thought
half so much upon poetry and understood it half so
well'.[33]

B.   THE RANGE OF EVANGELICAL READING

The extent to which evangelicals shared the literary
taste of their contemporaries is revealed not only
in analysis of their criticism but also through
examining the range of their secular reading.
Notwithstanding some heart-searching evangelicals
seem to have read much the same works as the more
cultured of their fellows.
      This is most obviously seen in their
acceptance of classical literature which many
evangelicals read for relaxation. John Mason Good
and Isaac Taylor junior devoted time to translating
the classics, producing work praised in the
evangelical press.[34] It was readily assumed by
evangelicals as by the world at large that education
should be classical. At the same time however there
was considerable unease about classical study,
expressed both by those who like a Methodist
Magazine reviewer could see little justification for
it, and by those who enjoyed it: Joseph Kinghorn,
a keen classicist, admitted, maybe to appease his
unsympathetic father, that the classics did nothing
to feed the hungry soul and thus compared un-
favourably with the Scriptures.[35] A correspondent
of the Christian Observer complained that they did
not prepare dying men to face eternity. Moreover,
they were liable to inculcate false ideas: their
morality was antagonistic to that of Christianity
which had very different standards of heroism,

while they propagated an 'absurd' and 'untrue'
religion.[36] An <u>Eclectic</u> reviewer was concerned lest
a taste for the classics should mitigate evangelical
disgust at idolatry, still prevalent on the mission
field.[37]
Attempts made to dispel this unease reflect
the evangelical constraint to explain everything in
explicitly religious terms. It was argued that
those who studied classical languages were thereby
equipped to read some of the original Scriptures.
A knowledge of the classics enabled preachers to
follow St. Paul's example and appeal to the educated
classes; it was therefore a necessary evangelistic
tool. More particularly classical descriptions of
pagan societies could serve the cause of religion
since they revealed to the percipient or well-
instructed reader the deplorable state of a world
without Christ; they were 'irrefragable witnesses
for Christ', making clear

> the utter insufficiency of man for his
> own happiness; the natural cravings of
> the human heart after an infinite good
> ... Where we would ask, except in the
> Sacred Scriptures, is the aching void
> of the natural heart more forcibly
> illustrated, than in the soberer
> reflections of Horace?[38]

Yet these claims are little more than <u>ex post facto</u>
justifications. Evangelical attempts to legitimise
classical literature within the immediate terms of
their theology are unconvincing.
Some of the other reasons given for classical
study, however, reveal the extent to which
evangelicals accepted the assumptions of their day.
Far from regarding the classics as opposed to
Christian ethics, some asserted the traditional view
that classical training was conducive to morality.
'Shall we abandon the classics' Robert Hall asked

> and devote ourselves to the perusal of
> modern writers, where the maxims inculcated,
> and the principles taught, are little,
> if at all, more in unison with those
> of Christianity? ... While things
> continue as they are, we are apprehensive
> ... that we should gain nothing by
> neglecting the unrivalled productions
> of genius left us by the ancients, but a
> deterioration of taste, without any

> improvement in religion ... Until a
> more Christian spirit pervades the world,
> we are inclined to think that the study
> of the classics is, on the whole,
> advantageous to public morals, by
> inspiring an elegance of sentiment and
> an elevation of soul, which we should seek
> for in vain elsewhere.[39]

Many evangelicals shared Hall's view that the
classics could not be rivalled as sources of good
taste. The Eclectic Review regarded them as the
'most precious gems of human genius' and argued
that they contributed significantly to the sum of
human happiness.[40] Christian Observer contributors
maintained, admittedly in the face of criticism,
that the cultivation of morals was not the sole end
of human existence: the study of the classics, a
source of profound philosophy and insight into
human nature, had proved to be the best way of
cultivating taste and imagination. Supremely
important though religious and moral knowledge was

> are we therefore to hold in contempt
> the blessings of civilization and
> secular knowledge? Is the cannibal of
> New Zealand in more enviable circumstances
> than civilized man, supposing both to be
> on a level in regard to Christian
> principles?[41]

Belief in the values of civilization provided for
the continued acceptance of classical literature
regardless of theological qualm.
　　Qualms were often overcome too when
evangelicals turned their attention to the work of
the major dramatists, most notably Shakespeare,
for while evangelical theology demanded the
anathematization of the theatre, it did not militate
so categorically against the reading of plays.
Drama as a literary form was sanctioned by
Scriptural precedent.[42] One of the worst characteristics of theatrical production, the contaminating
company, was eliminated when plays were read in
the safe seclusion of the home. Moreover, without
the glamour and glitter of costume and scenery,
and the immediacy of acting, much of the
captivating and seductive appeal to the passions
was lost. A play could be read soberly and, with
preceptoral help, its values could be dispassion-
ately compared with those of the faith. Approached

in this way drama was no more dangerous than any
other literary genre. The Eclectic Review
constantly stressed that it revered dramatic writing
although despising the theatre, while Hannah More
maintained that to reject such 'pure' works as
Racine's Athalia and Milton's Comus merely on
account of their form would be 'an instance of
scrupulosity which ... no well-informed conscience
could suggest'.[43]
    But not all plays were 'pure' and so some
evangelicals while acknowledging their genius felt
bound to criticise them. One unusually vituperative
Eclectic reviewer maintained that it would have been
better for English morality had Shakespeare never
been born.[44] A Christian Observer contributor who
admitted that drama was 'one of the highest kinds of
mental gratification' objected to his plays because
they were neither predominantly moral nor Christian
and tended to excite the passions.[45] 'No high grand
virtuous religious aim beams forth in him',
complained Richard Cecil, 'A man, whose heart and
taste are modelled on the Bible, nauseates him in
the mass, while he is enraptured and astonished by
the flashes of pre-eminent genius'.[46] According to
another minister his works were a 'mass of
fascinating mischief'.[47] But in the opinion of many
evangelicals the fascination outweighed the mischief
and rather than condemning they sought to excuse
Shakespeare: he had lived in a barbarous age;
the most offensive passages were not original but
had been forced upon him by the exigencies of
theatrical production.[48] While some evangelicals
complained as did Johnson about Shakespeare's
morals, others chose to follow another Johnsonian
tradition and stressed the bard's understanding of
people: 'Next to the Bible', commented Lord
Teignmouth, 'no author has so well anatomized the
human heart, and exhibited the workings of the human
passions'.[49] The Eclectic Review regularly
applauded Shakespeare's talent while Wilberforce
maintained that to read his work was almost his
'greatest treat'.[50] At eighty-six Hannah More
wrote a poem proclaiming his pre-eminence even over
Milton:

> Did ever Milton all your thoughts engage?
> And make you laugh and weep in the same page?
> Did Virgil ever weep, like good King Lear,
> That he a daughter had? I greatly fear
> Milton's a mighty man above this earth,
> Too great for jollity - too high for mirth.[51]

The high seriousness of evangelical theology,
asserted by Miss More in her didactic prose, did
not always prevail over literary sensibility. All
the world, commented a <u>Christian Observer</u> correspondent, reads Shakespeare ...[52]
... Almost all the evangelical world read
poetry. Devotional pieces were printed in every
number of the <u>Evangelical Magazine</u>, while volumes
of poetry were regularly reviewed in both the
popular and the more cultured evangelical press.
Biographies record numerous instances of
evangelicals who, even if they read little other
literature, delighted in poetry, wrote it, or urged
their children to memorise it. Quotations in
articles, sermons, and books reveal a widespread
familiarity with works such as Edward Young's
<u>Night Thoughts</u> and Cowper's <u>The Task</u> which, with
<u>Paradise Lost</u> and the Psalms, served to sanction the
genre. Its acceptability derived in part from its
subject matter. Poetry lent itself to meditative
introspection and religious reflection more readily
than did other genres. Descriptive poetry was
unlikely to instil immoral ideas or to inflame the
passions. On the contrary since the study of
nature was a means of grace, it could be used to
stir devotion. Religion and poetry, J.W. Cunningham
argued, seemed made for each other, for religion
enhanced perceptions of beauty and sublimity, the
proper subjects of poetic taste.[53]
Cunningham's argument reveals how congenial
neo-classical assumptions about the nature of poetry
were to evangelical modes of thought. Believing
that God's first intention was to instruct his
creatures the <u>Christian Observer</u> readily approved of
a genre which according to Aristotelian definition
should have a moral effect. It regularly quoted
Johnson's formula

> If the object of poetry is to instruct
> by pleasing, then every poetical effort
> has a double claim upon the attention
> of the Christian observer. For we are
> anxious that the world may be instructed
> at all rates, and that they should be
> pleased where they innocently may.[54]

The <u>Eclectic Review</u> was equally classical if less
didactic. It maintained that 'the design of poetry
must be to please, to gratify the imagination and
to touch the softer feelings', 'the office of
poetry is, not to teach, but to warm and elevate the

mind'.[55] Neo-classical critics had taught that
what was naturally interesting, truly poetic, and
therefore pleasing, was not the mundane and the
particular, but the idealised and the sublime. The
evangelical periodicals, believing that ignorance
of evil was bliss, were happy to concur:

> if the end of poetry be to relax and
> recreate the mind it must be attained
> by drawing away the mind from the low
> pursuits and sordid cares, from the
> pains and sorrows of real life, at
> least whatever is vulgar and disgusting
> in them, to an imaginary state of
> greater beauty, purity and blessed-
> ness.[56]

In clearly Platonic tones an Eclectic reviewer
declared that the aim of art was to be 'perfectly
like the perfect model that we may suppose nature
to have imperfectly copied'.[57]
    Their sympathy with classicism led some
evangelicals to be critical of modern poetry.
Crabbe's genius was praised but he was criticised
for his 'low and confined subjects' and his tendency
to portray life at its worst rather than its
best.[58] The Evangelical Magazine condemned the
'glut of poetical romances and eastern tales'
produced by Scott, Southey, Byron, and Moore,
which attracted readers by their 'extravagant
fictions' and 'romantic heroes' rather than by
'brilliant descriptions' and 'chaste delineations':

> They are calculated to amuse but not
> to instruct - to gratify a sickly taste
> but to impart no good counsel - to
> display pathos without exciting sympathy
> - to describe manners, but to inculcate
> no morality - in fine to pourtray (sic)
> character without affording a solitary
> example worthy of imitation.[59]

Similarly the Baptist Magazine deprecated 'stories
of war and blood - of furies and fiends - of knights
and castles - of dreams and sprites', and objected
to the 'demoralising pages' of modern poetry, which
was also sometimes criticised even by the more
cultured papers: an Eclectic reviewer commented
'There is a great deal of modern poetry, that is
ill-adapted to make its readers either the wiser,
the better, or the happier'.[60]

But not all evangelical reviewers condemned
modern poetry for some regarded it as superior
to that of the past.[61] Unquestionably the most
popular contemporary poet in evangelical as in
other circles was Sir Walter Scott, whose early
work in particular enjoyed long laudatory reviews
in both the Eclectic Review and the Christian
Observer.[62] 'There are some parts of the poem that
are quite inimitable', wrote William Wilberforce
of The Lady of the Lake, regretting only that there
was not 'much of a moral'.[63] Other evangelicals
shared his disappointment but it did not stop them
delighting in Scott's depiction of medieval life
and manners, his versification, his evocation of
sympathy, his realistic characterisation ...
Their reaction was summed up by Hannah More who
declared ecstatically of Rokeby

> Beautiful passages are numerous, and
> there are a thousand graces which I
> shall delight to dwell upon ... I am
> not disposed to be critical when I
> read poetry, where pleasure is the
> prevailing feeling as it ever must be
> in reading Scott.[64]

Pleasure prevailed too for many evangelical readers
of the works of Robert Southey. One Christian
Observer critic reported that he read Roderick with
'extra-ordinary pleasure' while others maintained
that no living poet had equal ability to refresh
and charm the mind; Southey was a 'true genius'
who gave dignity, interest, and an air of reality
even to subjects 'essentially and hopelessly
fictitious'.[65] The Eclectic Review was more
critical of Southey's wild flights of fancy which
infringed the canons of neo-classical taste,
complaining that the poet used myth and allegory
and lacked feeling on religious subjects. Nevertheless its reviewers too found much to praise in
his works.[66]
   Far less attention was paid by the evangelical
press to poets more centrally within the romantic
tradition, Coleridge, Shelley, and Keats. But
little space was accorded to them in the Edinburgh
Review whose condemnation of Wordsworth is well-
known. The Eclectic Review was initially critical
of the Lake poets on neo-classical grounds, and
looked for the early demise of the new school;
later reviewers however, notwithstanding their
dislike of Wordsworth's unpoetic subjects and

'imbecilities of style', acclaimed his poetry as
the source of 'some of our highest pleasure'.[67]
Jeffrey's disgust at The Excursion was not shared
by James Montgomery who wrote a complimentary
review of the poem for the Eclectic.[68] The
Christian Observer did not review Wordsworth's
poetry but some of its readers, Jane Venn and Henry
Thornton, appreciated it, as did Hannah More who
'could not believe that these noble Miltonic lines
had been written by a man whom the reviewers had
been assailing for years'.[69] This ultimate
evangelical compliment was also paid by John Styles
who maintained that Byron for all his genius had
not left to posterity works comparable to those of
Milton - and Wordsworth.[70]
     Byron, whose works sold extensively and whose
private life gave rise to much prurient gossip,
was by far the most controversial of the romantic
poets. His play Cain was threatened with prosecution for blasphemy and even the Edinburgh Review,
by no means generally antagonistic to him,
complained that 'his writings have a tendency to
destroy all belief in the reality of virtue':

> We have not been detractors from Lord
> Byron's fame, nor the friends of his
> detractors; and we tell him - far more
> in sorrow than in anger - that we verily
> believe the great body of the English
> nation - the religious, the moral, and
> the candid part of it - consider the
> tendency of his writings to be immoral
> and pernicious - and look upon his
> perseverance in that strain of
> composition with regret and
> reprehension. We ourselves are not
> easily startled, either by levity of
> temper, or boldness, or even rashness
> of remark; we are moreover, sincere
> admirers of Lord Byron's genius - and
> have always felt a pride and an interest
> in his fame. But we cannot dissent from
> the censure to which we have alluded ...[71]

In the light of such comments the Eclectic Review's
criticism of Byron does not appear exceptional.
Indeed its reviewers praised highly the early
cantos of Childe Harold's Pilgrimage, The Giaour,
and The Corsair, and when Lara was published
expressed pleasure at the appearance of another
Byronic poem.[72] Later reviews as in the secular

press were increasingly critical but compliments
continued to be paid to Byron.[73] Eclectic reviewers
on the whole disagreed with those who believed that
Byron's poems spread moral contagion:

> If in any degree they may lessen our
> abhorrence of vice, by making our
> sympathy predominate over principle,
> rather than by counteracting its
> influence, they at the same time,
> deepen our conviction of the miseries
> inseparably connected with a departure
> from virtue ... It is but justice to
> say, that there is nothing, so far as
> we recollect, in his poems, which
> displays any design, or which is in
> itself calculated to corrupt the
> virtuous mind, to raise a guilty glow
> of pleasure, or to delude the imagin-
> ation into a love of splendid crime.
> There is, at least, a highly moral
> lesson to be deduced, if the readers
> please, from his poetry.[74]

The Christian Observer reviewer of The Giaour agreed
with this, acknowledging that Byron never attempted
to suggest that vice brought happiness. But the
four reviews of Byron's poems in the Christian
Observer tended to be more critical than those in
the Eclectic Review, although readers' attention
was drawn to some 'truly beautiful passages'.[75] The
popular periodicals, maybe some of the detractors to
whom Jeffrey referred, were unwilling to grant Byron
any accolade and certainly did not hold to the view
that his work was comparatively innocuous. The
Baptist Magazine admitted that only the blind and
bigotted would deny Byron's genius, but it refused
to praise him.[76] The Evangelical Magazine likewise
acknowledged his genius but condemned him for
prostituting his gifts, for spreading profanity and
corruption, and for perpetrating false and morbid
views of human nature.[77]
    Whether or not they approved of him evangelic-
als like their contemporaries were fascinated by
Lord Byron, after whom J.W. Cunningham apparently
named a daughter.[78] Lord Teignmouth devoted
sixteen lines of a poem on nature and grace to him,
eulogising his 'matchless art' and urging him to add

                    ... to a poet's fame
    The brightest honours of a Christian's name!

> Why suffer sceptic gloom thy mind to cloud,
> And robe thy blazing genius in a shroud?[79]

Others, refusing to believe that a man would
willingly choose misery, assumed that he was ripe
for conversion and acted accordingly: John
Sheppard, a clothier from Frome whose wife had
recently died, sent Byron a copy of a prayer for his
redemption discovered in her private papers.[80] On
Byron's own death the Christian Observer printed
'Observations on the character, opinions and writings of the late Lord Byron' which spanned four
issues, while at Holland Chapel, Kennington, John
Styles preached a sermon on Lord Byron's Works
Viewed in Connexion with Christianity and the
Obligation of Social Life: Styles urged his
listeners to read only those parts of Byron's works
which the wise and the good had not denounced; to
recommend total abstinence would, he admitted, be
futile.[81]

The confessed inability of a leading preacher
to dissuade his congregation from reading such
literature is highly significant. M.J. Quinlan's
claim that good evangelicals did not read Byron
clearly lacks adequate foundation.[82] In particular
it should be noted that Styles was addressing an
Independent congregation. Matthew Arnold's stereo-
type of the uncultured dissenter has all too often
been uncritically accepted with the result that even
so competent a critic as R.D. Altick untypically
makes erroneous statements:

> While ... the Christian Observer gave
> prominent space to reviews of The Lady
> of the Lake, Crabbe's Borough and the
> first cantos of Childe Harold,
> dissenting periodicals such as the
> Eclectic Review paid little or no
> attention to current secular
> literature, except by way of condemn-
> ation.[83]

The allegation would be more accurate if directed
at the Evangelical or Methodist Magazines but the
Eclectic Review was both more comprehensive in its
coverage and more complimentary in its criticism
than was the Christian Observer. If as has been
suggested Anglicans were more accommodating than
dissenters over some public amusements, the same
was not necessarily true of polite literature whose
cause the Eclectic was anxious to further. The

negative attitude of the popular press, while clearly reflecting an important facet of dissenting
opinion, should not be over-emphasised: the
periodicals' failure to review secular works is no
proof of their subscribers' refusal to read them.
Indeed the Methodist President of 1825 would hardly
have issued so extensive a warning against 'the
irreligious and insidious influence, which pervade
so much of the literature, and especially so many
of the periodical works, of the day', had he not had
reason to fear that the rank and file were in danger
of falling.[84] It seems improbable that the members
of Holland Park were unique among dissenters in
indulging in proscribed reading. How widely Byron
and other such authors were read cannot of course
be determined. Nevertheless a study of biographies,
of the <u>Christian Observer</u>, and of the <u>Eclectic
Review</u>, reveals that there was a solid stratum
within evangelicalism which shared in the literary
interests of the day to a far greater extent than
has generally been recognised.

C. EVANGELICALS AND THE NOVEL

The extent to which the evangelical rank and file
shared in the changing tastes of the day is most
clearly revealed in their attitudes to the novel,
once the most objectionable of all literary genres.
In December 1800 the <u>Evangelical Magazine</u> had
published a 'Spiritual Barometer; or a scale of
the progress of sin and of grace'. Towards the
positive pole it was calibrated with the attributes
and practices thought to characterise those destined
for 'glory' and 'dismission from the body', while
at the other extreme, graded in degrees of
depravity, were the activities of those assumed to
be heading heedlessly to 'death' and 'perdition'.
'Love of novels' was among the most heinous of
sins, more damning even than attendance at the
theatre ...[85]
     Thus to condemn narrative prose while approving
narrative poetry was clearly inconsistent, and
<u>Eclectic</u> reviewers sought to differentiate between
the two: the enjoyment of poetry demanded effort
on the readers' part; the novelist in contrast
made no demands upon his readers. There were more
bad novels than bad poems for epic and dramatic
poetry, being subject to known rules, demanded a
degree of skill in their exponents: 'The
circumstantials of prose are the essentials of

verse'.[86] It followed that

> The effect of novel-reading is more
> deleterious than that of poetry,
> because the excitement is in general
> more powerful; and the novelist
> relies more simply on the passion of
> curiosity for producing gratification,
> than the poet does, who seeks to please
> by more refined means.[87]

Underlying such rationalisations was the fact
that the novel was not an accepted genre. Narrative
poetry was approved by association; the novel,
being a new medium, was _infra dig_. Novel criticism
was in its infancy and criteria of excellence were
not yet established. Thus objections to the novel
had been widely voiced in the latter half of the
eighteenth century, critics fearing that novel-
reading created false expectations in young girls
and aroused their passions, disinclining them in
Mrs. Barbauld's words for the 'neglect and tedium
of life'.[88] Initially therefore evangelical
complaints were merely reiterations of the qualms
of others, heightened by the fear that a girl's
soul and not just her respectability and temporal
well-being was at stake. If novels were to be read
at all, Hannah More maintained 'we should be
tempted to give the preference to those works of
pure and genuine fancy, which exercise and fill the
imagination' rather than to those which 'by
exhibiting passion and intrigue in bewitching
colours, lay hold too intensely on the feelings'.
Fairy tales and the _Arabian Nights_ being concerned
with remote and imaginary worlds did not mislead as
did modern novels, which evangelicals in common
with others dismissed as 'intoxicating stimulants'
productive of 'artificial' and 'injurious'
excitement.[89]

By the third decade of the century the more
general distrust of the novel was largely effaced,
although it was still regarded as a poor sister of
the more established genres. 'The times seem to
be past' proclaimed a _Quarterly_ reviewer in 1821
'when an apology was requisite for condescending to
notice a novel': whereas novels had once been
highly improbable, portraying vice favourably, and
engaging the passions, they had now changed to
become vehicles of morality.[90] Evangelical
reviewers disagreed. When Sir Walter Scott died the
Methodist Magazine wrote of his novels, the

popularity of which had done much to make the genre
respectable, 'Their capital defect is, that they
appear to have been written without any moral
aim'.[91] Christian Observer contributors protested
that Scott misrepresented religion, and that his
novels, while not licentious, were far from positively moral.[92] Novels might have improved but by
effectively denying that sin, an affront to God,
had dire consequences, they misled their readers
in matters of ultimate importance. Moreover even
the least objectionable novels were criticised for
engrossing more time than could legitimately be
devoted to relaxation by those accountable to God
for the use of every moment. 'Had he written
before the Flood' Hannah More wrote of Scott

> all would have been well ... A life of
> eight hundred years might have allowed
> of the perusal of the whole of his
> volumes; a proportionate quantity in
> each century would have been delightful:
> but for our poor scanty threescore years
> and ten, it is too much ...[93]

Above all evangelicals continued to oppose novel-
reading because, long associated with loose living
and the circulating library, it had acquired the
irrevocable stigma of worldliness: 'If we are not
to think, to feel, to act, and to perish, with the
world' argued a Christian Observer correspondent
'let a deep and wide interval yet exist between the
habits of pleasure of the two parties'.[94]
But not even evangelicals were proof against
the power of Walter Scott. In 1817 the Christian
Observer noted that novel-reading was practised to
a considerable extent even in the religious world
and on more than one occasion it blamed Scott for
this: 'The habit of novel-reading introduced into
many families where it did not formerly prevail,
by means of Sir Walter Scott's publications, has
always appeared to us so pernicious and alarming
that we have never ceased to remonstrate against
it'.[95] Such virtuous indignation was not altogether
justified for while many contributors were hostile
to the novel, some, including the editor's son,
Tom Macaulay, justified the reading of certain
classes of fiction.[96] The Macaulay children had
free access to their father's library and thus read
widely and avidly in literature of all kinds
including novels.[97] Further evidence of permis-
siveness comes from the Eclectic Review: its

contributors examined a number of novels, and while
some spoke derogatively of the genre, 'a species
of literature which, with rare exceptions, we have
not submitted to the drudgery of reading', 'a
class of works which has but doubtful claim on our
notice', it was by no means condemned out of hand.[98]
On the contrary reviewers admitted that 'To the
authors of fictitious narratives the literary world
is certainly indebted, for some of the most sublime
and useful works in poetry or prose', and suggested
that the skill needed to write prose narrative was
such that 'the performance, though it be but a
tale, will appear to deserve no mean rank among the
efforts of genius'.[99] In particular reviewers,
including those most uneasy about the novel, were
convinced of Scott's genius, although some voiced
regret that he did not put his undoubted talents to
better use.[100] If not positively moral, Scott at
least eschewed the libertinism of his predecessors,
while he was regarded as a far greater writer than
his contemporaries:

> ... seeing that the constant demand
> for such works necessitates a supply
> of some kind ... we will not dispute
> that a service is rendered to the
> lovers of light reading, by writers of
> superior talent ... who furnish the
> public with amusements more deserving
> of the name of intellectual, than the
> generality of novels.[101]

More positively, several reviewers spoke very
highly of Scott's achievements, acclaiming his
talents and whetting their readers' appetites by
quoting at length from his works. His plots were
criticised

> but such is his faculty of identification,
> so perfectly to the life are his
> characters drawn, coloured, grouped, and
> put into action, and with such veritable
> circumstance does he surround them,
> that we are insensible to deficiencies
> in his fable, that would be fatal to any
> less powerful spell than that by which
> he contrives to enthrall us ...[102]

Comments like this make plain the problems
which evangelicals faced. Eclectic reviewers were
in varying degrees convinced by the traditional

arguments against novel-reading. There was moreover much in Scott's writings of which they
disapproved. Yet they acknowledged his moral and
aesthetic superiority over other novelists past and
present, and, so lured, succumbed to his spell.
Their difficulty was explicitly stated in 1833:
'in perusing works of this class', a reviewer
wrote of a novel by Mrs. Hall, 'we too often find
ourselves forced to admire what we cannot approve;
pleased, interested, fascinated by the perusal,
and dissatisfied with ourselves on reflecting what
has so much pleased us'.[103] The dilemma found
typical expression in William Wilberforce, who was
glad when he finished reading Peveril of the Peak:
'this class of writing is too interesting: it
makes other studies insipid, or rather other light
reading; but yet much to be learned from this
class of writings ...'[104] The last statement
represents Wilberforce's attempt, conscious or
subconscious, to justify and account for his
interest. Thus when he read The Fortunes of Nigel
he commented

> It is strange how much Nigel has haunted
> me while reading it. In spite of all my
> resistance and correction of the illusion
> by suggesting to myself that the author
> may order events as he pleases, I am
> extremely interested by it. But I think
> it is partly because I consider it all as
> substantially true, giving the account
> of the manners and incidents of the day.[105]

But the books appealed to more than a purely
academic interest in the past and Wilberforce was
not wholly convinced by his own explanation. In
the last resort he was unable to justify the reading
he enjoyed so much. While he continued to delight
in Scott's writings and noted with satisfaction any
Christian emphases, he lamented the general absence
of 'moral or religious object':

> They remind me of a giant spending
> his strength in cracking nuts. I
> would rather go to render up my
> account at the last day, carrying up
> with me The Shepherd of Salisbury
> Plain than bearing the load of all
> these volumes, full as they are of
> genius.[106]

Hannah More's tract, <u>The Shepherd of Salisbury Plain</u>, was one of many religious tales which flooded the market in the first thirty years of the nineteenth century, a period which saw the effective birth of the religious novel. Indeed if some evangelicals were seduced into novel-reading by Sir Walter Scott, far more were led onto the downward track by Miss More and her successors. Unlike the Waverley novels, religious fiction was reviewed in all the evangelical periodicals, and, particularly in its infancy, received considerable approbation. The <u>Evangelical Magazine</u> was exuberant that the tables were now being turned on the devil:

> because the enemy of mankind hath
> dressed Vice and Licentiousness in
> these engaging forms, must we
> therefore wholly surrender them to
> his service? By no means. Rather
> let us restore them to the cause of
> Virtue and Religion.[107]

'With great pleasure we announce and recommend this publication', wrote the <u>Eclectic Review</u> of a widely acclaimed novel by Harriet Corp; 'She ... embodies her instructions in a form which must attract attention'.[108] The <u>Christian Observer</u> quoted several pages from another work by the same author to encourage young people to read it: they would do so with pleasure and profit.[109]

But religious novels also provoked criticism which became increasingly marked as their production escalated in the years after the Napoleonic wars. The term 'novel' was one of such disapprobation that evangelicals were initially loath to apply it to a Christian work: in 1806 the <u>Evangelical Magazine</u> wrote of John Satchell's <u>Thornton Abbey</u> 'Were this work written on any other subject than religion, we should not hesitate to call it a <u>Novel</u>, in the form of Letters: but that name has been too much degraded to be admitted into religious literature'.[110] There was considerable unease about mixing sacred and secular. Momentous religious truths should surely not be presented in so gaudy a garb: in 1823 the <u>Baptist Magazine</u> protested 'we cannot help calling in question the propriety of stating ... divine principles, or sacred influence, through the plot of a romance ...'[111] Also questioned was the propriety of producing fiction for adults. Stories were for children; the <u>Eclectic Review</u> was therefore

Faith and Fancy

> unwilling to believe, what seems indeed
> implied in the practice of many useful
> writers, that in addressing <u>men</u> and
> <u>women</u> of any class, it is really
> necessary, or really desirable, to
> tickle their ears, and lure their eyes
> with tales and pictures.[112]

The underlying assumption was that 'tales and
pictures' were merely sugar to the pill. Believing
that religious truth was conceptual, evangelicals
communicated it not on the whole through narrative,
but within the framework of narrative - through
long and sermonic comments and conversations. Too
much narrative was regarded as not only inappropriate but also counterproductive. The <u>Christian
Observer</u> feared that some might read religious
fiction for the plot and the incidents, vicariously
sharing the experiences and emotions described, but
skipping the moral lessons and religious
observations.[113] Thus, it praised one novel
because it was '<u>not</u> novelish in its character; its
incidents being few and simple, and only as pegs for
the moral'.[114] Similarly in a review of <u>Coelebs in
search of a Wife</u> it affirmed 'It may be very true
that novels are mischievous; but we cannot allow
this work to be called a novel ... the preceptive
parts are not choked with incidents'; 'Mrs. More
with her lively imagination, must have felt some
difficulty in preventing her <u>Coelebs</u> from de-
generating too much into matters of plot and
incident, of which she has admitted only so much as
seemed necessary for her higher purpose'.[115] Paradoxically the <u>Christian Observer</u> was giving highest
praise to those novels that made least use of the
genre's potentiality.
That the novel was not factually true was a
further cause of concern to some evangelicals and
gave rise to casuistry such as that described in
the <u>Evangelical Magazine</u> of 1805: 'to avoid the
offence some well-meaning Christians have taken at
fictitious narrative, the Author, like the
celebrated Bunyan, hath told his pleasing story as
a dream'.[116] A few evangelicals clearly had very
rigid ideas about what was 'true': a reviewer of
Mrs. Sherwood's <u>Stories explanatory of the
Catechism</u> complained that events illustrative of
catechetical teaching were unlikely to occur in the
right order.[117] Such bizarre objections were rare,
but concern for authenticity was sufficiently widespread to provoke the multiplication of tales

'founded on fact'. These were praised more highly
than mere fiction, but were not free from censure:
in 1825 the Baptist Magazine pronounced 'We are
jealous of these little tales founded on fact - not
knowing how far they are so - and we think an
intelligent child should be encouraged, in every
instance, to ask "is it true?"'[118] The Eclectic
Review, catering for the more educated, recognised
that even reputable histories were but 'fictions
founded upon fact', suggested that verisimilitude
was more important to a story than factual truth,
and argued that a work could be both fictional and
true.[119] Nevertheless it was generally accepted
that fact was more potent and edifying than fiction.
Virtuous characters in fiction, the Christian
Observer pointed out, might or might not be
imitable; certainly there was no obligation on the
reader to emulate them as there was in the case of
lives of real people.[120] Moreover testimonies and
memoirs were believed to provide authoritative
evidence of the activity of God, which fiction by
definition could not supply.[121] 'The God of
truth' the Baptist Magazine argued 'cannot be so
fully expected to use the creations of fancy, as he
may be the correct relations of his own righteous
acts and gracious operations'.[122] It was a mystery
to some evangelicals why people should want to read
the inventions of fiction when real life accounts
were just as exciting. In 1827 the Evangelical
Magazine hailed a set of biographies with the
comment 'There would be little occasion for works
of fiction, were a due attention paid to the
narratives of those who have actually figured on
the stage of life'.[123]
　　Underlying all such criticisms of fiction and
attempts to woo evangelicals from the novel was the
nagging fear that religious novel-reading might be
accompanied by the same ill effects as ordinary
novel-reading, over-excitement, an unwillingness to
read more serious matter, and an insatiable thirst
for fiction. The Christian Observer maintained that
'though occasional stimulants may be salutary,
they cannot with impunity become our daily food'.[124]
From the beginning there was concern lest religious
fiction proliferated: thus the Eclectic Review of
1806 praised Thornton Abbey but feared 'a serious
calamity, if the success of the present work should
let loose a pack of religious novels upon the
public'.[125] By the 1820s its fears were realised
and protests against a continuing inundation of
religious fiction became increasingly common in all

evangelical periodicals. An Evangelical Magazine
reviewer would have given one book unqualified
praise had he not been afraid that the increase in
religious fiction would prevent the study of real
history and would imperceptibly encourage the young
to read dangerously worldly novels.[126] The same
prevalent fear that people would progress from
religious novels to secular novels, and hence
become more worldly and less religious, was voiced
by the Methodist Magazine when it spoke disparaging-
ly of

> ... those religious novels which
> abound in the present day, and which
> threaten very extensively to pervert
> the taste of our youth. In the books
> to which we refer, evangelical sentiment
> is mixed up with flippant and
> fictitious narrative, which is only
> calculated to induce a habit of novel-
> reading, and to render the mind
> indifferent to sober truth and fact.[127]

But despite all their unease and antagonism
the reviewers felt unable totally to condemn such
novels. Christ had taught in parables. The need
to provide wholesome reading matter for evangelical
youth remained as did the initial evangelistic
incentive:

> ... it seems pretty clear that, while
> the rage for that kind of reading,
> which gratifies an irregular appetite
> and a distempered fancy, continues so
> inordinate, the only choice left to
> the friends of wisdom, is, to encounter
> folly on its own ground, and to make
> their way to the understanding by
> addressing themselves to the
> imagination.[128]

When the aim was laudable, critics could not but
approve. In any case they often enjoyed the books
themselves. Although he disapproved of tales, a
Baptist Magazine reviewer confessed that he had
derived considerable pleasure from Procrastination;
or the Vicar's daughter.[129] The ambivalence of the
reviewers' position over religious as over secular
novels was reflected even within individual reviews.
Many started by condemning the genre and then
proceeded to exempt from censure the particular

novel under review. The Eclectic Review's analysis
of Dunallan: or Know what you judge: a story
commenced 'We still think the light viands now so
much in request, a bad substitute for the more
healthy, spiritual food of our forefathers ...'
But the reviewer acknowledged that it was a novel-
reading age and if fictions were to be read 'their
being made subservient to moral or religious lessons
cannot be held criminal'. He admitted that tales
could have good effects upon their readers and
'when religious truths are recommended by the
charms of graceful fiction, and kept, at the same
time, in their genuine purity, we should not know
exactly in what terms to express our disapprobation'.[130]
     Ultimately the reviewers had no option but to
accept the religious novel because the evangelical
public for which they wrote liked it and made
profitable its increasing production. This state
of affairs was regretfully acknowledged by the
Eclectic Review of 1832 when it lamented that
whatever it said would be disregarded: 'Our
recommendation they scarcely need, nor would the
public wait for it. Our interdict would not be
respected. Tales the public will have ...'[131]

D.   THEOLOGY AND CULTURE

One question remains: how did evangelicals reconcile their love of literature with their theology?
On the one hand literature appeared to be sanctified
by divine example. God had shown

> That it is not only innocent, but
> laudable, to consecrate the powers of
> taste and fancy to his glory, by
> himself condescending to use the
> language of poetry, and the most
> splendid and impressive imagery, in
> his revelation of mercy to a sinful
> world.[132]

Moreover imaginative reading had particular merit in
evangelical eyes as a domestic occupation, well-
suited to those who shunned more public amusements:
'It is peculiarly gratifying' commented an Eclectic
reviewer, 'to find a taste for elegant literature,
and a susceptibility to the chaste and quiet
pleasures of the home circle, prevailing among the
higher classes ...'[133] More positively many

evangelicals regarded literature as an adjunct of
civilization, whose advance was thoroughly congruent
with the concerns of religion: far from associating
imagination with an appeal to the passions they
legitimised the study of literature as a non-
sensual pleasure which might stem the grossness of
sensuality. The Christian Observer was therefore
critical of Quaker proscription of poetry and other
arts:

> We are fully persuaded that a well-
> regulated attention to the study of
> the fine arts may prove beneficial
> to the mind in a variety of ways, and
> that they are so far from being in
> themselves hostile to the great
> interests of religion, that in them
> religion herself may often find a
> powerful, because engaging assistant.
> The fierceness of animal nature is
> as unfavourable to the growth of
> religious principle as the dense
> darkness of natural ignorance. If
> elegant pursuits, then, have but the
> power which has been assigned them of
> taming the natural .fierceness of man,
> of tending to subordinate his physical
> to his intellectual powers, they are
> surely thus far not opposed to the
> spirit and purposes of religion, but
> rather the contrary.134

But if much could thus be said in favour of
literature there was on the other hand much that
could be said against it. Most polite literature,
commented John Foster, was hostile to Christianity.
Few essayists or imaginative writers showed any
real awareness of eternity; indeed they kept
silent about Christian doctrines which, if true,
were of seminal importance to man's eternal well-
being. The values inculcated and the assumptions
made about true greatness, goodness, and happiness
were often antipathetic to Christianity. Yet so
appealing was literature that these were often
communicated with peculiar force,

> as if an eloquent pagan priest had been
> allowed constantly to accompany our Lord
> in his ministry, and had divided with
> him the attention and interest of his
> disciples, counteracting of course, as

far as his efforts were successful,
the doctrine and spirit of the
Teacher from heaven.[135]

'Dieu sera clément envers le génie', maintained Mme.
Necker, and was duly reprimanded by Hannah More,
'The wisest and best stand in as much need to be
redeemed by the blood of Christ, and to be
sanctified and guided by the Holy Spirit, as the
most illiterate and the most unworthy'.[136] Poetry
and art were not, as some had suggested, roads to
God for 'the wounds inflicted by sin could not be
healed by the grace of composition'.[137] By
acclaiming the works of Scott and others, evangelicals seemed to be underplaying the all-importance of
religious considerations; the Christian Observer
therefore spoke out against the tendency 'too widely
acted upon among professed Christians and the men
of this world, to meet as friends in the neutral
temple of Genius'.[138]

But such objections did little to mitigate
evangelicals' overriding belief in the inherent
value of much secular literature. The Christian
Observer logically argued that unless all non-
religious works were to be banned worldliness of
sentiment could not be regarded as an adequate
reason for prohibition, and ingenuously revealed
its true motives by admitting that it would 'regret
the necessity of urging a doctrine which should
tear us from Shakespeare and Corneille ... Happily
religion exacts ignorance of nothing that is really
worth knowing'.[139] An Eclectic reviewer faced up
to the problem more squarely:

We deeply lament the grossness which
so far deteriorates their high
qualities, as to exclude a large portion
of our wealthiest literature from the
staple of safe and commendable reading.
Still they must, to a certain extent,
be studied by all, who are anxious to
ascertain the finest characteristics
of English style, or the complete
range of English genius.[140]

Implicitly or explicitly many evangelicals assumed
that literature like art furthered civilization in
ways independent of religion. But this left them
with an insuperable problem, most clearly
articulated, if not resolved, by John Foster, who
concluded his discussion of the subject with the

crucial question:

> Under what restrictions then ought the
> study of polite literature to be
> conducted? ... I can only answer as I
> have answered before. Polite literature
> will necessarily continue to be the grand
> school of intellectual and moral
> cultivation. The evils therefore which
> it may contain, will as certainly affect
> in some degree the minds of successive
> students, as the hurtful influence of the
> climate, or of the seasons, will affect
> their bodies. To be thus affected is
> part of the destiny under which they are
> born, in a civilized country. It is
> indispensable to acquire the advantage;
> it is inevitable to incur the evil ...141

No statement more clearly reveals evangelicals'
acceptance of culture, and their failure to
reconcile it theologically with their faith.

NOTES

1. Josiah Pratt, op. cit., p. xxv. A type-
written list of c.240 volumes from Cecil's library
is deposited at Ridley Hall, Cambridge.
2. ER i series i (1805), prospectus; iii
series i (1829), preface. Cf. CO ix (1810), preface.
3. BM iv (1812), pp. 339-43.
4. Pollok (1798-1827) was temporarily famed
for his poem, The Course of Time, described in DNB
as his 'one permanent contribution to literature'.
His fellow Scot, the better-known Montgomery (1771-
1854), a Moravian, was a regular Eclectic reviewer.
5. MM liii (1830), p. 833. Cf. EM i series
xxvi (1818), p. 519; xxix (1821), p. 473; ii
series iv (1826), p. 472, but note also the praise
of poems on Scriptural subjects in the same
volumes.
6. CO xiv (1815), p. 329.
7. EM ii series i (1823), p. 21.
8. BM xv (1823), p. 112.
9. CO xii (1813), p. 734.
10. ER ii series vi (1816), p. 380.
11. Corp, Sequel ..., pp. 112ff.
12. ER ii series ii (1814), pp. 236-37.
13. J. Styles, Lord Byron's Works Viewed in
Connexion with Christianity ... (1824), pp. 14-16.
14. MM xlvii (1824), p. 171, from instruction

Faith and Fancy

to the Irish RTS.
15. ER i series viii (1812), p. 616.
16. BM iii (1811), p. 384.
17. W.C. Booth, The Rhetoric of Fiction (1961),
pp. 140–41.
18. ER i series x (1813), pp. 280, 377.
19. Ibid. viii (1812), p. 917.
20. CO xiii (1814), p. 666. Cf. Knutsford,
op. cit., p. 335.
21. CO xi (1812), pp. 91–105, 587–606, 654–75.
22. CO iv (1805), p. 516; viii (1809), pp.
109ff.; xi (1812), p. 752; xiii (1814), pp.
657ff.; xxiii (1823), p. 697; A. Roberts (ed.),
op. cit., pp. 29–30.
23. E.g. EM i series xxi (1813), p. 28;
xxii (1814), p. 146; xxiv (1816), p. 392 and for
sympathy towards the impoverished xxvii (1819),
p. 463; xxviii (1820), p. 422.
24. MM xlvii (1824), p. 824.
25. B. Willey, The Seventeenth Century Background (1934, 1962 edn.), pp. 189–92, 261–66.
26. T.P. Bunting, op. cit., i, p. 139; ER i
series ix (1813), pp. 226ff. The popular periodicals criticised ineffective attempts at allegory but
argued that it could be 'an eminent and useful means
of religious instruction', a case substantiated by
reference to Bunyan (e.g. EM i series xiv, 1806,
pp. 562–63).
27. Davie, op. cit., lecture ii.
28. CO vii (1808), p. 332.
29. CO xxxiii (1833), pp. 671ff.; Clarke
(ed.), op. cit., i, pp. 44ff.
30. ER i series vii (1811), pp. 185–205,
334–50, reprinted in Foster, Critical Essays i;
Quarterly Review v (1811), pp. 40–61; Edinburgh
Review xvii (1811), pp. 429–65.
31. CO viii (1809), pp. 781–92; xi (1812),
pp. 781–97; Quarterly Review ii (1809), pp. 146–54;
vii (1812), pp. 329–42.
32. J.R. de J. Jackson (ed.), Coleridge: the
critical heritage (1970), pp. 6–7. Cf. J.O. Hayden
(ed.), Scott: the critical heritage (1970), p. 6;
J.E. Barcus (ed.), Shelley: the critical heritage
(1975), p. 14; L. Madden (ed.), Robert Southey:
the critical heritage (1972), p. 106.
33. Ibid., p. 210.
34. On Mason Good's translation of De Rerum
Natura see ER i series ii (1806), pp. 603–10,
686–97, and for Taylor's Herodotus BM xxi (1829),
pp. 198–99.
35. MM xl (1817), p. 139; M. Wilkin, Joseph

Kinghorn of Norwich (1855), p. 72. Cf. J. Gilbert
(ed.), op. cit., i, pp. 318-19 where Mrs. Gilbert
noted that her husband, classical tutor at Rotherham
College, was 'desirous of exchanging a life of cold
classical study, which is extremely unfavourable to
the growth of personal piety, for the edifying
duties of a pastor'.
  36. CO xxxi (1831), pp. 652-60.
  37. ER ii series xxvii (1827), pp. 439ff.
  38. ER i series i (1805), pp. 485ff.; MM
liii (1830), p. 834.
  39. The Miscellaneous Works and Remains of
Robert Hall (1846), p. 446.
  40. ER ii series iv (1815), pp. 355ff.;
xvi (1821), pp. 121ff.; xx (1823), pp. 413ff.
  41. CO xxxii (1832), pp. 84-85; xxxiii
(1833), p. 789.
  42. EM i series xxix (1821), p. 238 refers to
Job and Canticles.
  43. More, Preface to the Tragedies ..., pp.
41-45; ER i series ix (1813), pp. 185-86; ii
series i (1814), pp. 631-44; xiv (1820), pp. 87-
88. Cf. CO xii (1813), pp. 228-29.
  44. ER i series iii (1807), p. 77.
  45. CO vii (1808), pp. 326-29.
  46. Josiah Pratt, op. cit., p. 100.
  47. CO xvi (1817), p. 217.
  48. ER i series iv (1808), p. 621; ii series
ii (1814), p. 70; xii (1819), p. 350. Cf. CO xxv
(1825), p. 282.
  49. Teignmouth, op. cit., ii, p. 306;
F. Brady and W.K. Wimsatt (eds.), Samuel Johnson:
selected poetry and prose (1977), pp. 301-07.
  50. ER i series x (1813), pp. 558-59;
ii series v (1816), p. 90; xv (1821), p. 473;
R.I. and S. Wilberforce, Life ..., iv, p. 204.
  51. Thompson, op. cit., p. 372.
  52. CO vii (1808), p. 388.
  53. J.W. Cunningham, On the Genius and Works
of Cowper in Grimshawe (ed.), The Works of Cowper
(1835), vi, pp. xxiiff.
  54. CO xi (1812), p. 376; xiii (1814),
p. 254; xviii (1819), p. 667.
  55. ER ii series xxv (1826), p. 242; xxviii
(1827), p. 47. Note the ER's complementary
refrain: 'To profit mankind a poet must please
them, but unless he profits them at the same time
he cannot please them long' (i series vii, 1811,
p. 21).
  56. Ibid. viii (1812), p. 1241.
  57. ER ii series iv (1815), p. 477.

58. CO x (1811), pp. 502-11; ER i series
viii (1812), pp. 1240-53.
59. EM i series xxvi (1818), p. 206, but the
EM praised the 'elegant and interesting fragments'
from Southey, Coleridge, Wordsworth and Lockhart in
The Keepsake for 1829 (ii series vi, 1828, p. 524).
60. BM viii (1816), p. 81; ER ii series xv
(1821), p. 182.
61. Ibid. vi (1816), p. 489, where it was
argued that the average quality of modern poetry
was higher than in any previous period; CO xxvii
(1827), p. 296.
62. E.g. ER i series iv (1808), pp. 407-22;
vi (1810), pp. 578-602; vii (1811), pp. 672-88;
ix (1813), pp. 587-605; CO ix (1810), pp. 366-89;
xi (1812), pp. 29-33; xiv (1815), pp. 750-60.
63. R.I. and S. Wilberforce, Life ..., iii,
pp. 459ff.
64. W. Roberts, op. cit., iii, p. 390. Miss
More had a standing order with her bookseller for
all new volumes of Scott's poetry.
65. CO ix (1810), p. 367; xi (1812), p. 384;
xiv (1815), pp. 592-616.
66. ER i series ix (1813), p. 101; ii series
i (1814), pp. 431-36; iii (1815), pp. 354-66;
vi (1816), pp. 196-204; xvii (1822), pp. 421-22;
iii series ii (1829), pp. 251-59.
67. Early criticism can be found in ER i
series iv (1808), pp. 35-43; v (1809), pp. 192-93,
and later appreciation in ii series vi (1816), pp.
4ff.; xii (1819), pp. 62ff.; xiv (1820), pp.
177ff.; xv (1821), p. 182.
68. Ibid. iii (1815), pp. 14ff.; Edinburgh
Review xxiv (1814), pp. 1-30.
69. Quoted M.G. Jones, Hannah More (1952),
p. 225; Stephen, op. cit., p. 40; Meacham, op.
cit., p. 54.
70. Styles, Byron's Works ..., p. 29.
71. Edinburgh Review xxxvi (1822), p. 447.
72. ER i series viii (1812), pp. 630-41;
x (1813), pp. 523-31; ii series i (1814), pp. 416-
26; ii (1814), pp. 393-98.
73. Ibid. iv (1815), pp. 94-96; v (1816),
pp. 269-75, 595-99; vii (1817), pp. 292-304;
viii (1817), pp. 62-66, 291-92; ix (1818), pp. 555-
57; x (1818), pp. 46-54; xii (1819), pp. 147-56;
xv (1821), pp. 518-27; xvii (1822), pp. 418-27.
74. Ibid. i (1814), pp. 422-23.
75. CO xi (1812), pp. 376-86; xii (1813),
pp. 731-37; xiii (1814), pp. 245-57; xvi (1817),
pp. 246-59.

76.   BM xxii (1830), p. 385.
77.   EM i series xxx (1822), p. 192;   ii series ix (1831), pp. 190, 196.
78.   Louisa Byron Cunningham has born 29 November 1816.   Six years later Cunningham wrote to Byron denying that he was the model for De Rance, Cunningham's tale of a profligate, of which Byron had never heard (R.E. Prothero, ed., Byron's Works: Letters and Journals vi, 1901, pp. 153-54).   When Byron's illegitimate daughter, Allegra, died, the Harrow Church vestry refused to endorse the plaque which he had designed for her grave, lest the perpetuation of her name harm schoolboys' morals, a fear common to evangelicals and highchurchmen alike (pp. 70-72);   that Cunningham nevertheless wrote to Byron in praise of Cain is seen by Trollopian sources as proof of his 'flunkeyism', an interpretation criticised by Elisabeth Jay who notes that Cunningham 'may well have been able to appreciate Byron's poetic gift whilst deploring the poet's manner of life' (op. cit., p. 204).
79.   Teignmouth, op. cit., ii, p. 212.
80.   Prothero (ed.), op. cit., v, pp. 488ff.
81.   Styles, Byron's Works ..., p. 29, preached 4 July 1824;   CO xxv (1825), pp. 79-87, 151-58, 214-22, 281-88.
82.   M.J. Quinlan, Victorian Prelude (1941), p. 180.
83.   Altick, op. cit., p. 117.
84.   J. Entwisle and J. Bunting, The Annual Address of the Conference of the Methodist Societies ... (1825), p. 9.
85.   EM i series viii (1800), p. 526.
86.   ER iii series ii (1829), p. 162.   Cf. ii series vii (1817), pp. 312-13;   xv (1821), pp. 280ff.;   xxix (1828), pp. 145-48.
87.   Ibid. xxv (1826), p. 445.
88.   Quoted W.F. Gallaway, 'The Conservative Attitude toward Fiction', Publications of the Modern Language Association of America lv (1940), p. 1054. Cf. J.T. Taylor, Early Opposition to the English Novel (1943);   I. Williams, Novel and Romance 1700-1800:   a documentary record (1970), pp. 1-24.
89.   H. More, Hints towards Forming the Character of a Young Princess (1805), Works (1818 edn.) x, p. 173;   Moral Sketches (1819), pp. 238-49; ER i series viii (1812), pp. 605-06;   ii series vii (1817), pp. 309-36;   CO xiv (1815), pp. 512-17, xvi (1817), pp. 298-301, 371-75, 425-29;   MM xlii (1819), pp. 606-09.
90.   Quarterly Review xxiv (1821), pp. 352-57.

91. MM lvi (1833), pp. 17-18.
92. CO xxxii (1832), p. 814; xxxiii (1833),
pp. 478-82.
93. W. Roberts, op. cit., iv, pp. 204-05.
94. CO xvi (1817), p. 301.
95. Ibid., p. 64; xxii (1822), p. 158;
xxxii (1832), p. 819.
96. CO xv (1816), pp. 784-87. Cf. xvi (1817),
pp. 230-31. The CO refrained from reviewing any of
Scott's novels until the thirty-ninth was published
in 1822; while much of the review was devoted to a
reasoned condemnation of novel-reading, Scott's were
regarded as the best of 'mere novels' (pp. 157-72,
237-50).
97. Trevelyan, op. cit., i, pp. 30-36, 130-32.
98. ER ii series xiii (1820), p. 526; xv
(1821), p. 280.
99. ER i series ii (1806), p. 140; ii series
xii (1819), pp. 429-30.
100. Ibid. xiv (1820), p. 268.
101. Ibid. xii (1819), p. 423.
102. Ibid. xviii (1822), p. 163.
103. ER iii series ix (1833), p. 41.
104. R.I. and S. Wilberforce, Life ..., v, pp.
268-70.
105. Ibid., p. 133.
106. Ibid., p. 254.
107. EM i series xiii (1805), p. 515; xx
(1812), p. 395.
108. ER i series v (1809), pp. 972-73.
109. CO vi (1807), pp. 522-26.
110. EM i series xiv (1806), pp. 514-15.
111. BM xv (1823), p. 111.
112. ER ii series ix (1818), pp. 61-62.
113. CO xi (1812), pp. 713-14.
114. CO xxx (1830), p. 432.
115. CO viii (1809), pp. 109, 111; xxiii
(1823), p. 648.
116. EM i series xiii (1805), p. 270.
117. Ibid. xxvi (1818), p. 477.
118. BM xvii (1825), p. 124.
119. ER ii series xiii (1820), pp. 276-77, 349:
'Whether the story be real or not, it is all true'.
120. CO xxv (1825), p. 162.
121. See for example ER iii series ii (1829),
p. 87 'We are unwilling to consider this story as
a mere fiction ... It disturbs the satisfaction
which we must feel at meeting with so pleasing a
delineation of the power of religion, to recollect
that the case is suppositious and ideal; that being
totally destitute of the character of evidence, it

must fail to convince: it may illustrate, but it can prove nothing'. Cf. ii series vii (1817), p. 313.

122. BM xv (1823), p. 385.
123. EM ii series v (1827), p. 342.
124. CO xxx (1830), p. 432.
125. ER i series ii (1806), p. 1030.
126. EM i series xxvi (1818), pp. 208-09.
127. MM xlvii (1824), p. 693.
128. ER i series viii (1812), p. 924.
129. BM xvii (1825), p. 173.
130. ER ii series xxiii (1825), p. 462.
131. ER iii series vii (1832), p. 346. Cf. CO xxxiv (1834), p. 731 'Complaints are made by some of our readers that we are much too abstinent as regards works of fiction'.
132. CO xxvii (1827), p. 298. Cf. ER i series i (1805), p. 488.
133. ER ii series xx (1823), p. 275.
134. CO xxiii (1823), p. 294.
135. J. Foster, On Some of the Reasons by which Evangelical Religion has been Rendered Less Acceptable to Persons of Cultivated Taste (1805, 1st American from 3rd London edn., 1807), pp. 78-79.
136. W. Roberts, op. cit., iv, pp. 144ff.
137. H. More, An Essay on the Character and Practical Writings of St. Paul (3rd edn. 1815) i, p. 289.
138. CO xxxii (1832), p. 597.
139. CO xii (1813), p. 229.
140. ER ii series xxv (1826), p. 565.
141. Foster, Cultivated Taste ..., pp. 169-70.

Chapter Nine

FAITH AND THOUGHT

Foster's famous essay On Some of the Causes by
which Evangelical Religion has been Rendered Less
Acceptable to Persons of Cultivated Taste is the
most extended explanation of intellectual alienation from evangelicalism, and, emanating from
within the evangelical fold, the most damning
indictment of the movement as essentially anti-
intellectualist.

Foster believed that evangelicals forfeited
intellectual respect because the faith of some,
being purely emotional, was mindless, while the
mental horizons of others were limited by some two
or three over-emphasised doctrines which, they
assumed, explained everything. Even when belief
was more balanced, distinctive dialect and grotesque
gestures rendered objectionable religious statements
which the educated might have accepted if expressed
in the language of Dryden or Pope. Foster
recognised that there was no easy remedy for this,
for as long as evangelicalism was practised and
preached by the ignorant and uncultured, the impression given of the faith to the intelligentsia would
be unavoidably degrading:

> ... unless miracles are wrought, to
> impart to the less intellectual disciples
> an enlarged power of thinking, the
> evangelical truth must accommodate
> itself to the dimensions and unrefined
> habitudes of their minds ... Insomuch
> that if there was no declaration of the
> sacred system, but in the forms of
> conception and language in which they
> declare it, even a most candid man
> might hesitate to admit it as the
> most glorious gift of heaven.[1]

But the intellectual poverty of evangelicalism was not, according to Foster, just circumstantial. He complained that some Christians made no attempt to redress their ignorance and even gloried in it, attributing

> a kind of merit to their indifference
> to knowledge, as if it were the proof
> or the result of a higher regard for
> religion. If a hint of wonder was
> insinuated at their reading so little
> and within so very confined a scope,
> it would be replied that they thought
> it enough to read the Bible; as if it
> were possible for a person whose mind
> fixes with inquisitive attention on
> what is before him, even to read the
> Bible without at least ten thousand
> such questions being started in his mind
> as can be answered only from sources of
> information extraneous to the Bible.
> But ... this reading of the Bible was
> no work of inquisitive thought ...
> Those who have no wish for anything
> like a general improvement in knowledge,
> have no disposition for the real
> business of thinking, even in religion ...[2]

What really annoyed Foster was the complacency and arrogance characteristic of those who neither acknowledged nor sought to extend their limited understanding

> as if it comprised everything which it
> is possible, or which it is of
> consequence, for any mind to see in the
> Christian religion. They were like
> persons who should doubt the information
> that incomparably greater numbers of
> stars can be seen through a telescope
> than they have ever beheld, and who
> have no curiosity to try.[3]

Foster's bitter condemnation of his fellow evangelicals invites scrutiny: to what extent were men of 'cultivated taste' to be found in evangelical circles? Were evangelicals as opposed to learning as he seems to imply? How far were they prepared to question known verities, to reformulate their beliefs as a result of new discovery?

A. THE PLACE OF LEARNING

That evangelicalism produced some able men cannot
be doubted for their thought and taste were such as
to gain them recognition outside purely evangelical
circles. Among the Anglicans there was Richard
Cecil, described by the highchurch British Critic
as 'a very profound and original thinker', James
Stephen, whose 'great natural talents' were praised
by Henry Brougham, and his neighbour Henry Thornton,
whose book on paper credit was still regarded as
outstanding by J.S. Mill half a century later.[4] A
number of Evangelicals, spurred by a belief in the
value of hard work, achieved university distinctions,
most notably Isaac Milner, whose degree result was
starred 'incomparabilis', and Samuel Lee, a
carpenter's apprentice who, having taught himself
Greek and Hebrew, made some progress in Chaldee,
Syriac, Samaritan, Persian and Hindustan before
being sent to Cambridge at CMS expense in 1813.[5]
Evangelical senior wranglers at Cambridge included
the future missionary, Henry Martyn, Francis
Wollaston, later Jacksonian Professor, and his
successor in that chair, William Farish, Professor
of Chemistry.[6] Dissenters could boast of Robert
Morrison, a LMS missionary appointed East India
Company translator on account of his unusual fluency
in Chinese, of the shoe-maker scholars William
Carey and Samuel Drew, and of that unrepentant
bibliophile Adam Clarke, a collector of rare books
and first editions, who was elected to various
learned societies and appointed by Royal Commission
to revise Rymer's Foedera.[7] In addition there was
a small group of extremely able dissenters who
earned the respect and frequently enjoyed the
friendship of the literary elite of the day, men
such as Isaac Taylor junior whose work so excited
the young Marian Evans, and Josiah Conder of the
Eclectic Review, an intimate correspondent of
Robert Southey.[8] There was BFBS secretary Joseph
Hughes, a friend of Coleridge who wrote to him
'Having no-one in the circle of my acquaintance who
is at once competent and interested in religion
theologically, I had additional pleasure in the
opportunity of conversing with you'.[9] And above all
there was Hughes' fellow Baptist Robert Hall, a
man who not only enjoyed Coleridge's respect but
was described by the Quarterly Review as an
'absolute master of English', a thinker whose
talents were 'surpassed by those of very few men
in his time'.[10]

But if these men and others, as their
obituarists were to claim, 'gave to the winds the
notion that earnest piety was necessarily associated
with feeble intellect', the dissenters among them
frequently shared Foster's sense of alienation from
their fellow nonconformists.[11] Josiah Conder had
no doubt that the Eclectic Review was not properly
appreciated:

> The times are against it, and its
> enemies are very numerous, among
> those who ought to be its friends.
> It is thrown away upon the Dissenters.
> They prefer the Evangelical
> Magazine and the Congregational ...
> I am continually receiving
> testimonies to its character from
> those who are without ...[12]

Their non-evangelical friends similarly differentiated between the intellectual elite and other
evangelicals: Coleridge complained to Hughes of
'the undervaluing of, – nay the suspicious aversion
to, – all intellectual practice among so many truly
pious Christians'.[13] The justice of his charge
was admitted even by the popular press. The
Evangelical and Methodist Magazines acknowledged
the lowly birth of their readers and the educational
deficiency consequent upon this, but referred too,
often sadly, to the contempt with which many
evangelicals regarded learning: 'It is a sentiment
but too generally embraced by a certain class of
conscientious serious Christians, that divine
teaching is totally incompatible with human
literature ...'; 'It is much to be regretted that
many serious persons are prejudiced against
learning ...'[14] Confessing that the 'religious
world' largely ignored the Eclectic Review, the
Evangelical Magazine argued that the work deserved
wider support.[15]
   The prejudice which operated against learning
was deeply rooted in the fundamental tenets of
evangelicalism and as such influenced the thinking
even of its most able men. Reacting against the
intellectualism of much eighteenth century religion,
evangelicals had from the beginning stressed that
the purely intellectual route to salvation was a
cul-de-sac: 'Do not suppose' wrote Simeon

> that the faith of Christ is bare
> assent to truths which you have been

> taught by your parents, or that it is
> that kind of conviction that is founded
> upon a consideration of evidence, such
> as you would feel respecting any common
> report which was substantiated to your
> satisfaction ...

He revived the Lutheran distinction that 'Assent is
an act of the understanding only: but true faith is
a consent of the will also, with the full con-
currence of our warmest affections'.[16] Hence the
agonising of many potential evangelicals who had
considerable intellectual comprehension of the faith
for an 'interest' in the blood of Christ, an
emotional and practical acceptance of the personal
implications of belief.[17]
    To the attaining of such an interest
intellectual ability was totally irrelevant: the
most learned divine, relying on his intellect alone
in his quest for truth, might reason his way into
Unitarianism; the most ignorant and illiterate
could enjoy the benefits of saving faith. Among
less educated evangelicals the belief that intellectual competence was no prerequisite for discipleship, that 'in the wisdom of God the world by wisdom
knew not God', was easily transmuted into the
complacent ignorance so deplored by Foster.
Commenting upon his book, an Evangelical Magazine
contributor argued that men of taste had always been
opposed to the 'preaching of the Cross': contemporary rejection of evangelicalism by the educated
merely proved that modern religion was true to the
primitive model. Now as before God was displaying
his 'glorious and discriminating grace'.[18] The
socio-economic antagonism between privileged and
unprivileged was thus inverted to take theological
form as the latter argued that ultimately the
greater birthright was theirs.
    Some of the more educated were moved by faith
to forego some of their privileges. The arguments
levelled against other secular activities were
marshalled with added force against learning:
mental pursuits were particularly destructive of
religious impressions for they demanded total
absorption: unlike the manual worker the student
could not constantly think on God. His 'literary
duties, which require intense devotion of mind,
necessarily call off his thoughts in a great
measure from dwelling on heavenly objects'.[19] So
precarious was religious faith that even the most
legitimate studies could weaken piety and interrupt

private devotion. 'Christ' commented the Rev. Legh
Richmond 'has often been crucified between classics
and maths'. Evangelical fathers wrote to sons at
university urging them to work hard but at the same
time to refrain from putting too much store by
academic attainments: what should it profit a man
to become senior wrangler and lose his own soul?[20]
Even where personal religion was not apparently
threatened evangelicals sometimes eschewed intellectual pursuits believing that they were called to
make better use of their short and accountable time
on earth. The individualistic ethos of evangelicalism combined with a narrow conception of religion
to preclude any real awareness of the church as a
corporate body whose different members had different
tasks. Evangelicals' linear scale of values and
overwhelming sense of religious need militated
against academic study, as against any activity
which did not obviously contribute to the salvation
of the world. 'How little honour is it to be the
best chemist in Europe in comparison with being a
useful minister of Christ', wrote John Venn to the
scientist Francis Wollaston, 'What comparison can
there be between saving a soul and analysing a
salt!'[21]
Josiah Conder, whose aim was to unite religion
and learning in the pages of the Eclectic Review,
would probably not have engaged in such qualitative
evaluation. But even he was forced to conclude that
knowledge was a dispensable commodity, 'entirely
unconnected with the permanent realities of the
soul':

> 'As for knowledge it shall vanish
> away'. I certainly would not remain
> willingly ignorant of any of the
> wonders of natural science or human
> wisdom; I would not part with the
> thirst for knowledge, which is as
> essential a concomitant of mental
> health, as the appetites are of
> physical vigour. But shut out as
> the greater part of society are from
> intellectual pursuits, often being
> compelled to sacrifice them to the
> considerations of duty, it would be
> discouraging to think that on this
> account they would suffer any material
> loss.[22]

'However desirable and useful in various respects

learning may be' wrote Richard Cecil, 'it is not
essential to the Christian'.
'I have met with poor and illiterate men, who
having the grace of God in their hearts, could state
the doctrines of the Gospel with admirable distinction and accuracy'.[23] Inherent in Cecil's statement
was the qualification upon his thesis. Illiterate
some Christians might be, but to live the life of
faith they had to familiarise themselves with 'the
doctrines of the Gospel'. And as a doctrinal faith
evangelicalism both demanded and engendered abstract
thought. In a later essay, published in 1820,
On the Evils of Popular Ignorance, Foster propounded
the view that some intellectual aptitude was a prerequisite of conversion. The uneducated, he
believed, were governed solely by sense impressions,
were interested only in the immediate, responded
only to that which was palpable, and were incapable
of abstract thought. In these circumstances he
could not conceive how they could respond to
religion. Inability to think in abstractions and
aversion to intellectual exercise would prevent
them from apprehending religious truth: language
of atonement would be meaningless to them; their
concern for the immediate would prevent them from
seeing that the welfare of the soul was important;
their lack of mental exercise would debar them from
the practice of self-examination ...
Foster's conclusions derive largely from his
inability to appreciate or even to conceive of a
non-intellectual approach to life, and possibly too
from personal experience of failure in the pulpit.
Nevertheless overstated though some others believed
his case to be, his emphasis on the role of the
intellect in the life of faith was in tune with
much evangelical thought.[24] Evangelicals might
condemn a purely intellectual approach to religion,
but they were equally critical of forms of faith
which seemed to them to appeal only to the heart
and not to the head: Catholicism whose 'senseless
ceremonies and foolish pageants' aroused men's
senses and passions, was dismissed by John Burder
as providing 'little or no food for the mind of
man'.[25] Its presumed teaching that ignorance was
the mother of devotion was contrasted with the
evangelical emphasis upon 'religious knowledge',
a familiarity with the doctrines and duties of the
faith thought to be essential for salvation.[26]
Similarly the novelist Mrs. Sherwood criticised her
father, a characteristically eighteenth century
Anglican, because his religion centred upon emotive

'benevolence' rather than on doctrinal affirmation:

> I do not think that his ideas of
> doctrine were over clearly defined;
> neither he nor my mother had any
> distinct ideas of human depravity:
> hence neither of them until the very
> last, could see all that the Saviour
> had done.[27]

The frequently repeated charge that evangelicalism,
particularly in its Methodist forms, was anti-
doctrinal is therefore totally fallacious. Those
who were received into full Wesleyan connexion
had not only to testify to their conversion and
call to preach, but also to undergo a public oral
examination on 'all the Doctrines preached by
Methodists', listed by Adam Clarke as original sin,
the divinity of Christ, the atonement, justification
by faith, the witness of the Spirit, Christian
perfection, and the eternal duration of rewards and
punishments.[28] Fiducia was not an alternative to
assensus but a corollary of it.
    It followed that evangelicals were anxious to
further their theological understanding: periodical readers were urged to undertake regular study,
the Methodist Magazine listing in 1808 forty-six
authors whom it regarded as most worthy of
attention.[29] Biographies reveal that many read
voraciously in theology, while some built up
substantial libraries.[30] Not only professional
theologians but also laymen puzzled over complex
theological problems: on 23 April 1823 the popular
tract writer John Vine Hall read Luke x 21-22 and
was beset by 'perplexing thoughts concerning the
personal distinctness between Father, Son, and
Holy Spirit'.[31] Some such queries were submitted
to the popular periodicals which provide clear
proof that their first readers were intellectually
more competent than is generally assumed. The
Evangelical Magazine in particular was not aimed at
theological illiterates. On the contrary its
doctrinal discussions demanded a fairly high level
of ratiocination, and in some cases presupposed
knowledge of Hebrew. Articles in the Baptist and
Methodist Magazines were shorter and less analytical:
nevertheless discussions such as that on the pre-
existence of the human soul necessitated abstract
thought.[32] Methodist hymnbooks, as E.E. Kellett has
pointed out, were learned volumes.[33] Evangelicalism
was too doctrinal to be as mindless as Foster had

once suggested.

The encouragement which evangelicalism as a doctrinal faith gave to intellectual activity is most clearly revealed within Quakerism, for among Friends evangelicals were the intellectuals. Their theological interests were condemned by the quiet- ist branch of the movement in language paradoxically reminiscent of that employed by evangelicals against others as 'carnal wisdom', 'head knowledge', 'outward learning', and 'empty profession'. 'This anti-intellectualism' writes the Society's most recent historian, 'was a persisting trait of quietism, and one of its main lines of demarcation from evangelicalism'.[34] The true Quaker way, quietists such as Sarah Grubb believed, was to wait in emptiness and passivity upon the Holy Spirit who would make himself known in mystical experience and inner revelation. J.J. Gurney's concern with the doctrinal formulations of the Society, and campaigns for Biblical instruction in Quaker schools were therefore regarded with intense suspicion as 'human efforts'. To busy oneself with such matters, with Biblical and other studies, was to inhibit the Word of God which came in the waiting and the quietness. Gurney, notes his biographer,

> recognised the importance of concepts
> as aids to and instruments of Christian
> experience, whereas Sarah Grubb was
> truly convinced that insight and verbal
> messages are given directly from the
> Lord ... She could not accept Gurney's
> ordered sermons, clearly reflecting his
> careful study of the Bible and years
> of systematic thought about the basic
> principles of Christianity, as anything
> other than superficial, creaturely
> compositions, devoid of the true fire.[35]

Central to the dispute between Sarah Grubb and Gurney was the latter's typically eighteenth century claim that God worked through human means. It was commonly assumed that miracles were phenomena characteristic of the first age of the church only, divine endorsements of the authority of Christ passed on to his first disciples; in subsequent eras the God who had once worked through miracles utilised human skills. While the charismatic movement of the late 1820s challenged this belief, the vast majority of evangelicals continued to uphold it and indeed seemed not to conceive that any

other might be possible. In 1828 Henry Venn of the
CMS preached a university sermon on 1 Corinthians
xiv, the most extensive New Testament discussion of
glossolalia - but made no reference to any
charismatic understanding of the chapter. On the
contrary he defined spiritual gifts as those
abilities and intellectual powers which were
necessary in every age, and argued that the acquire-
ments in which the Corinthians were exhorted to
excel were those that academic study produced.[36]
The gift of tongues, bestowed spontaneously at
Pentecost because of the exigencies of the time, was
that linguistic proficiency which subsequent generations were charged to acquire through diligence.
Thus the **Christian Observer** urged its readers to
remember

>   that we are under an ordinary, not an
>   extraordinary, dispensation of the
>   Spirit; and that we cannot attain,
>   but by his blessing on our diligent
>   research, that knowledge which in the
>   miraculous ages was conveyed by
>   immediate inspiration.[37]

'Divine assistance' a Methodist proclaimed 'never
supersedes the use of means. On the contrary, it
is never promised in any other way'.[38]
     Evangelicals' belief that God worked through
human means served as a significant incentive to
study. When in 1796 the young Jabez Bunting founded
'A Society for the Acquirement of Religious
Knowledge consisting of young men of the Methodist
connexion in Manchester', he and his fellow members
affirmed

>   It is at once our absolute duty and our
>   invaluable privilege, to cultivate, by
>   every means in our power, the rational
>   and moral faculties, with which God has
>   graciously endowed us ... The supply of
>   the means is the requisition of the duty.[39]

Illiteracy it was sarcastically asserted was not a
qualification for ministry. Like so many gibes
against wilful ignorance this was directed not only
against evangelicals but against Catholics: whereas
the Catholic priest whose primary task was to
administer the sacraments was respected because of
his office and need be no more able than his flock,
the respect accorded to an evangelical cleric was

directly proportional to his performance in the
pulpit from which he was expected to deliver sermons
which he had himself composed. To this end, the
Baptist Magazine asserted, study was necessary:
since the age of miracles was past, men could no
longer expect to preach by inspiration.[40]
     Intellectual competence was demanded not only
by the nature of the task but also by the expectations of the clientele: only 'growing men', it
was claimed, could gain and retain the respect of
congregations in an increasingly learned age.[41]
Both the Eclectic Review and the Baptist Magazine
noted with concern that as ministers who could
command intellectual respect died, children of
dissenting homes turned to the more cultured
establishment.[42] Methodists felt that they had yet
more cause for anxiety: as the men to whom they
preached availed themselves of educational opportunities so, Joseph Sutcliffe pointed out,

> an unlettered pastor with a provincial
> accent sounds but ungracious on their
> ear. The evangelical clergy, the polish
> and good learning of many dissenters,
> place Methodism in a contest very
> different from former years.[43]

From outside evangelicalism James Mackintosh
observed that

> a party which has hitherto not only
> neglected but rather despised or
> dreaded knowledge, has been compelled,
> by the literary spirit of the age,
> to call in literature to their aid:
> their new followers of a higher class
> require elegance.[44]

     The pragmatic nature of such arguments should
not be overemphasised for they presuppose that the
spirit of an educated age was already reflected
within evangelicalism both among those who had grown
up within the faith and among new converts. The
call for cultured preachers was a response to
changes that were already taking place. Thus the
Baptist Magazine of 1810 was concerned to point out
that the 'prejudices unfavourable to learning'
were fast declining: contemporary dissenters
valued an educated ministry.[45]
     The statement was maybe too sanguine for
periodical writers regularly appealed for funds for

poorly supported academies, and produced articles
justifying ministerial education to those still
sceptical of its value. The frivolity and high
spirits of some students gave rise to much murmuring
among those who feared that learning rather than
piety was becoming the qualification for ministerial
office. In reply the proponents of education denied
that they were aiming to 'make' ministers, and
claimed that they were merely concerned the better
to equip those already assumed to possess ministerial gifts.[46] While the practice of appointing
untrained men, which had escalated during the
revival, continued particularly within Methodism,
the arguments in favour of training fell on fertile
ground. By the late 1820s the demand for a
Wesleyan Theological Institution was gaining
strength and was approved at Conference of 1834,
the chief opposition deriving not from anti-
intellectualism but from dislike of autocratic
centralization.[47] Some old dissenters continued to
study at Scottish Universities, and some in the
homes of respected ministers who sometimes found
themselves running embryonic academies; increasingly others were sent to colleges, some long-estab-
lished, many others owing their foundation to the
revival. Ad hoc though this preparation might be
its strength was recognised by Anglicans who shared
the dissenting consciousness of denominational
competition. Evangelicals were painfully aware
that their university educated ordinands, unlike
dissenters, had no theological training, and they
increasingly recommended that men should undertake
some theological study prior to accepting a
living.[48]
       There was some debate as to what constituted
proper ministerial training. While some students,
then as always, wished to restrict their courses to
subjects of obvious future utility, there was
considerable feeling that ministers should
experience a wider education: 'in these days of
refinement and science, something more is necessary
in order to acquire attention, than a bare knowledge
of Scriptural doctrines'.[49] The Christian Observer
confessed to a 'romantic attachment' to the
traditional form of university education.[50] Believing that Christians should do their duty in the
place in which they were called, Evangelicals argued
that students were accountable to God for the
diligent pursuit of prescribed studies. At the
very least they would thereby learn self-discipline.
Claudius Buchanan commented on the tendency of his

fellow students to give up mathematics, 'I am
inclined to believe, that were I an eminent saint,
I should be a good mathematician, a good linguist,
a good Scripturalist', while an undergraduate who
asked Simeon whether it was not his religious duty
to read the Bible and to pray rather than continue
to study classics and maths was given very short
shrift.[51]
     While dissenters, frequently faced with the
task of constructing a ministerial training course
from scratch, laid greater emphasis on subjects
relating to theology, the curricula of dissenting
academies, printed in the <u>Evangelical Magazine</u>,
were far from narrow. The classics were regularly
included, and among other subjects taught in various
places were Hebrew, Chaldee, Syriac, and French,
various branches of maths, physics, chemistry, and
astronomy, history and geography, <u>belles lettres</u>
and philosophy...[52]
     The benefits of a general education were less
readily proffered to those who served abroad. In
the early years of evangelical overseas expansion
there was some feeling that missionary education
was an unnecessary luxury. At a meeting of
Anglicans at Rauceby in 1795 some argued that the
'grand requisites' of a missionary were not to be
conferred by education, and if possessed superseded
the need of scholastic preparation. The apostles
had not been so trained. Those present apparently
assumed that education was essentially classical,
and hence not directly relevant to mission among
the uncivilized.[53] Their ignorance of the
situations in which missionaries were to serve was
responsible for much of the recurrent tension
between the latter and their sponsoring societies.
In contrast David Brown, who as chaplain to the
East India Company had first hand experience of
the mission field, wrote to Simeon in 1789:

> You will be aware that zeal and grace,
> though essentials are not the only
> requisites on this occasion. They must
> be men of general knowledge, and possess
> such a share of science, as may make
> their conversation interesting to the
> learned Brahmins, who will only be
> communicative in proportion to the
> returns made them by those with whom
> they converse. There should also be
> a natural propensity to languages.[54]

The value of an extensive and accurate knowledge of
languages, ancient and modern, could not be gain-
said for the production of vernacular Bibles was
an essential part of the church's missionary task.
Shoddy and summary translations were totally unacceptable for those concerned for 'God's honour and
the glory of his Word' maintained that 'so sacred
a work ought to be done as well as possible'.[55]
Brown's belief that missionaries should be
'men of general knowledge' was also increasingly
accepted as charismatic enthusiasm was tempered by
a belief in means, and as the societies were forced
through experience to recognise that evangelism
abroad was not rewarded by easy conversions.
Moreover, for all Simeon's influence at Cambridge
no graduate presented himself to the CMS until 1815;
the few volunteers for the mission field were men
of low social status who lacked the educational
qualifications which Anglicans at least were
accustomed to assume in ordinands for home service.[56]
The assumption that such men could be sent abroad
in zealous ignorance was replaced by the diametrically opposed belief that spiritual training should
be accompanied by social and academic education.
Thus, in a paper on the 'Best means of preparing
missionaries for their work' delivered at an
interdenominational gathering in 1820, Jabez
Bunting argued that potential missionaries should
know 'what the heathen are, what modes of address
suit them' and should be given 'general preparatory
knowledge, suited to the intended station'. History,
natural philosophy, astronomy and geography should
be included among their studies, thus enlarging
their minds, while their social experience should be
augmented by removal from 'their own sphere, by
introduction into proper society ...'[57] In 1825 a
Language Institution was founded in London which
aimed, by providing lectures and a library to
acquaint men with the languages, manners, customs,
and opinions of those whom the missionary societies
sought to influence. The individual societies too
began to make some provision for their own
candidates: substantial pressure for the Wesleyan
Theological Institution came from the missionary
society, while in 1826 the CMS established a
seminary at Islington. In an early lecture
delivered there Daniel Wilson expounded upon the
advantages which educated missionaries, always
assuming they were men of faith, enjoyed over their
uneducated colleagues.[58]
Education was not merely valued for those who

were to engage in full-time Christian service. On
the contrary evangelicals gave their support to a
wide variety of educational organisations. Carey,
Kinghorn, Taylor senior and Baines junior participated in literary societies in the towns in which
they lived, and for purposes of scholastic discussion were happy to mix with men of very varied
religious creeds.[59] Other dissenters recommended
that libraries should be set up at churches.[60] Many
evangelicals contributed either to the BFSS or to
the National Society, depending upon their belief
about the nature and place of religious instruction
in a syllabus, and similarly supported either
University College London or the supposedly more
godly institution in the Strand, and in some cases
both.[61] The Evangelical Magazine recorded the
establishment by dissenters of societies to finance
the education of ministers' children and of grammar
schools at which they might safely be educated.[62]
     The multiplicity of these efforts to further
post-elementary as well as basic education constitutes a serious challenge to the common assumption
that evangelicals were concerned only to enable men
to read the Scriptures and regarded any subsequent
education as undesirable. To argue in this way
is to misinterpret the refusal of some evangelical
authorities to teach writing in Sunday Schools.
W.R. Ward has stressed that within Methodism the
debate over writing was but one of many foci of the
ongoing conflict between those who wished to assert
connexional and pastoral authority, and those who
wanted to continue the flexibility of local and lay
autonomy to which the revival had given rise.[63] In
a battle born of social divisiveness and centring
on the exercise of power the real issue was not
what the schools should teach but who should control
their syllabi and practice. The Sunday School
writing debate was admittedly less a pretext for
the assertion of power than the otherwise similar
Leeds organ controversy, for the question raised
was more obviously a matter of serious principle.
But the principle under discussion was not the
value of literacy but the proper use of Sunday.
Those who opposed the teaching of writing on
Sundays did not on the whole object if children
learnt to write on other days of the week. Their
stance paralleled that of those Evangelicals who,
on Sundays only, refused to despatch or open mail,
read papers, travel, visit, or engage in business.
The Methodist Magazine stressed that to teach
writing on the Sabbath was to legitimise the

teaching of trade on the Sabbath.[64] Convinced in
the decades following the French holocaust that
England's continued well-being was contingent upon
the strict observance of Sunday, evangelicals
prohibited any activity that was not immediately
concerned with the worship of God, regardless of
its inherent merit, and the scarcity of other
opportunities for its prosecution. Nothing mattered
in comparison with the need to avert the outpouring
of divine wrath which they were sure would be
visited upon a nation whose neglect of the Sabbath
was symptomatic of its deep-seated spiritual
malaise.

If concern for the well-being of the nation
militated against the teaching of writing on
Sundays, it was one of the factors which led
evangelicals to encourage and participate in
elementary education on other days of the week, for
education was lauded as conducive to morality and
as a preservative of public order. While the mere
confinement of children who might otherwise roam the
streets contributed temporarily to this, the lessons
taught were assumed to instil an appreciation of
English social organisation and a willingness to
maintain it. While sanctioning indoctrination this
assumption derived from a belief in human rationality for evangelicals adhered to 'the intellectualist
assumption that working men were the victims of
false ideas'.[65] Their certainty that if men were
taught to reason they would be better Christians
and better citizens caused them enthusiastically
to advocate education for the lower classes at a
time when some of their contemporaries were still
regarding it with fear and suspicion.

Their beliefs similarly inclined Evangelicals
to the progressive side in the ongoing debate on
girls' education. Refusing to school their
daughters exclusively in 'worldly accomplishments',
they considered at length in the <u>Christian Observer</u>
of 1808 what form of female education should
properly be adopted as an alternative. In common
with many of their contemporaries, some contributors
were uneasy about teaching girls 'severe' or
'scientific' subjects, metaphysics, logic, the
classics, which might vitiate female tenderness and
delicacy. On the other hand there was considerable
support even for such studies and the belief that a
girl's mind should not be trained was firmly
repudiated. Such training was regarded as essential
for both long and short term purposes. On women
lay maybe the most vital of all tasks, the up-

bringing of young children; since Evangelicals
sometimes hesitated before sending their children
away to school, the mother's responsibility was
correspondingly greater. Moreover, insistence upon
the values of home society gave rise to the belief
that a woman should be a genuine companion to her
husband, who might otherwise lack opportunities for
thoughtful talk. While not expected to be his
intellectual equal, his wife should at least be
able to converse intelligently with him. In any
case confining her activities to the home, a woman
whether married or not, needed some mental stimul-
ation to prevent her time hanging upon her hands.
It would be cruel, Hannah More commented, for
parents to insist upon a retired life without
qualifying their daughters for that retirement.
Religion and mental cultivation alone could equip
women of standing for such a life.[66]
        The juxtaposition here as elsewhere of
'religion' and 'mental cultivation' is indicative of
the high premium which evangelicals placed upon
learning. While frequently recommended as a
preservative against worldly or sensual temptation,
its value as an antidote to Regency raffishness was
not merely negative but derived from its peculiar
concordance with Christianity, its suitability
for a being destined for eternity. Indeed so
congruent were faith and study that evangelicals
tended to regard a love of books in youth as a mark
of potential spirituality. The writers of memoirs
and obituaries frequently noted with approbation
that their subjects had been addicted to reading as
children, isolated from and uninterested in the
childish play of their fellows.[67] As a counterpart
to this conversion often served as an incentive to
bookish pursuits. Taught to eschew the pleasures
of the world and the flesh, to find enjoyment at
home rather than in society, evangelicals developed
a taste for reading, and, many claimed, found that
faith facilitated thought. 'Why now' exclaimed one
of Rowland Hill's exemplary characters, 'it appears
... as though I had been all my days without brains,
while I was living without grace'.[68]
        Hill's character, however, exercised his brains
on religious subjects alone, as did others who
likewise lauded the value of intellectual activity.
The potentially limited connotations of evangelical
terminology are revealed in the title of Edward
Bickersteth's book, The Christian Student, a synonym
for the student of theology. A restriction of
interest to subjects of religious utility was

implicitly encouraged by influential leaders like
Thomas Scott who announced in 1779 'for these last
two years I have scarce opened a book but upon
religious subjects', and by the most widely
circulated periodicals, the contents of which were
almost exclusively theological.[69] On the other
hand genuine interest about a wide range of subjects
was evinced by the Eclectic reviewers. Between
January and June 1828, six months chosen at random,
non-theological reviews dealt with Irish history,
coins and medals, volcanoes, indigestion, Hayti,
Celtic antiquities, classical and legal textbooks,
Columbus, the U.S.A., a journey through India,
'mental and moral science', the North Coast of
Africa, travels in Sicily, South African monarchs,
Austria, the mortality and 'physical management'
of children, the Sandwith Isles, the Peninsular war,
the history and philosophy of science, and botanical
geography ...
    That the Eclectic Review went some considerable
way towards increasing its readers' general
knowledge is, given its terms of reference, only to
be expected. The Christian Observer did little in
this respect, its non-theological reviews being
primarily concerned with literature, and philosophical studies on the nature of the mind, which it
reviewed at considerable length. But its propriet-
ors were of a higher station in life than those of
the Eclectic Review and could perhaps assume that
their readers had enjoyed a general education and
were in receipt of secular reviews in a way that
the dissenters and editors of the popular press
could not. It is significant, in contrast, how
much general information was communicated by the
latter. The belief that every phenomenon in nature
testified to divine planning meant that astronomy
and geology, botany and mineralogy, anatomy and
zoology, were regarded as properly religious studies.
While much of the writing about these subjects was
too subsumed in theological didacticism to
constitute proof of genuine intellectual curiosity,
the extent to which it acted as a stimulant to
wider interests must not be underestimated. Even
the Methodist Magazine, which confessed to
exclusively religious concerns, conveyed some
general knowledge under the sectional headings 'The
Works of God Illustrated' and 'The Word of God
Displayed'. More comprehensively, the Evangelical
Magazine's analyses of every Biblical jot and
tittle gave rise to wide-ranging investigations:
in 1802 under the title 'The Natural History of the

Fox or Jackall' it sought to determine which species
was described in Scripture and in so doing conveyed
much information about the habits of the animal
kingdom.[70] Similarly the Baptist Magazine printed
a long series of 'Philosophical Reflections' for
its younger readers in the hope of making them more
aware of the profuseness of God's provision for
man's every need: thus in April 1821 in the 24th
article in the series it illustrated divine care in
mundane matters by discoursing at length on the
properties and use of iron.[71] In particular the
popular periodicals mirrored the practice of the
secular reviews in devoting much space to tales of
travel and accounts of the geography and customs of
other lands. If the prevalence of these testifies
in part to the impetus given to intellectual
inquiry by the missionary movement, the evangelical
counterpart to exploratory expeditions, the interest
evoked was not purely pragmatic. In these as in
articles on many other subjects it is clear that
faith provided the initial justification for
studies which soon proved to be absorbing in their
own right. Joseph Kinghorn's interest in Egyptian
mythology, the works of Zoroaster, Rabbinical
literature, and Hebrew accentuation, went way
beyond their utility in Biblical study.[72]

Faith provided too the justification for
studies which bore little relation to Biblical
matters, for many evangelicals assumed that the
subordination of the senses to the mind legitimised
intellectual pursuits of almost any kind. 'We feel
a desire to know, and we are highly gratified by
knowing' wrote H.F. Burder, and listed among The
Pleasures of Religion the study of

> the history of the ages which are
> past, and of the generations now
> mingled with the dust - the character,
> the manners, and the transactions of
> other nations, in distant parts of
> the world, contemporary with
> ourselves - the scenery and the
> products of countries we never
> expect to visit - the natural
> history of the various tribes of
> animals peculiar to their respective
> climates and elements - the laws
> which regulate the phaenomena of
> the heavens and the earth, and the
> ocean - and the treasures of science,
> reduced by the wisdom of enlightened

men, to systematic forms, and applied
to purposes of practical utility.
Pleasures arising from sources such
as these are interdicted by no law;
and when they do not unduly engross
the mind, so as to impede the
performance of incumbent duties,
they are not only allowable, but
desirable.[73]

Their practice suggests that others shared his
enthusiasm, for obituaries and memoirs often contain
tantalising hints about the intellectual inclinat-
ions of other evangelicals concerning whom little
else is known: despite the paucity of his formal
education Lawrence Butterworth composed a Greek
grammar and was working on Greek etymology at the
time of his death in his late teens; Rev. Joseph
Webb, who also died young, gained great pleasure
from linguistic research, investigating the origins
of the English language in Anglo-Saxon and Gothic
sources; their fellow Baptist, the Rev. William
Anderson, taught himself French, for a short time
studied Italian and German, and read voraciously not
only in theology but also in history, philosophy,
politics, and political economy ...[74] That the
writers of brief memoirs saw fit to mention these
non-theological concerns is significant, for it
points to a respect and even approval of certain
secular studies on the part of their readership.
Their accounts reveal too that evangelical
apprentices and ministers commonly snatched time
from sleep in order to study, a course of behaviour
invariably regarded as commendable. Recollecting
his life and times in an autobiography which is
clearly the product of an alert and interested
mind, Thomas Jackson recorded that as a young
minister, preaching some nine times a week and
travelling extensively, he would sometimes rise at
3,00a.m. to study Greek; in addition he managed to
read between thirty and fifty volumes per annum,
mainly thick theological tomes, but also a variety
of classical and literary works.[75] A recent
biographer has suggested that Thomas Coke, the
effective founder of Methodist missions, was widely
read for a man so extensively involved in administration.[76] The point can be made yet more aptly
of other evangelicals, manual workers and travelling
preachers, who lacked Coke's initial educational
advantages. The extent of evangelical intellectual
activity can only properly be judged against the

plumbline of opportunity. While there was clearly
a strand of anti-intellectualist feeling within
evangelicalism, there can be no doubt that many
evangelicals, far from resting complacently in their
ignorance, did more than might be expected to
redress it.

B. THE LIMITS ON CURIOSITY

Foster's argument that evangelicals were intellectual philistines is seriously weakened by the
evidence that faith often provided an incentive for
study which many evangelicals thoroughly enjoyed.
Clyde Binfield, however, properly distinguishes
between men 'of great learning' and men 'of
extensive information', and in a series of cameos
of nineteenth century nonconformity suggests that
dissenting ministers could usually be placed in
the latter category: they possessed 'good second-
class minds'.[77] While, as he rightly implies, this
level of competence should not be underrated, it is
nevertheless clear that an antiquarian delight in
the accumulation of knowledge and the ability to
juggle with ideas and arguments did not of themselves preclude that blinkered outlook on life
which Foster so despised. It is therefore necessary
to determine the extent to which evangelicals
displayed an open-minded curiosity, a willingness
to reformulate and adjust ideas, and above all that
love of truth for its own sake which R.W. Dale
believed they so signally lacked.
    Such a task is fraught with difficulty for it
is almost impossible for the historian so to
assimilate the framework of thought of a previous
age as to be able accurately to assess what
constituted open-mindedness for those operating
within it. The temptation and danger is to regard
as truly open-minded those whose views correspond
most closely to those of our own society. Yet
this is to overlook the originality of men who
developed new ideas which subsequent generations
were to reject, and it certainly does less than
justice to those who thought deeply within the
context of certainties which their descendants can
no longer accept.
    A further difficulty relates to the emotional
distance between the nineteenth and twentieth
centuries, for now it is not easy to empathise with
the intensity of feeling characteristic of doctrinal
dispute in the nineteenth century. Yet to ignore

or underestimate the agony of mind which such
debates occasioned is to fail in historical
understanding. Doctrine was too sensitive and too
important an issue for dispassionate discussion;
challenges to faith were matters of eternal life
and death, threats operative at the deepest level
of personality: 'It is not to be endured' wrote
Hannah More 'to hear questions on which hang all
our hopes and fears speculated upon as if they were
a question of physics or history'.[78]
While the threats posed thus precluded some
intellectual investigation, it would be wrong to
suggest that evangelicals were antagonistic to all
new thinking. The Christian Observer explicitly
condemned readers who wished to eschew the study of
Hebrew because it laid open to question matters
which from childhood they had regarded as sacred:
'no thinking man will allow this to be any argument
against improvement in Biblical any more than in
any other science. The immutable interests of
truth can never suffer from knowledge well
applied'.[79] Individuals regularly encouraged others
to show them where their interpretation of
Scripture was questionable.[80] Indeed it was part
of evangelical belief in the importance of the
Bible that every attempt be made to ascertain its
correct meaning, and that new, even uncongenial,
ideas be accepted once they were proved to have
Scriptural authority. The process was facilitated
by the increasing rejection of a rigidly systematic
approach to the Bible, a rejection which W.R. Ward
suggests derived in part from the influence of
enlightenment thought.[81] Old dissenters' repudiation of the strict logic of hyper-Calvinism and
the enunciation of an unsystematic moderately
Calvinist creed in the early years of the nineteenth
century testify to the willingness of evangelicals
within specified limits to rethink and reformulate
their beliefs.
Those limits concerned the nature of the Bible.
While evangelicals were prepared to accept some
textual amendations as a result of modern scholarship at no point did they grant the premises of
German criticism. The authenticity of the Trinitarian verse was sometimes questioned but the
sacrosanctity of the vast bulk of Scripture was
regularly upheld.[82] The Bible was a book unlike all
other books, the final and authoritative statement
of God to man. The approach to it should therefore
be different from that commonly adopted for to
question the Bible was to question God, to go beyond

the bounds set for human enquiry: 'No learning, no research, however profound and extensive, can atone for that levity of criticism which treats the records of human salvation as of any authority less than divine', commented the Methodist Magazine, 'The greatest injury that can be done to any man, is, to impair his confidence in that testimony which God hath given concerning his Son'.[83]

It needs to be stressed that evangelicals were not alone in thus repudiating the methods of Biblical criticism. The British Critic, Anglican equivalent of the Eclectic Review, and the Christian Remembrancer, highchurch counterpart of the Observer, shared their horror at the 'awful corruption of Christianity' which the Eclectic maintained had taken place in Protestant Germany.[84] The Christian Remembrancer in particular was well-supplied with epithets with which to denounce 'the erroneous tendency ... of neological sophistries' and, specifically, 'the neological blasphemies of Mr. Milman's History of the Jews', which 'unhallowed volume' it wished to see immediately withdrawn.[85] Works such as Milman's which described Abraham as 'an independent sheik of Emir' and implied that the Biblical account was not altogether accurate were condemned by evangelicals and highchurchmen alike. The authenticity of Scripture, the Critic maintained, in an argument characteristic of the previous century, was confirmed by miracle and fulfilled prophecy; its testimony to providential intervention should be taken into account by any subsequent historian as categoric fact.[86] Milman's 'sadly irreverent predilection for secondary causes and human agency' was therefore criticised by the Christian Remembrancer on the grounds that Jewish history, being 'one continuous and stupendous miracle ... is not ... to be viewed in the same light as the ordinary narratives of the profane historian'.[87] Highchurchmen also shared evangelical apprehension as to the consequences of the new thinking, the Critic reproving Niebuhr for questioning that all humanity was derived from a single pair:

> If Adam had not sinned, Christ had not
> died: and we cannot see that the Gospel
> holds out the death of Christ as being
> of any avail, except to the descendants
> of Adam ... In this critical and
> philosophical age, we warn the incautious
> reader of history against entering upon

> speculations, which may end in ruining
> his faith; and against adopting notions
> concerning his first parents, which may
> lead him to doubt concerning his
> Redeemer.[88]

As H.J. Rose's increasingly abrasive attack upon
Bretschneider similarly reveals, deep-rooted fears
of Biblical criticism were by no means restricted
to evangelicalism.[89]
    The most conservative reaction does however
appear to have been exclusively evangelical.
Notwithstanding their general belief in the
importance of human means, some evangelicals tended
increasingly to deny that these had been operative
in the writing of Scripture. The Record attacked
Milman for describing a Scriptural passage as a
poem 'treasured up with religious care among the
traditions of the tribes', and for failing to
recognise that it was preserved 'by the command
of the Spirit who spoke through the mouth of
Jacob'.[90] If human means were minimally employed
in the writing of Scripture, it followed that there
was little need to investigate the circumstances
of Biblical writers before reaching conclusions
about the meaning of 'God's Word'; correct understanding was better facilitated by a knowledge of
the Author. In contrast the doctrine of verbal
inspiration played no part in highchurch apologetic,
and was explicitly repudiated by some reviewers
who referred without embarrassment to 'the Book
which contains his Word'.[91] 'It seems now to be
understood' commented the British Critic approvingly
in 1829,

> that the writings of prophets and
> apostles are to be interpreted just
> as we should interpret the writings
> of other men; that these writings
> differ from other compositions only
> in this, that their meaning whenever
> it can be discovered, will conduct us
> into all necessary truth; but that,
> in the endeavour to discover that
> meaning, we must resort to the same
> methods which help us to find the
> sense of all other ancient authors.[92]

It has of course to be admitted that apparent
challenges to the Bible were more threatening to
evangelicals, who equated Scripture with the faith,

than to highchurchmen who had an alternative source
of support and authority in the Church. Nor did the
Record speak for all evangelicals. But the Christian Observer opted out of the conflict, fearing to
print even for purposes of refutation the 'fallacious' interpretations of the neologists.[93] And even
the Eclectic Review, which rejected the Record's
teaching, nevertheless proved less capable of meeting the Germans on their own ground than some
highchurch critics. Like the British Critic the
Eclectic recognised that there was some good in the
work of Schleiermacher, accepted the possibility
of error in non-doctrinal matters, and acknowledged
that the Gospels might share some common source
materials. The Eclectic's review, however,
comprised lengthy quotations and inconclusive
discussions on vaguely related topics, whereas the
British Critic attempted logically to repudiate
some of Schleiermacher's suggestions, and produced
an intellectually respectable discussion of the
synoptic problem.[94] According to another Eclectic
reviewer, Mühlenfels' suggestion that the Jews
fashioned God after their own image could be met
by 'quiet reference to the letter of Holy Writ', a
response which reveals the failure even of one of
the more educated evangelicals to understand the
basic presuppositions of German theology.[95]

Similar limitations in evangelicals' interest
and understanding can be identified in a study of
their response to the new geology. Again criticism
must be qualified for the Eclectic was in tune with
much contemporary opinion when it questioned whether
Lyell had really proved that all change was
uniform.[96] But whereas the Critic, which shared
its doubts, recognised the scientific calibre of
The Principles of Geology and provided a long and
clear precis of Lyell's arguments, the Eclectic
reviewer quickly dismissed Lyell's views and proceeded to give unqualified praise to Andrew Ure's
attempts to reconcile Scripture and geology.[97]
Such attempts, while enjoying some highchurch
sympathy, met with antagonism from the Critic which
argued that 'the conclusions of geology, in its
present imperfect state, cannot be reconciled with
the Mosaical history of the creation'; to seek a
premature agreement was to the detriment of both.[98]
Convinced that science and religion would ultimately
prove compatible, a reviewer nevertheless maintained
that the former should be approached with minds
'wholly unfettered by the trammels of any pre-
conceived opinions' and opposed the practice of

pursuing scientific investigation 'by continual
reference to the cosmogony of Moses'.[99]
    It is here that evangelical comments on geology
are most open to criticism. Assuming that the Bible
was encyclopaedic in function, many evangelicals
regarded the 'cosmogony of Moses' as indisputable
fact. A Methodist reproved the editors of the
otherwise praiseworthy Cabinet Cyclopedia for a lack
of deference to Scripture and quoted Cowper's lines

> Some drill and bore
> The solid earth, and from the strata there
> Extract a register, by which we learn,
> That He who made it, and revealed its date
> To Moses, was mistaken in its age.[100]

Others were more prepared to consider the new
scientific ideas but their obsessive interest in the
way in which they could be related to Scripture
resulted in much unscholarly discussion. Whereas
the Christian Remembrancer criticised the author of
Mosaical and Mineral Geologies for seeking to defend
the Bible while ignorant of geology, the Christian
Observer seemed unaware of the inadequacy of
Higgins' knowledge.[101] The editors gave space to
numerous contributions by George Bugg who, admitting
he was no geologist, nevertheless rejected the
theories of scientists in favour of his own which he
regarded as more concordant with Genesis.[102]
Admittedly the paper refused to endorse all his
opinions and his tirades met with much critical
response. But notwithstanding their assertions to
the contrary, even those who challenged him tended
to share his assumption that the Bible gave scientific guidance, and themselves suggested how the two
sorts of evidence be reconciled. The lengthy
debates in the Christian Observer thus focused upon
matters such as the possibility of a long time-gap
between Genesis i 1 and Genesis i 2.[103] The desire
to comprehend and defend the Bible precluded wider
scientific interests.
    Evangelicals' insistence on viewing everything
through Biblical spectacles seriously inhibited
the development of their thinking. If much intellectual inquiry was rendered irrelevant because the
Bible had already given all the answers, even the
study of subjects on which it had not proclaimed
so categorically was limited by the belief that
everything could and should be explained within a
narrowly Biblical framework and according to the
Biblical model. Many evangelicals therefore

believed that history should be studied to throw
light upon 'the ways of God to man', and the
subject was regularly praised as a means of illustrating and confirming Christian doctrine:
according to the Baptist Magazine it showed 'that
righteousness exalteth a nation' and that 'sin is a
disgrace to any people'; Thomas Morell whose
history books were much praised in the evangelical
press suggested that the fall of Troy was a comment
on James iv 1.[104] This sort of approach inevitably
stifled intellectual inquiry for those who insisted
on drawing improving lessons from their material
were more interested in the uses to which it could
be put than in the academic questions which it
prompted. Indeed Hannah More admitted as much for
she was an inveterate opponent of the attempt to
invest history - or any other subject - with
autonomous value:

> While every sort of useful knowledge
> should be carefully imparted to young
> persons, it should be imparted not
> merely for its own sake, but also for
> the sake of its subserviency to higher
> things. All human learning should be
> taught, not as an end but a means; and
> in this view, even a lesson of history
> or geography may be converted into a
> lesson of religion.[105]

While Miss More's works gained widespread
popularity, one or two of the more scholarly
evangelicals disagreed with her views. Foster was
predictably cynical about the moral utility of the
study of history, while another Eclectic reviewer
recognised, as Miss More did not, that the doctrine
of Providence was a matter of belief, not of
observation:

> We see the agency of Providence so
> indefinitely varied, capable of aspects
> and interpretations so different, so
> many points of intersection and counter-
> action between Divine volition and human
> volition, and, in the vast majority of
> cases, so mournful a preponderance of
> evil, that we cannot profess, from such a
> survey alone, to support the doctrine in
> question.[106]

A didactic approach to history was repudiated by

Adam Clarke, whose pamphlet on the death of
Professor Porson, Charles Simeon's life-long bête
noir, reveals a genuine interest in establishing
an accurate record of events, regardless of whether
or not they yielded improving lessons.[107] His
concern for accuracy was shared by his fellow
Methodist, Thomas Jackson, a prolific biographer,
whose caution in tracing developments of thought and
character when there were few private papers extant
caused him to frown upon the uncritical methods of
others:

> I was astonished to find how often
> writers copy from one another without
> inquiry, improve upon one another's
> mistakes and misrepresentations ...
> In this manner history and biography
> have too often been written; their
> authors being more anxious to interest
> their readers by startling narratives,
> than by a record of that which is
> strictly and literally true.[108]

Jackson's criticism was directed neither
exclusively nor even primarily at evangelicals.
Concern for documentary evidence was in its infancy
and in a pre-Ranken age literary and moralistic
approaches to history were both more common and more
acceptable than they were later to become. If
Clarke and Jackson were therefore in some respects
ahead of their age, their fellow evangelicals were
not out of accord with it when they demanded that
history be written from a moral and religious
standpoint. In a generally discriminating analysis
of Gibbon's strengths and weaknesses, the Eclectic
Review criticised his religious scepticism, but so
too did the Quarterly, which recommended the
destruction of those volumes likely to prove harmful, a course of action which the evangelical
periodical refused to sanction.[109] It was no
evangelical but Robert Southey who wrote

> For the want of religion there can
> be no comparison. The more religious
> an historian is, the more impartial will
> be his statements, the more charitable
> his disposition, the more comprehensive
> his views, the more enlightened his
> philosophy. In religion alone is true
> philosophy to be found; the philosophy
> which contemplates man in all his

relations, and in his whole nature;
which is founded upon a knowledge of that
nature, and which is derived from Him
who is the Beginning and the End.[110]

Such statements serve as a useful corrective
to any over-severe condemnation of evangelical
writing of history. Nevertheless the parallel
between the mass of evangelicals and their contemporaries must not be over-emphasised. When Southey
and others argued that historians should be
religious, they were opposing those who trampled on
that which was traditionally regarded as holy, and
who wrote snidely and sceptically about the aims
and actions of (Protestant) church and churchmen.
But they did not believe that secular history should
become nothing but a branch of theology.

The difference in approach is most clearly
revealed in the <u>Edinburgh Review</u>'s criticism of
two evangelical works. In 1806 a reviewer objected
to the loose conception of proof perpetrated by the
anonymous author of <u>An Historical View of Christian-
ity</u>, a study which sought to confirm the truth of
revelation by reference to the writings of ration-
alist historians: Christ had taught that the
kingdom of heaven resembled a grain of mustard seed
and Gibbon had shown this to be true by describing
the rapid spread of Christianity, an argument which
the reviewer quickly pointed out no more proved the
truth of that faith than the rapid diffusion of its
doctrines confirmed that of Islam.[111] A similar
tendency to ignore conflicting evidence and interpretation was a cause of complaint against Hannah
More, who claimed that in pre-Christian days the
Jews alone maintained 'that great truth, of there
being <u>only one living and true God</u>', and asserted
that geographically and commercially Judea was
'most conveniently situated for pouring forth that
light of truth':

It may not be so easy ... to make a
child understand completely how Judea
was the most favourable position for
the dissemination of a new religion.
We think, that the finger of a child
would point at least as readily either
to Egypt, the native soil of so many
ancient deities; or to Arabia, whence
Islamism has been spread to the banks
of the Ganges upon one side, and to the
foot of Mount Atlas at the other.[112]

The reviewer's translation of 'light of truth' into 'a new religion' is illuminating. His misreading of 'most' as a superlative, rather than as a synonym for 'very', does not altogether vitiate his complaint: he apparently expected the author to engage in an objective comparative study. Hannah More in contrast started from the presuppositions of faith. To consider the religious advantages of other lands would have seemed to her a singularly fruitless exercise. All that was necessary was to ascertain why the deity so wisely selected Judea. Evangelical belief in the superiority and originality of Christianity informed all attempts to argue that this was the case.

Evangelical histories were criticised not only on account of their weakness in argument, but also for their inadequacy as the theological works which they purported to be. The reviewer did not dispute Miss More's belief that the ways of God could be identified and explained but dismissed as 'very whimsical' the specific examples she gave, for Miss More believed that the historian should seek to identify the activity of God in each and every event studied. She therefore managed to reduce the deity to a being politically comprehensible, scheming as might any human manager: by divine condescension the Red Sea nearly reached the Mediterranean as a stimulus to ancient trade; it was separated from it, however, so as to encourage exploration. Moreover, as the <u>Edinburgh Review</u> noted, in explaining exactly how God worked his purpose out she made him ultimately responsible for human wickedness.[113] Indeed Miss More's failure to recognise the age-old problem of the causation of evil is but one indication of the simplistic nature of much evangelical writing: life past and present was assumed to be easily explicable within the framework of the evangelical scheme; there was little room for the accumulation of 'grand questions to be asked ... in eternity'.[114]

The phrase was Foster's. Eschewing any attempt to explain everything in simplistic fashion, he recognised that there was much in life that was incomprehensible and inexplicable, and rejoiced in the belief that it was man's eternal destiny gradually to move towards fuller understanding. But his intellectual curiosity, his conviction that 'one object of life' was the formulation of 'grand questions', was, as he bitterly recognised, not widely shared within evangelicalism. It has been the argument of this chapter that in condemning his

fellow evangelicals as lacking all interest in
intellectual matters, Foster and those who thought
like him were grossly overstating their case.
Evangelicalism did much to encourage a love of books
and an interest in study. Indeed it can be proposed
that its weakness in argumentation was in part a
product of its success in spreading intellectual
interests among its rank and file, for some of those
who contributed to the religious press were probably
self-taught thinkers tackling subjects beyond their
competence. But while evangelicalism successfully
encouraged men to read and to study, Foster was
right to affirm that it did not on the whole produce
open-mindedness and a questioning mentality. On
the contrary the movement was often embarrassed by
its intelligentsia and did not altogether know how
to harness the abilities of its most thoughtful men
for the furtherance of the faith. While those who
threw their energies into the elucidation and
translation of the Biblical text, and even into the
accumulation of miscellaneous knowledge were praised
for their efforts, those who sought to explore the
imponderable mysteries of life and death, to question the nature of their beliefs, were revered -
and frequently rebuked. Several of the most able
had, like Foster, reasoned their way into evangelicalism from Arianism and Socinianism, but they were
not encouraged to continue the process of questioning once safely within the household of faith.[115]
Thus, notwithstanding its respect for Foster, the
Baptist Magazine showed little sympathy for his
philosophical discussion of matters which it assumed
to be straight-forward.[116] Foster's fellow Baptist
Joseph Kinghorn recognised the moral and intellectual difficulties inherent in Christianity and
maintained that any thinking man had to face up to
them, but the patriarchal Andrew Fuller dismissed
as presumptuous his queries concerning the morality
of a deity who created and called to account a race
he knew would rebel.[117] The fear that men who asked
such questions might, like Adam Clarke, propound
unorthodox answers obsessed a school which believed
that its existence depended upon doctrinal purity,
and which sought at any cost to avoid heresy.[118]
Thus not even Richard Cecil, whose originality of
mind combined with undoubted orthodoxy, escaped
censure. There were murmurings within and without
John Street Chapel that his sermons, designed to
meet the interests of an educated congregation,
were, however stimulating, insufficiently evangelical: one hearer, a 'pious clergyman', commented:

> Mr. Cecil is a very wise preacher.
> He is a second book of Ecclesiastes.
> Yet I would like him better and he
> would do more good, if he were rather
> a second Epistle to the Romans.[119]

In the eyes of most evangelicals the apostolic
proclamation of gospel truth was so comprehensive
as to render unnecessary any further quest for the
meaning of life.

NOTES

1. Foster, _Cultivated Taste ..._, pp. 13ff.
2. Ibid., p. 21.
3. Ibid., pp. 23-24.
4. _British Critic_ iv (1828), p. 257;
H. Brougham, _Speeches_ (1838), i, pp. 402-14 (Brougham
believed that Stephen's inadequate education had
precluded the proper polishing of his talents, but
nevertheless described his pamphlet, _War in Disguise_
(1805), with which he disagreed, as 'brilliant and
captivating', a work of 'extraordinary merit');
J.S. Mill, _Principles of Political Economy_ (1848,
1909 edn.), p. 515. For the view that Clapham
contributed to the development of the mid-Victorian
intelligentsia and the Bloomsbury Group see N.
Annan, 'The Intellectual Aristocracy' in J.H. Plumb
(ed.), _Studies in Social History, a tribute to_
G.M. Trevelyan (1955).
5. _DNB_ adds that, the reputed master of
eighteen languages, Lee was appointed in 1819 to the
chair of Arabic, in 1831 to that of Hebrew. Milner
was President of Queens, sometime Jacksonian
Professor of Natural and Experimental Philosophy,
Mathematical Professor and University Vice-
Chancellor. His close friend Joseph Jowett was
Regius Professor of Civil Law, while another
evangelical James Scholefield became Regius
Professor of Greek.
6. Hopkins, op. cit., ch. vii; F.W.B.
Bullock, _Evangelical Conversion in Great Britain_
_1696-1845_ (1959), p. 193. Among the wranglers were
W. Carus, J.W. Cunningham, W. Dealtry, H. Venn
Elliott, T. Gisborne, F. Goode, C.J. Hoare,
E. Hoare, W. Jowett, W. Mandell, M. Preston,
T. Sowerby, T. Thomason.
7. The first volume and part i of the second
bear his name. He was a fellow of the Antiquarian
Society and of the Royal Asiatic Society, an
Associate of the Geological Society of London, and

a member of the American Historical Institute. For
further indications of his scholarly interests see
A List of Manuscripts formerly in the possession of
the late Dr. Adam Clarke; on sale ... by Baynes
and Son (1836); A Historical and Descriptive
Catalogue of the European and Asiatic Manuscripts
in the Library of the late Dr. Adam Clarke ...
(1835); A List of Manuscripts, English, Irish,
French, Icelandic ... formerly in the possession of
... Dr. A. Clarke (1836). Drew who was illiterate
at the time of his conversion published metaphysical
works of such calibre that he was awarded an A.M.
by Marischal College Aberdeen; the Baptist missionary Carey was appointed Professor of Bengali at
the government sponsored civil service college of
Fort William, published a grammar and translated
into English some Bengali literature; the author
of a Chinese grammar, linguistic treatises, and a
three volume Dictionary of the Chinese Language,
Morrison was to bequeathe his substantial Chinese
library to University College London.
    8. Southey who was scathing of the general
intellectual standard of evangelicalism (Quarterly
Review iv, 1810, p. 507), corresponded with and
praised the work of the evangelical poets James
Montgomery and Henry Kirke White, and was complimentary about the standard of the Baptist Library
at Bristol: K. Curry (ed.), New Letters of Robert
Southey (1965), i, pp. 213, 439, 482; ii, pp. 12ff.,
50; C.C. Southey (ed.), The Life and Correspondence
of Robert Southey (1849-50), iii, pp. 59ff., 92ff.,
256ff.; G.S. Haight (ed.), The George Eliot Letters
(1954-56), i, pp. xliii, 63-64, 93, 98, 174; ii, pp.
305, 441. The Taylor family were cited by Francis
Galton in his Hereditary Genius (1869), pp. 190-91.
    9. Coleridge wrote to a third party of 'that
worthy and enlightened man, the Revd. Joseph
Hughes', whom he thanked in almost obsequious tones
for giving him spiritual help: E.L. Griggs (ed.),
Collected Letters of Samuel Taylor Coleridge (1956-
71), i, pp. 116, 247-48; iii, pp. 35-36, 463, 472ff.;
v, p. 300; vi, pp. 1048ff. Cf. Leifchild, op. cit.,
p. 465.
    10. Quarterly Review xcv (1832), pp. 100ff.
Cf. British Critic xiii (1833), pp. 292, 325:
'There probably is not a man in the kingdom capable
of feeling the slightest interest in the manifestations of intellect, virtue, and religion, who is
not familiarly acquainted with the name of Robert
Hall. His published specimens of Pulpit Oratory
were some of them at least, of such surpassing

235

splendour and power, that they took at once an
elevated station in our standard theological
literature, and placed their author beyond all
dispute among the great and commanding spirits of
the age'.
  11. Good Words vi (1865), pp. 681-88, refer-
ing to Taylor, Foster, Hall and the Scottish Thomas
Chalmers.
  12. Conder, op. cit., pp. 224, 248. Cf.
J. Gilbert (ed.), op. cit., i, p. 98.
  13. Griggs (ed.), op. cit., vi, pp. 1048ff.;
Leifchild, op. cit., p. 466.
  14. EM i series xii (1804), pp. 492ff.; MM
xxxi (1808), pp. 612-13.
  15. EM i series xv (1807), p. 567.
  16. Quoted Hennell and Pollard (eds.), op.
cit., pp. 86, 92.
  17. E.g. Bateman, Wilson ..., i, pp. 8-29;
EM i series ii (1794), pp. 78-79, 405.
  18. Ibid. xvii (1809), p. 15.
  19. CO ix (1810), p. 720; xiv (1815), pp. 79-
80; xxii (1822), pp. 474-75, 623-26; xxv (1825),
pp. 358-59.
  20. Grimshawe, op. cit., pp. 579ff., 618.
Cf. Townsend (ed.), op. cit., pp. 23ff.; Pearson,
op. cit., ii, pp. 41-42.
  21. Hennell, op. cit., p. 52. Cf. Carus,
op. cit., p. 722.
  22. Conder, op. cit., p. 97.
  23. C. Cecil (ed.), Original Thoughts on
Various Passages of Scripture being the substance of
sermons preached by the late Rev. Richard Cecil,
A.M. (1848), p. 649.
  24. For criticism of Foster's book see EM i
series xxviii (1820), p. 467. His difficulties in
preaching are outlined in Ryland's biography.
  25. Quoted ER ii series ix (1828), p. 555:
'since ... man is a rational creature, it may be
expected, that a true system of religion will
recognise and be suited to this his character'.
  26. EM i series xii (1804), p. 227; MM xxxv
(1812), p. 68; CO xxx (1830), p. 248.
  27. S. Kelly (ed.), The Life of Mrs. Sherwood
... (1854), pp. 47-48.
  28. Clarke (ed.), op. cit., ii, pp. 95-96.
  29. MM xxxi (1808), pp. 471-73.
  30. Ward, op. cit., p. 57 records that the
Wesleyan solicitor, Thomas Allan 'a man forgotten
by history' and 'a scholar by instinct' 'left a
theological library to Conference which bore comparison with those of Dr. Williams and Sion College'.

31. Newman Hall (ed.), op. cit., p. 132.
32. See e.g. MM xxiii (1800), pp. 22-28.
33. Kellett, op. cit., p. 108.
34. E. Isichei, Victorian Quakers (1970), p. 19.
35. Swift, op. cit., pp. 173-74.
36. H. Venn, Academical Studies Subservient to the Edification of the Church (1828) based on the text 'Seek that ye may excel to the edifying of the church'.
37. CO xxv (1825), pp. 143-44. Cf. ER iii series x (1833), p. 44.
38. MM xxxi (1808), p. 613. Cf. EM i series viii (1800), p. 520.
39. T.P. Bunting, op. cit., i, pp. 57-58.
40. BM v (1813), p. 199; xvii (1825), pp. 108-09; CO xvii (1818), pp. 159-60.
41. EM i series iv (1796), p. 362; xiv (1806), p. 70.
42. ER iii series vi (1831), pp. 492-94; vii (1832), p. 138; BM xxv (1833), pp. 7-8.
43. W.R. Ward (ed.), The Early Correspondence of Jabez Bunting (1972), p. 192. Letter dated 26 December 1828,
44. R.J. Mackintosh (ed.), Memoirs of the Life of the Right Honourable Sir James Mackintosh (1835), i, p. 408.
45. BM ii (1810), p. 441; xvi (1824), p. 126.
46. Ibid. iv (1812), pp. 436-38; v (1813), pp. 199-201; xxv (1833), pp. 6-10; MM liv (1831), pp. 382-84; EM ii series xi (1833), p. 307.
47. Ward, op. cit., pp. 160-61.
48. R. Cecil, Ms Diary, p. 12f., dated 26 August 1804; CO xxxii (1832), pp. 49-58.
49. EM xv (1807), p. 305.
50. CO xxxii (1832), p. 51.
51. CO xvi (1817), p. 514; A.W. Brown, op. cit., pp. 35-36. Cf. Carus, op. cit., pp. 433, 843ff.
52. E.g. EM i series xxv (1817), pp. 363-64 (Rotherham); xxix (1821), pp. 431-32 (Idle); ii series iii (1825), pp. 341-42 (Blackburn); iv (1826), p. 345 (Homerton); v (1827), p. 302 (Cheshunt); vii (1829), pp. 371-72 (Highbury); ix (1831), p. 356 (Western). For a detailed study of individual academies see H. McLachlan, English Education under the Test Acts being the History of the Nonconformist Academies 1662-1820 (1931).
53. Carus, op. cit., pp. 108ff.
54. Ibid., pp. 75ff.
55. Jackson, Watson ..., p. 575.

56. Stock, op. cit., i, ch. vii.

57. T.P. Bunting, op. cit., ii, pp. 174ff.

58. BM xvii (1825), pp. 396-98; CO xxvi (1826), pp. 563-64, 568-69.

59. S. Pearce Carey, William Carey (1923, 1934 edn.), p. 66; Wilkin, op. cit., pp. 277ff.; J. Gilbert (ed.), op. cit., i, p. 47; Binfield, op. cit., p. 81.

60. EM i series xx (1812), p. 346; xxiv (1816), p. 505; MM xlii (1819), p. 609.

61. The EM welcomed both institutions (ii series ii, 1825, p. 338; vi, 1828, pp. 309, 354, 553; xi, 1833, p. 161). The CO while not initially hostile to University College gave a far more cordial welcome to Kings (xxv, 1825, p. 395; xxviii, 1828, p. 407; xxix, 1829, p. 317), and when challenged stressed that it had never defended 'that creature of Brougham's creation' (xxxi, 1831, p. 577). The Record predictably condemned Gower Street as latitudinarian and liberal and rejoiced in its teething troubles (e.g. 7 July 1831; 11 March 1833).

62. EM i series xiv (1806), p. 70; xv (1807), p. 529; xviii (1810), p. 494; xx (1812), p. 78.

63. Ward, op. cit., pp. 137-40.

64. MM xlvii (1824), pp. 762-64.

65. Ward, op. cit., pp. 12, 278.

66. More, Coelebs ..., ii, p. 420.

67. EM i series i (1793), pp. 89ff., 177ff.; ii (1794), pp. 3ff.; BM xxi (1829), pp. 181ff.

68. R. Hill, Village Dialogues iv (1803), pp. 127ff.

69. Scott, op. cit., pp. 185-86.

70. EM i series x (1802), pp. 403-04.

71. BM xiii (1821), pp. 157-58.

72. Wilkin, op. cit., pp. 240, 285, 449, 474.

73. H.F. Burder, The Pleasures of Religion (1823), p. 13.

74. BM vii (1815), pp. 221-31; xx (1828), pp. 489-92, 537-40; xxv (1833), pp. 445-50, 489-92.

75. Jackson, Recollections ..., ch. vi et passim.

76. J. Vickers, Thomas Coke, Apostle of Methodism (1969), p. 321.

77. Binfield, op. cit., p. 190.

78. Quoted M.G. Jones, op. cit., p. 232.

79. CO xxv (1825), pp. 144-45.

80. Scott, op. cit., p. 216; Carus, op. cit., p. 674; Venn, Sermons ..., iii, p. 370.

81. Ward, op. cit., p. 17.

82. Simeon believed that 1 John v 7 was a

later interpolation (Hennell and Pollard, eds.,
op. cit., pp. 46, 58), as from its inception did
the ER (i series vi, 1810, pp. 62-71, 155-64; ii
series xiv, 1820, p. 382; iii series i, 1829, p. 506;
iii, 1830, p. 169).
   83. MM 1 (1827), p. 763.
   84. ER ii series xxix (1828), p. 523; British
Critic iv (1828), pp. 178ff.; vi (1829), pp. 469ff;
viii (1830), pp. 308ff.; Christian Remembrancer
viii (1826), pp. 65ff.; ix (1827), pp. 637ff.,
677ff.
   85. Ibid. xii (1830), pp. 224, 285, 679;
xiii (1831), p. 288.
   86. British Critic vii (1830), pp. 376-78,
388, 395, 401; The Record, 30 November, 3, 7, 28
December 1829.
   87. Christian Remembrancer xii (1830), pp.
283, 679.
   88. British Critic iv (1828), pp. 370-71.
   89. Christian Remembrancer ix (1827), pp. 637-
44, 677-91.
   90. The Record, 3 December 1829.
   91. Christian Remembrancer xii (1830), pp.
283ff.; British Critic ii (1827), p. 398; iv
(1828), pp. 172-73.
   92. Ibid. v (1829), pp. 359-60.
   93. CO xxix (1829), pp. 719-20; xxx (1830),
p. 252.
   94. British Critic ii (1827), pp. 347ff.;
iv (1828), pp. 149ff.; ER iii series i (1829),
pp. 413-31.
   95. Ibid. iv (1830), p. 345.
   96. G. Himmelfarb, op. cit., pp. 70-78
stresses that in the 1830s 'Common sense and the
empirical evidence combined in favour of the idea
that violence and catastrophe, rather than an un-
deviating uniformity, was the message engraved upon
the rocks'.
   97. ER iii series vi (1831), pp. 75-81;
British Critic xi (1831), pp. 180-205.
   98. Ibid. vi (1829), p. 387ff. The
Remembrancer (xi, 1829, pp. 585ff.) reviewed Ure far
more favourably than did the Critic.
   99. British Critic xii (1832), p. 66.
   100. MM liii (1830), p. 689.
   101. Christian Remembrancer xv (1833), pp.
390ff.; CO xxxii (1832), pp. 742ff. Deep commitment to Scripture, literally interpreted, and in-
experience in logical debate could result in
bizarre but sincere arguments such as that put
forward in xxiii (1823), p. 695: 'On the

supposition that each of the six days of creation
extended to a period of 6000 years, Adam, who was
created on the sixth day, and lived only 930 years,
probably did not, as well as any of his posterity,
live to see a single Sabbath. Is it likely that
the Creator left man without that sacred institution
for several thousand years?'

102. CO xxviii (1828), pp. 236ff., 308ff.,
367ff., 428ff.
103. Ibid., pp. 98ff., 311ff., 628ff., 750ff.;
xxix (1829), pp. 91ff., 160ff.
104. EM i series xxi (1813), p. 426; ER i
series ix (1813), pp. 264ff.; BM xiii (1821),
pp. 205-06; xxii (1830), p. 198.
105. More, Female Education ..., iii, p. 127.
106. Foster, Critical Essays, i, pp. 174ff.,
192ff.; ER ii series ix (1818), p. 44.
107. A. Clarke, A Narrative of the Last Illness
and Death of Professor Porson ... (1808); Hopkins,
op. cit., pp. 12-13.
108. Jackson, Recollections ..., pp. 153-54.
Cf. 203-04 where he objected to the practice of
eliminating 'indelicate expressions' from new
editions of old works, thus subjecting accuracy to
the moral scruples of the day.
109. ER ii series v (1816), pp. 1-20, 180-201;
Quarterly Review xii (1815), p. 391.
110. Ibid. xxxvii (1828), pp. 197-98.
111. Edinburgh Review viii (1806), p. 273.
More concordantly with evangelical opinion the
reviewer questioned the prudence of familiarising
young people with the names and writings of infid-
els.
112. Ibid. vii (1805), pp. 91-100, a review of
Hints towards forming the character of a young
princess.
113. More, Hints ..., pp. 21-22, 203-11.
114. Ryland (ed.), Foster ..., i, p. 189.
115. Obvious examples are Thomas Scott (who
did not want to go on questioning) and Robert Hall
and John Mason Good who did.
116. BM xxv (1833), pp. 167-69.
117. Wilkin, op. cit., pp. 313-21.
118. Clarke's views on eternal sonship are
discussed by I. Sellers in the Wesley Historical
Society Lecture 1975, copy lodged in Dr. Williams's
Library. Had Clarke been less eminent he would
undoubtedly have been disciplined: future
ministerial candidates were expected to hold orthodox views on the subject.
119. T.P. Bunting, op. cit., i, p. 217; Josiah

Pratt, op. cit., pp. cxxi-ii. On Cecil's originality of mind, see J.H. Pratt, op. cit., pp. 22-25,
and J. Jerram (ed.), The Memoirs and a selection
from the letters of the late Charles Jerram (1855),
pp. 52, 264-65: 'He did not talk upon subjects as
other men did ... he viewed things with a different
eye, with deeper penetration, and on a wider
scale ... I never left him without receiving ideas
and impressions which I never had before'.

EPILOGUE

The man who more than most sought to break through
the constraints of accepted dogma was Edward Irving,
against the plumbline of whose thinking evangelical
attitudes to matters cultural and intellectual can
usefully be measured.

On the one hand, whereas Irving engaged in
pentecostalist denigration of the intellect,
evangelicals stressed its value. The contrast
between his missionary address and that of Jabez
Bunting is striking, for while the latter stressed
the importance of academic preparation if missionaries were to be adequately equipped for their task,
Irving denounced any reliance on human means and
human calculation.[1] Such thinking was closely
associated with premillenialist doctrine, for
expectations of the Lord's imminent return precluded
both long-term preparation for the evangelisation of
the world, and any optimism about man's role in this.
The continuing postmillenialist belief of many
evangelical leaders was therefore identified by
some opponents with 'notions of the march of mind',
against which Irvingite charismatics maintained 'a
belief in the positive rightfulness of ignorance,
which is conceived of as Apostolic, and through
which the Holy Ghost may speak without being dimmed
by mere human learning'.[2]

The widespread condemnation of pentecostalism
even by those evangelicals who shared Irvingite
unease over the spread of liberalism shows that
evangelicalism was far from being as anti-
intellectualist as is sometimes assumed. The
majority of evangelicals continued to assert the
priority of ratiocination over charismatic inspiration and from the beginning denominational leaders
sought to encourage this: writing of Methodism,
the form of evangelicalism most vulnerable to

242

pentecostalist fervour, W.R. Ward notes 'The great
defence of church order and preservative against
the revivalists was to unite sound learning with
vital religion'.[3] Both because of their belief in
the mode of God's operations and because of their
assumption that the nurture of the mind was more
godly than the satisfaction of the senses, evangelicals approved of bookish pursuits.

But if on the one hand comparison with
Irvingism reveals the extent of evangelical intellectualism, on the other it shows up its inadequacies. Irving should not be remembered merely by
his late aberrant pentecostalism. In the last few
unhappy months of his life, swept along by a movement over which he had lost control, he felt bound
to subject his intellect to the supposed dictates
of the Spirit, speaking in tongues. But in his
prime he was revered by the intelligentsia of
London: Coleridge, who regarded him as a major
attraction of his Thursday soirees, wrote to an
acquaintance 'You will like Irving as a companion
and a converser even more than you admire him as a
Preacher - He has a vigorous & (what is always
pleasant) a growing mind ...'[4]

Irving was a visionary of a type rarely if ever
nurtured by evangelicalism, a man even less prepared
than Foster and Kinghorn, Clarke and Cecil, un-
questioningly to accept the current teachings of the
church. Indeed he was highly critical both of
Scottish Presbyterians and later of English
evangelicals believing that their overriding intellectual interest in correct doctrine precluded an
openness of the whole personality to the Spirit of
God. In catechetical formulations truth was
'presented to the intellect chiefly', in the Bible
'to the heart, to the affections, to the imitation,
to the fancy, and to all the faculties of the soul'.
Yet the Bible was all too often relegated to a
source book of proof texts:

> The solemn stillness which the soul
> should hold before her Maker, so
> favourable to meditation and rapt
> communion with the throne of God, is
> destroyed at every turn by suggestion
> of what is orthodox and evangelical -
> where all is orthodox and evangelical;
> the spirit of the reader becomes lean,
> being fed with abstract truths and
> formal propositions ... Intellect,
> cold intellect, hath the sway over

heaven-ward devotion and holy
fervours.[5]

If like many would-be reformers Irving overstated his case, there is nevertheless much truth
in his suggestion that evangelicals valued the
intellect at the expense of other facets of the
human personality, and in consequence lacked the
vision to accept insights of the type which Irving,
ahead of his time, was seeking to communicate.
Like F.D. Maurice, who acknowledged his debt to
him, Irving was above all concerned to effect a
'realised theology', a theology which proclaimed
the Lordship of Christ over the present as well as
the future, over the whole of life and not just over
men's disembodied minds and souls.[6] Thus he argued
that from the beginning of time the Spirit of God
had been at work through natural means both in man
and in the world at large preparing the ground for
redemption.[7] Moreover he believed that the salvation of man far from being esoterically consummated
in the world to come, was integrally related to the
salvation of the natural and work-a-day world:

> as we grow to be redeemed by the power
> of Christ, working in us the law of the
> Spirit of life, we grow again to be
> lords and masters of the creature,
> and come to deliver it in a proportion-
> ate degree from its thraldom.[8]

To the disgust of the Baptist Magazine Irving was
therefore scathing of evangelical attempts to opt
out of the life of this world:

> is it for this that God sets men free
> from spiritual bonds, that they may
> build them prison walls and naked cells
> ... and leave the wilderness a wilderness
> still, and make the city a waste, and
> the fertile field a desolate waste ...
> That separation from certain honest
> customs of life, which is beginning to
> be introduced as parts of religious duty,
> the proscription of innocent mirth and
> well-timed hilarity, the violent philippics
> against the sports and amusements of the
> field, the proscriptions of that free and
> easy discourse which our fathers enter-
> tained, the formation of a religious
> world different from the other world, and

> the getting up of certain outward
> visible tests of a religious character,
> the proscribing of all books unless they
> expressly treat upon some religious
> subject; also your Moravian establish-
> ments, and Methodist dresses, and many
> other things which I could name, savour
> to me of the same ignorance and misuse
> of the creature which the Papists carried
> to its perfection ... In one word, all
> this is bondage, miserable bondage;
> the creation waileth to be liberated by
> liberated man. And shall redeemed man
> desert the redeeming of the creation?[9]

Irving's more positive approach to life in this
world was reflected in his Christology. His theological interests focused predictably not upon
Pauline theories of the Atonement, but upon
doctrines more obviously concerned with the earthly
Lordship of Christ, the Incarnation and the Second
Coming. His distaste for intellectual abstractions
caused him to repudiate a docetic sacrificial
offering in favour of a fully human Saviour,
energising living flesh and blood, 'in all points
tempted like as we are, yet without sin'. It was
Irving's interpretation of this last point which
caused the furore, resulting in his condemnation for
heresy. The question at issue, Irving explained,
was 'whether Christ's flesh had the grace of sin-
lessness and incorruption from its proper nature,
or from the indwelling of the Holy Ghost. I say
the latter':

> the precious truth for which we contend,
> is, not whether Christ's flesh (human
> nature) was holy - for surely the man
> who saith we deny this blasphemeth
> against the manifest truth - but whether
> during his life it was one with us in
> all its infirmities and liabilities to
> temptation, or whether, by the miraculous
> generation it underwent a change so as to
> make it a different body from the rest
> of the brethren. They argue for an
> identity of origin merely; we argue
> for an identity of life also. They
> argue for an inherent holiness; we
> argue for a holiness maintained by
> the Person of the Son, through the
> operation of the Holy Ghost.[10]

Irving's heresy was to become a later
orthodoxy. Current thought, however, as P.E. Shaw
has pointed out, 'in the interests of the divine
impaired the human nature of Christ'.[11] Thus even
Josiah Conder, one of the most cultured and open-
minded of evangelicals described Christ as coming
'so near to man that he even suffered being tempted'.
His biographer believed that this indicated a morbid
reaction against Socinianism which made Christians
of the period afraid of dwelling on the real and
complete humanity of Christ.[12] But evangelicals
were reacting against more than Socinianism. Their
failure to appreciate the humanity of Christ was
indicative of their inability fully to accept their
own humanity. Their subordination of passion, sense
and imagination to spirit and intellect was in part
a reflection of the thought of the day. But it was
reinforced by what K.S. Inglis has called 'the
evangelical schism between soul and body, between
the spirit and the world', a schism which evangelicals believed should characterise Christ's followers
as well as Christ himself.[13] Thus while they
accepted and enjoyed non-religious cultural and
intellectual pursuits to a far greater extent than
is generally recognised, they were never able
confidently to assimilate such worldly activities
within the framework of·their world-denying theology.
If a study of their practice does much to qualify
the traditional charge of philistinism, the failure
even of the most cultured evangelicals to reconcile
their enjoyment of the arts with their faith reveals
how substantial a schism still remained between
evangelicalism and culture.

NOTES

1. See above, pp. 26ff., 216.
2. A.L. Drummond, op. cit., p. 147; Rowdon,
op. cit., pp. 50, 52.
3. Ward (ed.), op. cit., p. 14.
4. Griggs (ed.), op. cit., v, p. 474. Cf. pp.
280, 286-87, 365, 368-69, 476-77, and for
Coleridge's unhappiness about Irving's later beliefs
vi, pp. 549-50, 554, 570-71, 677, 840.
5. E. Irving, The Oracles of God (1824),
pp. 13-14.
6. On Maurice and Irving see H.C. Whitley,
Blinded Eagle (1958), pp. 94-97.
7. E. Irving, Sermons, Lectures and Occasional
Discourses (1828), ii, pp. 604-86, one of a number of
lectures on the parable of the sower.

8. Ibid., p. 718.
9. Ibid., pp. 719-20; BM xxi (1829), p. 240.
10. Quoted Shaw, op. cit., pp. 22-24.
11. Ibid.
12. Conder, op. cit., p. 90.
13. K.S. Inglis, Churches and the Working Classes in Victorian England (1963), p. 305.

SELECT BIBLIOGRAPHY

In the interests of brevity the primary sources used
for this study are not cited here since full references are provided in the footnotes. A comprehensive list can be found in my thesis lodged in the
Library of the University of Keele. Autobiographies,
biographies and memoirs, which can be variously
classified as primary or secondary sources, are
central to any analysis of evangelicalism and
culture; some of the most illuminating are listed
in Section A of this bibliography. Section B
comprises secondary works which may be of interest
to those who wish to pursue the subject further:
they throw light upon the nature of evangelicalism
in the early nineteenth century, its beliefs, its
relationship to other forms of faith, the attitudes
its adherents adopted towards non-religious pursuits.
Also included are some few studies which fall outside the time-span of this book but which are of
obvious relevance to its main theme. The place of
publication is London unless otherwise stated.

A. AUTOBIOGRAPHIES, BIOGRAPHIES AND MEMOIRS (listed
       in order of subject)

Cecil, R. Memoirs of John Bacon esq. R.A. ... (1801)
Cox-Johnson, A. John Bacon R.A. 1740-99 (1961)
Tyndale, T.G. Selections from the Correspondence of
      Mrs. Ely Bates ... (Oxford, 1872)
Macdonald, J. Memoirs of the Rev. Joseph Benson
      (1822)
Birks, T.R. Memoir of the Rev. Edward Bickersteth
      (1851)
Bunting, T.P. The Life of Jabez Bunting D.D. ...
      (1859-87)
Ward, W.R. (ed.) The Early Correspondence of Jabez

Bunting (1972)
Burder, H.F. Memoir of the Rev. George Burder (1833)
Buxton, C. Memoirs of Sir Thomas Fowell Buxton bart,
    3rd edn. (1851)
Carey, S. Pearce William Carey, 8th edn. (1934)
Pratt, J. Remains of the Rev. Richard Cecil A.M.
    with a view of his character ... to which is
    prefixed a memoir of his life, 14th edn. en-
    larged (1854)
Charlotte Elizabeth, Personal Recollections (1841)
Clarke, J.B.B. (ed.) An Account of the Infancy,
    Religious and Literary Life of Adam Clarke,
    LL.D., F.A.S. (1833)
Aveling, T.W. Memorials of the Clayton Family (1867)
Conder, E.R, Josiah Conder, a memoir (1857)
Bateman, J. The Life of the Rev. Henry Venn Elliott
    M.A. (1868)
Smyth, C. 'William Farish 1759-1837', Magdalen
    College Magazine lxxvi (1937)
Ryland, J.E. (ed.) Life and Correspondence of John
    Foster ... (1846)
Ryland, J. The Work of Faith, the Labour of Love,
    and the Patience of Hope illustrated in the
    Life and Death of the Reverend Andrew Fuller
    (1816)
Vansittart, J. (ed.) Katharine Fry's Book (1966)
Gilbert, J. (ed.) Autobiography and Other Remains of
    Mrs. Gilbert, formerly Ann Taylor (1874)
Goode, W. Memoir of the late Rev. William Goode, 2nd
    edn. (1828)
Grant, B. The Dissenting World: an autobiography,
    2nd edn. enlarged (1869)
Morris, H. The Life of Charles Grant (1904)
Hare, A.J.C. The Gurneys of Earlham (1895)
Swift, D. Joseph John Gurney, Banker, Reformer and
    Quaker (Middletown, Connecticut, 1962)
A Biographical Sketch of Alexander Haldane of the
    Inner Temple Barrister-at-Law J.P. communicated
    to 'The Record' of 28 July 1882
Haldane, A. The Lives of Robert Haldane of Airthrey
    and of his brother James Alexander Haldane, 2nd
    edn. enlarged (1852)
Hall, N. (ed.) The Author of 'The Sinner's Friend',
    an autobiography (1865)
Miscellaneous Works and Remains of Robert Hall with
    a memoir of his life by Olinthus Gregory and a
    critical estimate of his character and writings
    by John Foster (1849)
Pearson, J. The Life of William Hey esq. F.R.S.
    (1822)
Townsend, J.H. (ed.) Edward Hoare M.A., a record of

his life based upon a brief autobiography
(1896)
Leifchild, J. Memoir of the late Rev. Joseph Hughes
A.M. ... (1835)
Oliphant, M. The Life of Edward Irving (1862)
Drummond, A.L. Edward Irving and His Circle (1937)
Whitley, H.C. Blinded Eagle (1955)
Jackson, T. Recollections of My Own Life and Times
(1873)
Rupp, E.G. Thomas Jackson, Methodist Patriarch
(1954)
Wilkin, M.H. Joseph Kinghorn of Norwich (1855)
Latrobe, C. Letters to My Children (1851)
Knutsford, Viscount The Life and Letters of Zachary
Macaulay (1900)
Milner, M. The Life of Isaac Milner ... (1842)
Roberts, W. Memoirs of the Life and Correspondence
of Mrs. Hannah More, 2nd edn. (1834)
Roberts, A. (ed.) Letters of Hannah More to Zachary
Macaulay containing notices of Lord Macaulay's
youth (1860)
Jones, M.G. Hannah More (Cambridge, 1952)
Jackson, T. The Life of the Rev. Robert Newton
(1855)
Grimshawe, T.S. A Memoir of the Rev. Legh Richmond,
4th edn. (1828)
Williamson, G.C. John Russell R.A. (1894)
Scott, T. The Force of Truth (1779)
Kelly, S. (ed.) The Life of Mrs. Sherwood (chiefly
autobiographical) ... (1854)
Carus, W. Memoirs of the Life of the Rev. Charles
Simeon ... (1847)
Brown, A.W. Recollections of the Conversation
Parties of the Rev. Charles Simeon M.A. (1863)
Hennell, M.M. and Pollard, A. (eds.) Charles Simeon
1759-1836 (1959)
Hopkins, H.E. Charles Simeon of Cambridge (1977)
Bevington, M.M. (ed.) Memoirs of James Stephen
written by himself for the use of his children
(1954)
Stephen, C.E. The First Sir James Stephen, letters
with biographical notes (Gloucester, 1906)
Stephen, L. The Life of Sir James Fitzjames Stephen
(1895)
Taylor, I. (ed.) The Family Pen, Memorials, Biogra-
phical and Literary of the Taylor Family of
Ongar (1867)
Teignmouth, Lord Memoir of the Life and Correspond-
ence of John Lord Teignmouth (1843)
Meacham, S. Henry Thornton of Clapham 1760-1815
(Cambridge, Mass. 1964)

Select Bibliography

Forster, E.M. Marianne Thornton 1797-1887: a
    domestic biography (1956)
Knight, W. Memoir of Henry Venn ... (1882)
Hennell, M.M. John Venn and the Clapham Sect (1958)
Jackson, T. The Life of the Rev. Richard Watson, 2nd
    edn. (1834)
Wilberforce, R.I. and S. The Life of William
    Wilberforce (1838)
──────────────────────── Correspondence of William
    Wilberforce (1840)
Wilberforce, A.M. (ed.) Private Papers of William
    Wilberforce (1897)
Bateman, J. The Life of the Right Rev. Daniel Wilson
    D.D. ... (1860)

B. FURTHER READING

Annan, N.G. 'The Intellectual Aristocracy', J.H.
    Plumb (ed.), Studies in Social History, a
    tribute to G.M. Trevelyan (1955)
Best, G. 'The Evangelicals and the Established
    Church in the Early Nineteenth Century',
    Journal of Theological Studies new series x
    (1959)
──────────── 'Evangelicalism and the Victorians',
    A. Symondson (ed.), The Victorian Crisis of
    Faith (1970)
Binfield, J.C.G. So Down to Prayers: studies in
    English nonconformity 1780-1920 (1977)
Bradley, I. The Call to Seriousness, the evangelical
    impact on the Victorians (1976)
Brilioth, Y. Three Lectures on Evangelicalism and
    the Oxford Movement (1934)
Brown, F.K. Fathers of Victorians (Cambridge, 1961)
Cunningham, V. Everywhere Spoken Against, dissent
    in the Victorian novel (Oxford, 1975)
Dale, R.W. The Evangelical Revival and Other Sermons
    (1880)
──────────── The Old Evangelicalism and the New (1889)
Davie, D. A Gathered Church, the literature of the
    English dissenting interest, 1700-1930 (1978)
Davies, H. Worship and Theology in England: from
    Watts and Wesley to Maurice (Princeton, 1961)
Fletcher, I. 'The Fundamental Principle of the LMS',
    Transactions of the Congregational Historical
    Society xix (1962)
Gladstone, W.E. 'The Evangelical Movement; its
    parentage, progress, and issue', British
    Quarterly Review lxx (1879)
Hennell, M.M. 'Evangelicalism and Worldliness 1770-
    1870', G. Cuming and D. Baker (eds.), Popular

251

Belief and Practice: Studies in Church History
   viii (Cambridge, 1972)
Hempton, D.N. 'Evangelicalism and Eschatology',
   Journal of Ecclesiastical History xxxi (1980)
Herbert, T.W. John Wesley as Editor and Author
   (Princeton, 1940)
Hewitt, G. Let the People Read: a short history of
   the United Society for Christian Literature
   (1949)
Jay, E. The Religion of the Heart: Anglican evang-
   elicalism and the nineteenth century novel
   (Oxford, 1979)
Kellett, E.E. Religion and Life in the Early
   Victorian Age (1938)
Kent, J. 'The Victorian Resistance: comments on
   religious life and culture 1840-1880', Victor-
   ian Studies xii (1968)
————————— 'A Late Nineteenth Century Nonconformist
   Renaissance', D. Baker (ed.), Renaissance and
   Renewal in Christian History: Studies in
   Church History xiv (Oxford, 1977)
Laqueur, T. Religion and Respectability: Sunday
   schools and working class culture 1780-1850
   (1976)
Malcolmson, R.W. Popular Recreations in English
   Society 1700-1850 (Cambridge, 1973)
Mathews, H.F. Methodism and the Education of the
   People (1949)
Mayo, R.D. The English Novel in the Magazines 1740-
   1815 (1962)
McDonald, H.D. Ideas of Revelation, an historical
   survey A.D. 1700 to 1860 (1959)
McLachlan, H. English Education under the Test Acts
   being the History of the Nonconformist Academ-
   ies 1662-1820 (Manchester, 1931)
Mineka, F.E. The Dissidence of Dissent: the
   Monthly Repositary 1806-1838 (Chapel Hill,
   1944)
Newell, A.G. 'A Christian Approach to Literature',
   The Evangelical Quarterly xxxii (1960)
————————— 'Early Evangelical Fiction', The
   Evangelical Quarterly xxxviii (1966)
Newsome, D. The Parting of Friends (1966)
Perrin, N. Dr. Bowdler's Legacy, a history of ex-
   purgated books in England and America (1969)
Pollard, A. 'Anglican Evangelical Views of the Bible
   1800-1850', The Churchman new series lxxiv
   (1960)
Rack, H.D. 'Wesleyanism and "the world" in the later
   nineteenth century', Proceedings of the Wesley
   Historical Society xlii (1979)

Reynolds, J.S. The Evangelicals at Oxford 1735-1871
    (Oxford, 1953)
Russell, G.W.E. The Household of Faith, portraits
    and essays (1902)
Sangster, P. Pity my Simplicity, the evangelical
    revival and the religious education of children
    1738-1800 (1963)
Scott, P. 'Cricket and the Religious World in the
    Victorian Period', Church Quarterly iii (1970)
Shepherd, T.B. Methodism and the Literature of the
    Eighteenth Century (1940)
Smyth, C. Simeon and Church Order: a study in the
    origins of the evangelical revival in Cambridge
    in the eighteenth century (Cambridge, 1940)
————— 'The Evangelical Movement in Perspective',
    Cambridge Historical Journal vii (1943)
————— 'The Evangelical Discipline', H. Grisewood
    (ed.), Ideas and Beliefs of the Victorians
    (1949)
Spring, D. 'The Clapham Sect: some social and
    political aspects', Victorian Studies v (1961)
Stephen, J. Essays in Ecclesiastical Biography
    (1849)
Walsh, J.D. 'The Magdalen Evangelicals', Church
    Quarterly Review clix (1958)
Ward, W.R. Religion and Society in England 1790-1850
    (1972)
Willmer, H. '"Holy Worldliness" in Nineteenth
    Century England', D. Baker (ed.), Sanctity and
    Secularity: Studies in Church History x
    (Oxford, 1973)

INDEX

Index

Index

Index